RESPECT

Other books by Sara Lawrence-Lightfoot

Worlds Apart: Relationships Between Families and Schools

Beyond Bias: Perspectives on Classrooms (with Jean Carew)

The Good High School: Portraits of Character and Culture

Balm in Gilead: Journey of a Healer

I've Known Rivers: Lives of Loss and Liberation

The Art and Science of Portraiture (with Jessica Hoffmann Davis)

RESPECT

An Exploration

Sara Lawrence-Lightfoot

A MERLOYD LAWRENCE BOOK

PERSEUS BOOKS
Cambridge, Massachusetts

Many of the designations used by manufacturers and sellers to distinguish their products are claimed as trademarks. Where those designations appear in this book and Basic Books was aware of a trademark claim, the designations have been printed in initial capital letters.

Copyright © 2000 by Sara Lawrence-Lightfoot
Published by Basic Books, A Member of the Perseus Books Group
First published by Perseus Books

A CIP catalog record for this book is available from the Library of Congress.

ISBN-13: 978-0-7382-0318-8   ISBN-10: 0-7382-0318-1

Text design by Greta D. Sibly

Books published by Basic Books are available at special discounts for bulk purchases in the United States by corporations, institutions, and other organizations. For more information, please contact the Special Markets Department at Perseus Books Group, 2300 Chestnut Street, Suite 200, Philadelphia, PA 19103; or call (800) 810-4145, x5000.

DHSB   25   24   23   22   21   20   19

For my mother
Margaret Cornelia Morgan Lawrence
who, by her lifelong example, has
showed us the reverence, witness,
and power of respect,
given and received

Acknowledgments

When the six "messengers" of *Respect* said "yes" to my invitation to join me in this project, they took a courageous leap of faith—one that required trust, generosity, and grace. They had no idea how their voices and experiences might be mined and molded to illuminate the dimensions of respect. Yet they opened their doors wide and let me watch their work, and they opened their hearts and minds to deep conversation and rich revelations. I am indebted to Johnye Ballenger, Dawoud Bey, Kay Cottle, Jennifer Dohrn, Bill Wallace, and David Wilkins, all amazing practitioners of respect.

As always, Wendy Elisabeth Angus, my esteemed assistant, contributed her deft skills, judicious counsel, and unerring support to this project, collaborating on every phase of the work. Merloyd Lawrence, editor extraordinaire, used her keen eyes and strategic restraint wisely. James Holland assisted me with discerning literature reviews and inspired me with his love of poetry. Kirsten Olson Lanier offered graceful and probing critiques of the narratives and responded with generosity and wisdom to all of my requests for help. I appreciate the wonderful work of this quartet.

During this project I was nourished by the support of my partner and muse, Irving Hamer, a beautiful listener, deep thinker, rigorous truth-teller, and loving soulmate. I'm so thankful to have him by my side, watching my back, and face to face. Every day my children, Tolani and Martin, teach me important and difficult lessons about resilience, resistance, empathy, and forgiveness, all central qualities of respect, all part of the dynamic and texture of life at home.

In my family of origin I also learned valuable lessons about the roots and symmetry of respect, around the dinner table and out in the world, in intimate conversations and public witness. I thank my loved ones all: Mom Margaret, Chuck and Mari, Paula and John, and their progeny. When I needed to hear myself talk, friends circled around. I am grateful for memorable conversations with Susan Berger, Sissela Bok, Maya Carlson, Tony Earls, Pat Graham, Ronne Hartfield, Linda Whitlock, and Marti Wilson.

I received excellent support and vigorous cheerleading from the folks at Perseus Books. I owe special thanks to Elizabeth Carduff for her gracious leadership; to Hilary Selby Polk for her efficient and patient guidance through every stage of publication; and to Faith Hanson for her fine copyediting.

Finally, I want to express my great appreciation to the Spencer Foundation, which generously supported this work. The Foundation's fellowship afforded me the time, space, and freedom to witness respect in all of its richness and beauty.

Sara Lawrence-Lightfoot
October 1998

Contents

No one of my generation—baby boomers now in our middle years—can possibly read the word **RESPECT** (in bold capitals) without hearing Aretha Franklin's searing declaration; her soul-stirring, heart-wrenching anthem. "R-E-S-P-E-C-T. Find out what it means to me . . . Show me, just a little respect." Aretha, the Queen of Soul, sings to her lover, demanding a little respect from the man who has demeaned her, diminished her, and made her feel small and worthless. But we have made it our song. We are beating the rhythm with our bodies, in heartfelt empathy, in total identification. We are pounding our feet, raising our fists, flashing our eyes, and singing along. Every party we go to, every time we crash or jam or jive, we put on Aretha's "Respect."

Aretha's anthem is a women's wail, but the men shout it out as loud as we do as they join the groove. Here we are—children of the sixties—serious students, dedicated activists, hanging-out hippies, irreverent beatniks—wearing black and thumbing our noses at authority, joining peace marches and growing our Afros, questioning power in all its guises. Here we are dancing "Respect," demanding it, claiming it. At other times, our longing sounds more like a prayer: "Please dear Lord, dear parents, dear teachers, show us a little respect! See us, hear us, pay attention."

Aretha's voice fades into a vision of a beautiful little East African girl whom I met in 1976 while traveling in Kenya. She is four years old and speaks four languages with astounding fluency. I meet her, ask her name, and she tells me, "I'm Tolani." I love the name, its lilting, musical sound, and decide immediately that if I ever have a daughter, I will name her Tolani. Much later I discover the name's meaning. In fact, it is a *West* African name, used by *both* boys and girls; and it means "one who gives respect *and* one who is respected." How I love its meaning, its promise of symmetry, as much as its music. You get respect when you give it. When my daughter arrives four years later, I name her Tolani, and hope that she will live both sides of this resonant equation.

Thinking about my small daughter's name sends me further back to my own childhood; to watching my parents operate in many spheres, observing the ways they treated everyone with the same even-handed generosity and deference whether conferring with a university president or greeting the gas station attendant. Whether they were listening to an elder's wise, weathered tales or deciphering the tangled story of a young child, there was always this clear-eyed, full attention.

When my father died in 1986, my brother gave the eulogy, his intimate, loving view of a very public man. Chuck's voice cracked as he recalled one of our father Charles's loveliest qualities.

> Charles had a natural air of authority about him. He commanded respect without ever asking for it. In high school, my rowdiest friends—the guys who stole hubcaps and crashed parties—were perfect gentlemen in my father's presence. They'd stand and say "yes, sir, Dr. Lawrence," and answer his many questions about school and home and where their parents and grandparents were from. It was much later that I realized Dad's secret. He gained respect by giving it. He talked and listened to the fourth-grade kid in Spring Valley who shined shoes the same way he talked and listened to a bishop or college president. He was seriously interested in who you were and what you had to say. And although he had the intellectual and physical tools to outmuscle a smaller person or mind, he never bullied. He gained your allegiance by offering you his strength, not by threatening to overpower you.

My mother Margaret shared her husband's quiet authority. I remember watching her at her work as a psychiatrist treating inner-city families at Harlem Hospital. I remember her sitting comfortably on a tiny child's chair, pulling play people and cars and balloons out of her large African bag. Sometimes she brought a loaf of her homemade "Maggie Bread" to be offered in bite-sized pieces for a hungry child. I remember the way a child responded with trust to her serious, nurturant gaze. The parents' bodies would relax as they listened to her soothing voice and began to appreciate the intelligence and bravery she saw in their son. Her reverent respect for the child and his family was always in evidence.

I suspect that my mother's "reverence" for her troubled and vulnerable young patients, and her understanding and empathy for their parents, is rooted in her own experience as a child. Not only was she respected by her own parents, but she felt empowered and honored by "the whole middle-class Negro community" of Vicksburg, Mississippi, where she was raised. This respectful embrace protected her from the ugly racism then poisoning encounters between whites and blacks in Vicksburg, and made young Margaret feel that she could do and be anything. In this southern city, where, as Margaret puts it, "white folks were totally irrelevant," she absorbed the attention and admiration of her elders and saw her future reflected in their eyes.

Margaret's certainty about her parents' undiluted respect for her did not mean that she was confident of their love. An older brother, called "Candy Man," with fair skin and golden curls had died eleven months before Margaret was born, but his idealized memory haunted the family forever. There was no way Margaret could compete with this dead brother. With her brown skin and dark eyes, she would never be as beautiful or as loved. Absent the love, she channeled her efforts into gaining her parents' respect; and they gave it in full measure: a constant, unswerving belief in her talents, her achievements, and her dreams. The respect was clear, unadorned. The respect was enough.

Despite this feeling of security, Margaret recognized that

her parents did not give one another the same kind of constant, devoted reassurance. As an only child she was much preoccupied with her parents' relationship. Their rage and distrust of one another was always smoldering just below the surface, always ready to ignite into painful words that split the air. Margaret absorbed the anguish, heard the disrespectful slurs, and promised herself that if marriage was in her grown-up future, she would choose a man who would not inflict such pain, and for whom she would feel both respect and devotion.

Many years later, on her wedding day, clinging to her father's strong arm, Margaret prepared to enter St. Mary's Church. She heard the solemn notes of the "Wedding March," noticed the packed pews of folks dressed in their best finery, spotted her handsome man standing tall as he waited for her at the altar, and was overcome with panic. On the precipice of promising herself to Charles, she was haunted and consumed by the echoes of her parents' marriage. Her mind filled with images of Mary kneeling to pray that her husband would not be unfaithful, the memory of going hand-in-hand with her mother in search of her father along the streets of Vicksburg, the sound of her father walking down the hall and shouting: "You white bitch!" Margaret dreamt of a union with Charles that was respectful and open and affectionate, a more equal, loving partnership. Later in life she told me, "Charles was my first companion. I was fascinated by hearing somebody else's thoughts and feelings. It was my *first* experience of expressed affection. You are not related to a person unless you say something about it and let the other person know how you feel. I remember holding back at first and getting some requests from Charles that I respond."

While Margaret's hopes for symmetry in her marriage were to be realized, disrespect was a constant shadow as she prepared for a medical career. At her first summer job after marriage, a research position at the Mississippi Department of Public Health, Margaret went to meet the director. "He immediately called me 'Margaret' . . . This was 1938 in Mississippi, and people did not immediately call each other by their first names." The director was making clear that despite her credentials from Columbia Medical School, she was a Negro talking to a white boss. "Charles was infuriated . . . He was so angry, he felt destroyed." Her new husband's rage and pain brought home to Margaret their already deep bonds. "For the first time, I knew what it was to be a wife and feel a kind of empathy with someone close to you . . . You feel something he does."

In facing these demeaning experiences early in marriage, my father was bolstered by a mighty memory: Mr. Pleasant McAdney, a prosperous farmer in Copiah County, whom no one—not even white folks—called by his first name. He would remember the way this proud farmer dressed when he went to town to do business: clean, neatly pressed overalls, a jacket, and a collar and tie. He would remember the firm stride, the silent, alert dignity that elicited respect from merchants and bank presidents, even when Mr. McAdney followed the status quo and went in by the back door.

The chapters that follow are fueled by all these potent early memories of respect: Aretha's audacious anthem, the double meaning of Tolani's name, my father's "natural authority," and my mother's capacity for empathy and healing attention. They are also haunted by the ghosts of disrespect: my maternal grandparents locked in a twisted love that left them feeling angry and diminished; and my parents'—Charles and Margaret's—early experiences of racial slurs, the shorthand symbols of a long history of oppression. In the background of many of the stories of respectful relationships in this book is someone like Mr. McAdney, refusing to succumb to slavery's legacy or other long shadows of disrespect. All these autobiographical echoes across the generations have inspired my interest in "respect"—its roots, its development, its expression—and shaped the way I understand and interpret its meanings.

My interest in exploring the underlying nature of respect is motivated by more than personal memories, however. I am also drawn to the concept because it holds increasing importance for public and private life today. When we worry about the deterioration of civility, street violence, the lack of decorum and safety in our schools, the invasions of privacy by the press, harassment in the workplace, and the dirty language and offensive gestures that fill our daily encounters, we often cite lack of respect as the reason that our social fabric is tearing. Likewise, when we suffer the private assaults of infidelity, emotional and physical abuse, even misunderstanding and isolation, we often see the roots of the pain as originating in disrespectful attitudes and behavior. Every morning the newspaper contains a story that echoes the words of Aretha's anthem: pleas for respect from people who have been violated, neglected, or ignored by loved ones, acquaintances, strangers, or public figures. Courts are filled with juveniles who have been thrown out of their homes and cast out of school for their delinquent behavior. The judge may or may not give them time in juvenile detention, but she will almost always give them a sermon on respect. In September, in almost every classroom across the country, teachers begin the year with admonitions and rituals that have respect as their central message. And parents lament the ways in which their offspring do not show them the respect that they remember giving to their parents when they were young.

Most of these references to respect—both public and private— are warnings about the catastrophic consequences that result when it is *absent*. We pay more attention to it when it is *not* expressed. But complaints about the loss of civility or the disrespectful attitudes that characterize contemporary society raise two questions. First of all, it is hard to know what is being used to measure the degree to which things are truly worse. Has there been a real and measurable deterioration of respect, or are we simply hearing the lament voiced by every generation as it confronts a reality so different from its own past, change that feels ominous and frightening? When we reach adulthood, do we put on the rosy glasses of nostalgia, conjuring up a time when parents had authority and children were respectful; when teachers were strict and their students obeyed? One of my colleagues, Joseph Featherstone, a social historian, claims—only half-jokingly—that adults in our society suffer from "A History of Amnesia," a profound ahistoricism that tends to romanticize the past and denigrate the present. We reminisce about a world that was stable and safe and civilized—when you could trust your neighbor, ride the subways at night with no fear, and believe what your children told you—all the while forgetting or ignoring the facts of the past, which, of course, included incidences of betrayal, crime, and deception. Undoubtedly, our stories express a complex of feelings, some rooted in real lived experiences, and others filtered through the haze of nostalgia.

The other, perhaps more interesting, question raised by our laments about the absence of respect in relationships, in the workplace, or in political life has to do with what we mean by the term. Although our views are no doubt both fluid and hybrid, traditional conceptions of respect still have a potent influence on the ways we judge our society. Respect is commonly seen as deference to status and hierarchy; as driven by duty, honor, and a desire to avoid punishment, shame, or embarrassment. Often our view does not involve individuals, as in "respect for property," for the law, the flag, or institutions. In many contemporary cultural views—calls for more respectful relationships in health care, urban planning, education, or the more strident calls for a civil society—we do not hear the voices of individuals; neither do we see any recognition of the painstaking work involved in nourishing respectful relationships. The traditional view of respect, though rarely expressed in its pure form, tends to be relatively static and impersonal. The remnants of this view survive today and shape our expectations, our apprehensions, and our disappointments.

In this book, I hope to shape a new view of respect. Usually, respect is seen as involving some sort of debt due people because of their attained or inherent position, their age, gender, class, race, professional status, accomplishments, etc. Whether defined by rules of law or habits of culture, respect often implies required expressions of esteem, approbation, or submission. By contrast, I focus on the way respect creates symmetry, empathy, and connection in all kinds of relationships, even those, such as teacher and student, doctor and patient, commonly seen as unequal. Rather than looking for respect as a given in certain relationships, I am interested in watching it develop over time. I see it not only as an expression of circumstance, history, temperament, and culture, rooted in rituals and habits, but also arising from efforts to break with routine and imagine other ways of giving and receiving trust, and in so doing, creating relationships among equals.

Respectful relationships also have a way of sustaining and replicating themselves. I would like to document how respect grows, the dynamic interactions that create and sustain the respect. Respect generates respect; a modest loaf becomes many. With that in mind, this book will examine how people work to challenge and dismantle hierarchies rather than how they reinforce and reify them, as well as the ways in which the context—the situation of healer and patient, teacher and student, photographer and subject—shapes the ways in which people engage in respectful relationships. Since the focus here will be on individuals, it will be important to consider how family roots, temperament, and life stories shape the ways in which they are able to become respectful and respected. Rather than the language of inhibition and constraint typical of a more old-fashioned view of respect, the voices in this volume will be ones of challenge and exuberance. Rather than the language of dutiful compliance, we will hear words of desire and commitment.

In *Respect,* I will emphasize relationships that are asymmetric; relationships that are characterized by contrasts in power, knowledge, and control between the participants. The more powerful persons in these relationships—the experts, the witnesses, the knowledge bearers—are those usually seen as on the receiving end of respect. The people whose voices you will hear, and whose actions you will see, however, each believe that it is impossible to do the work that they do without offering respect, creating a relationship with respect at the center. I purposely chose people, both black and white, who are articulate about the ways in which respect defines the character of their work.

In each of the six chapters of this book, I watch respect developing over time, sustained by past experience and continually reinvented in the present. Each chapter focuses on a different setting, from a childbed to a deathbed, from a studio to a law school lecture. Most important, I have sought, through each person's story, to reveal one crucial dimension of the term. With these six facets, or sources of illumination, I try to portray the many-splendored quality that we call *respect*.

The book opens with the drama of birth. Ten years ago, Jennifer Dohrn, a nurse-midwife, founded a birthing clinic in the South Bronx, the first built in the country especially designed to serve poor women, mainly black and brown. A radical political activist in her young adulthood, who often lived her life underground and took great risks in her fight for justice and equality, Jennifer chose midwifery as a way to bring a constructive mission and concrete skills to impoverished communities. Her work with women has *empowerment* as its central theme. In a situation where women often feel most vulnerable and frightened, when they feel disempowered and diminished by the rituals and technology of hospitals, when medical experts tend to take over and make all the decisions, Jennifer works to give women the knowledge and self-confidence to feel their full strength. As Jennifer puts it, "Birthing is a time when lots of family building takes place; when women feel strong and powerful."

Johnye Ballenger, a pediatrician with a private practice in Cambridge, Massachusetts, teaches residents at Children's Hospital, is on the faculty at the Harvard Medical School, and works one day a week at a community health center in Boston. Her message of respect is conveyed through her *healing* actions; her medium is her message. Her mission of respectful care echoes strong themes from a childhood in Kentucky—where she was raised by industrious and disciplined women who valued education and civility—her early devotion to Catholicism, and by a particular "legacy" that she inherited from enslaved ancestors.

A teacher of middle and high school students in an affluent suburb of Boston, Kay Cottle sees respect embedded in classroom *dialogue*, as she helps students learn how to ask good questions, value inquiry, listen to each other, and begin a habit of thoughtful reflection. To her, true dialogue combines heart and mind, "loving and thinking," and it always entails risk: the teacher and her students allowing themselves to be vulnerable in the safe haven of the classroom.

As an artist and photographer, Dawoud Bey creates larger than life-sized color portraits that allow us into the psyche of his subjects. For him, photography begins—always—with a "deep *curiosity*." Rather than the photographer being a "predator" and the camera being a barrier between artist and subject, Dawoud spends most of his energy creating relationships, listening to stories, and engaging in conversation. "I am endlessly curious," he says about the primary motivation that defines his respectful regard of people with whom he works. The process cannot be separated from the image. He explains his method using this equation: "If I want the pictures to have a more intense quality, then the relationships need to be more intimate and reciprocal."

At the Harvard Law School, an environment known for its hard-edged encounters, competition, and rivalry, David Wilkins stands out. The generations of students who have passed through his demanding, first-year course in civil procedure, speak of this professor with respect, as well as appreciation for the respect and attention he bestows on them. At the root of his unyielding devotion to "seeing his students whole" and "creating a classroom culture in which they can feel comfortable" is his own hard-earned fight for *self-respect,* his determination that none of his students will have to go through the pain he experienced as a very successful but often terrified law student at Harvard twenty years before. His journey of self-respect is haunted by a dark family legacy: a long line of extraordinarily bright and achieving men who never felt their full power, who always felt the emptiness and fraud that comes from deferring to others and never fully valuing themselves.

Respect then comes full circle, from the life-giving screams of birth to the terror and peaceful silence of death. Just as Jennifer Dohrn offers her strength to laboring women, helping them feel powerful and creative as they give new life, so Bill Wallace, an Episcopal priest, pastoral therapist, and AIDS activist, supports his patients during the great transition of death. His respect is conveyed through undiluted *attention*, watchful witness; "letting dying persons lead; listening to what they want, and how they want to be in this moment." His therapeutic and religious stance—attentive and compassionate—was wrested from a childhood of brokenness, sadness, and abuse, and from a determination to heal himself as he offers counsel and support to others.

Six windows on respect—*empowerment, healing, dialogue, curiosity, self-respect,* and *attention*—each one reveals a different angle of vision; each one illuminates different experiences. As I listen to these storytellers and observe them in action, I bring my own voice to the mix, echoing with my own history and associations and underlying the dimensions we explore. I also bring these voices together both in harmony and counterpoint, creating moments of dissonance and resolution that sharpen our understanding of the six forms of respect. As I talk with these teachers and healers, I feel as though we are in a hall of mirrors, seeing ourselves reflected in each other's eyes, hearing our conversations echoed in their stories. In order for us to explore the rich phenomenon of respect, we must ourselves engage in respectful dialogue, one built on relationships that move toward symmetry and intimacy. Our dialogue captures our full attention, allows us to take risks, explore silences, and challenge our inhibitions. The attentive, healing power of such a relationship, the life-enhancing glow of respect given and gained, is an experience I would wish for all my readers.

CHAPTER ONE

Empowerment

You who have stood at the bedposts
And seen a mother on her high harvest day
The day of the most golden of harvest moons for her.
You know being born is important.
You have seen this love's pay day
Of wild toiling and sweet agonizing
You who have seen the new wet child
Dried behind the ears, swaddled in fresh garments
You know that nothing else was so important to you.

—Carl Sandburg,
"Being Born Is Important"

T o be a witness to birth is not only to celebrate the labor and the harvest, the woman and the child. In that moment, we also feel and understand—with sudden force—the importance of our own arrival in the world.

Jennifer Dohrn, a nurse-midwife, witnesses many "high harvest days" in her work at the Childbearing Center that she founded and directs in the South Bronx. She knows that poverty haunts the lives of most of the women she serves, and she hears the sound of their desperate voices pleading for a better life for themselves, their children, and their babies not yet born. Yet she is more aware of the strength in the young mothers who come through the doors of the Center; their raw resolve, their unyielding dreams; their determination to make that better life for themselves and their families.

Jennifer works to capture their hope and their strength in preparation for one of the "most powerful moments of their lives": the birth of their babies. She wants them to experience in full the moment of birth, "when time stands still and nothing else matters." As an experienced midwife, Jennifer provides an oasis of respect and safety that allows women to be in touch with their bodies, take control of their care, and realize their own power to give birth and build a family. Jennifer works to create a safe place and example of care that will help young mothers feel both respected and *empowered*. She also hopes to create a synergy, a "circle of women" whose strength will be amplified by their collective quest.

A Queen's Place

The Childbearing Center is a gray faceless building sitting at the corner of Burnside and University Avenues, a busy cross-section in the South Bronx. It is surrounded by an array of small shops—most with English and Spanish signage—crowded next to each other: convenience stores, beauty parlors, luncheonettes, liquor stores, bridal shops, fast food joints, record stores, shoe repair shops. As I arrive by taxi, I am astounded by how much is squeezed into this bustling intersection. It is a bright spring day and the streets are filled with people, the teenagers pushing the season in shorts, halters, and sandals, the elderly folks still huddled in winter coats and hats. There is a simple sign over the front door of the Childbearing Center, in both Spanish and English, and a few posters in the window of mothers and babies, but from the outside the building seems dull, not particularly welcoming.

I ring the bell of the first of two locked doors and walk through at the sound of the buzzer. By the time I reach the second door, Jennifer Dohrn is standing there smiling broadly and opening her arms for a big hug. Behind the locked doors, there is a large reception area that is sunny and welcoming, more like a living room than a waiting area. A plump, burgundy velvet couch and love seat dominate the sitting area, in front of a batik hanging that fills the wall. Jennifer explains to me later that there is only "one rule" at the Center that everyone takes very seriously: children may not climb or sit on the couches. As a result, these welcoming, friendly couches barely show the wear and tear of the thirty-five families who pass through there daily. A big rocker sits out in the center of the room with extra seating provided by simple metal chairs that line the walls and look more like a typical hospital waiting room.

When Jennifer decided to spend three thousand dollars on this furniture and art, people thought she was "crazy," that it would be quickly damaged by careless families from the community who would not appreciate it anyway. Instead, the warm, peaceful decor seems to be the first sign of caring and respect to families that enter the space. The very pregnant mothers fall into the cozy corners of the couch as they wait for their appointments with the midwives. Their children gather in an adjoining playroom filled with toys and books, where they happily occupy themselves out of view but within hearing distance of their parents. There is a long reception area at one end of the room where families sign in, pick up their medical charts, make appointments, or receive referrals. A receptionist, who answers the phone with a friendly voice that does not seem to grow dull from routine, switches rapidly back and forth from English to Spanish.

Jennifer gives me a quick tour, which includes four examining rooms used interchangeably by the seven midwives who work there; a large meeting room, also with couches and chairs, where parents gather for educational sessions or to share information in support groups; a small kitchen for the staff; and a "family room" with a table, chairs, and yet another couch, where I first spotted the poster—of a handsome brown couple holding their newborn child—with the Carl Sandburg verse written below it. The two birthing rooms are somehow both cozy and high-tech, a cross between a large bedroom and a doctor's office. A queen-sized bed with a colorful quilt dominates the center of the room. There is a rug on the floor, prints on the walls, as well as comfortable chairs. The medical equipment is spare and pushed to the edges of the space. There is a full bathroom, which has a Jacuzzi bathtub that mothers often use during birthing. The gushing water is soothing and relaxing, easing the pain and tension of contractions.

In the second birthing room we greet a brand-new baby boy and his family. The mother, a pretty, lean Puerto Rican woman, is sitting in the bed propped up against a pillow with her hour-old son sleeping peacefully in her arms. The baby is rosy and perfect. A white knit hat covers his head, and a nightgown and light blanket swaddle his tiny body. The mother and child are surrounded by women: the baby's grandmother and three of her sisters, and five of the mother's sisters. They have all been present at the delivery, and they continue to hover around, watching, murmuring, and admiring the miracle in their midst. Although she must be exhausted, the mother's face shows only joy and pride. She smiles shyly as she says that she has decided to breast-feed this child, her second born. Her first son, now seven years old, was born in a hospital and was bottle fed. This time she is feeling more self-confident and wants to try breast-feeding because she believes that it will be "safer for my baby." Jennifer congratulates her on her decision as the women nod their heads in approval.

The midwife who worked through most of the night assisting the birth is dressed in a simple blouse, a loose-fitting skirt, and flat shoes. She moves quietly on the periphery, offering praise for the successful delivery and the beautiful baby, and blending into the group of women. Her pale white skin and her graceful skirt contrast with the light brown tones of the women and the tight slacks and bright sweaters that hug their bodies. I am awed by the sight of the tiny infant in his mother's arms and by the calm, life-giving spirit that seems to have settled around us. It feels both ordinary and amazing. By early afternoon the baby, his mother, and her entourage are heading home, four hours after the birth.

Jennifer and I leave the birthing room and head for her office, a small rose-colored oasis that she has recently painted and decorated. This is her asylum, a place to rest and think and gather herself at brief moments during her very strenuous and long workdays. There are plants and carefully chosen art, family photos, and favorite books. A Middle Eastern rug picks up the tones of the walls. An antique lampshade casts soft shadows on Jennifer's face.

Now that we are not moving, I take in the unusual beauty of this woman. Her eyes, both sad and smiling, look directly at me. Loose, irreverent brown curls frame her long, lean face. Huge exotic copper-and-bead earrings dangle down to her shoulders and make music when she turns her head. Her body is reed thin, strong and erect. Her hands move as she speaks, and the African bracelets that go halfway up to her elbow also make jangling noises. During a delivery, Jennifer always wears these earrings and puts on fresh makeup so that "when the baby arrives, his or her first view of life outside of the womb will be lovely."

Several women and children are sitting in the waiting room as Jennifer begins the morning clinic. On her way to the examining rooms, she greets the women individually, with a remark or a touch, and their faces brighten. Most of the families who come to the clinic are poor; some have had earlier experiences delivering their babies in hospitals; others have used the birthing clinic for all their children. Whether they are old-timers or newcomers, they all speak about the differences between the Childbearing Center and hospitals. "This is a place," says one, "where everyone cares; where they are always nice to you; where you feel safe." Another refers to the "kindness" and "respect" that she feels from the midwives and the way that the Center is a place where "the whole family is welcome." A third straightens up to her full height, pats her large belly, and exclaims proudly, "They do everything to give us knowledge so we can take care of ourselves." By contrast, these women speak about their experiences in hospitals as cold and disrespectful. "They do everything in their power to make you feel small and stupid."

When Jennifer started the Center ten years ago, she had just graduated from Columbia University with a degree in nurse-midwifery, and was determined to find a way to serve "the poor and people of color." The movement to create freestanding birthing centers apart from hospitals, with more options as to how birth was to be handled, had focused on middle-class and upper-middle-class communities. Poor communities were not seen as fertile ground for midwifery, and poor families were not perceived to be interested in, or trusting of, alternative practices. "But I believed," says Jennifer, "that centers should not be restricted to one segment of the population." The timing was fortuitous. Through a series of professional contacts, Jennifer collaborated on a large grant proposal to the Kellogg Foundation that allowed her to open a Childbearing Center in an inner-city community.

The South Bronx was chosen as the site because families there were being poorly served by traditional medicine, and because there was a health care center in place with which the Childbearing Center could affiliate. "Before the Center," says Jennifer, shaking her head, "one out of every three women in this community had no prenatal care. They had no access to the hospital clinic." The Childbearing Center would not only provide access to prenatal care for these women, it would also—through its affiliation with the health center—permit access to the whole health network. "A woman coming in pregnant could be directed to an ophthalmologist if her older child needed glasses; to the dentist if someone had a cavity . . . or to an obstetrician if there was a complication in the pregnancy."

For the first two years after the Center opened, Jennifer was the only midwife. There are now seven on staff, with an equal number of community workers who have been trained at the Center, who assist the midwives and serve as liaisons to the community. Jennifer explains, "The great majority of trained midwives in this country are white women from middle-class backgrounds. Although the midwives do not live around here, all of the community workers come from the communities we serve." Forty-five percent of the patients who come to the Center are Latino, largely from Puerto Rico and the Dominican Republic. Forty-five percent are African-American or of African descent, including from many African countries and the Caribbean, and 10 percent are Vietnamese refugees, most of whom have spent time in refugee camps in the Philippines, "suffering the worst kind of dislocation." Occasionally, one or two white women, who are part of a missionary group in the neighborhood, will walk through the door. This diverse population of patients has in common poverty and a wish to find a place where they will be received respectfully and where they will be able to get good care.

Over the years, the population has grown from a tiny, reluctant group of women who knew nothing about midwifery and were skeptical of its practices, to a large, vibrant group of families, many of whom have become staunch advocates of the cause. They have clearly come to trust the health care that they receive at the Center and to see the benefits of the natural birthing process that allows them to be in the midst of their families and take charge of their babies' births. They are drawn to the Center because they feel it is a place that "treats them with dignity." "The word on the street is that we are nice people," says Jennifer simply. "People feel, 'They are glad to see me. They care about me. They treat me with kindness.'" As one woman put it, elegantly poised on the big burgundy couch, "They treat me like a queen." Remembering that woman, Jennifer describes how "triumphant" she looked, how "regal" she appeared sitting there in her sweat suit and sneakers. "Here she was feeling strong and beautiful, fully in charge, rather than feeling she was an animal in the hospital being disrespected."

This Is About You

The first woman that Jennifer sees during the morning clinic is a thirty-eight-year-old black woman, who looks much younger than her years even though she is suffering from a terrible cold and "exhausted" by being eight and a half months pregnant. This is Sharon's third baby (the first two are girls) and she reports that this has been her most difficult pregnancy. She is feeling miserable, sneezing, wheezing, and coughing, as she makes her way into the examining room. Jennifer sits at a small desk and Sharon drops heavily into the chair directly facing her. She gives Jennifer her medical chart, on which she has already recorded her weight and temperature. Jennifer says later that one of the primary goals of their work at the Center is to help women learn to be "in charge" of their care. In an effort to "eliminate the passivity" that is typical of patients within the hierarchies of traditional medicine, she encourages the women to "get involved." They not only participate and make choices about their own care, they are also urged to read their own medical charts. "If there are any secrets in the chart," says Jennifer adamantly, "then you're not giving the right care. Everything I know they should know. This is about *them* not me."

This focus on empowerment is central to Jennifer's practice and shapes the rituals and policies at the Center. "A woman must feel . . . this is about *you*. *Your* body. *Your* baby. *You* are at the center. *You* are problem-solving, learning, asking questions. *You* can decide. I want to give knowledge—through classes, groups, teaching, mentoring, reading—so that they can make good and informed choices."

When Jennifer is settled at the desk, she looks directly at Sharon, strokes her arm gently, and exclaims, "Now, I'm yours. You have my full attention. How are you?" "Terrible!" says Sharon, barely able to stop coughing long enough to respond. She digs out the Tylenol and Sudafed from her pocket and drops them on the desk. "This stuff is not working. I have all this mucus coming out of my nose . . . my eyes are dripping all the time." Jennifer is purring sympathetically. She opens Sharon's chart to check her weight gain (during the pregnancy she has gained 38 pounds; her weight is now up to 170), and then—using a circular moving chart—she calculates the length of pregnancy (thirty-eight weeks and six days). "Is the baby moving okay?" Jennifer asks. "Contractions?" Holding her belly, Sharon nods. "Everything is fine. I just feel awful." Jennifer switches gears. "How are things at home? Do the girls have a place to go when you go into labor?" "My mom's at home," says Sharon. "Besides," she adds dead seriously, "I'm going to have it on a weekend. That's my plan." Jennifer bursts out laughing, but Sharon holds firm. "My other two babies arrived on the weekend . . . so that's what's going to happen this time."

A pause in the conversation is followed by a question that seems to be part of an ongoing dialogue between them. Jennifer's voice is gentle and beseeching. "So you're thinking about the breast?" Sharon is still but her voice seems to squirm a bit. "Yeah, *thinking* about it." "I said *thinking*," teases Jennifer. Then I hear a familiar mantra. "It's your decision. . . your baby." Sharon clasps her breasts and offers a line of mild resistance. "Well I don't even have enough up here. I'm not big enough." Now Jennifer sounds both reassuring and didactic. "Everyone makes enough milk for their baby. Even if you just do it for a few weeks, the baby will be immunized. Our kids need to be protected." Jennifer's voice fades; she has said enough. This is *Sharon's* baby.

After taking her blood pressure (which is "perfect" at 90 over 50), Jennifer asks Sharon to climb up on the examining table.

The expectant mother moves with difficulty, first grunting as she pulls down her sweatpants, then hauling herself up on the high table. Her belly is perfectly round; the dark brown skin is stretched smooth. Her cornrows fan out in a circle behind her head. She looks worried as Jennifer uses a tape to measure her stomach. "I have two knots," she warns when Jennifer begins to feel for the baby. "It is not two heads, I assure you," says Jennifer with a big smile. Then moving her hand over Sharon's belly, she reports, "Well, the back is here, the butt is here. This is the elbow . . . the shoulder. I'm still feeling the baby as near seven pounds." Then, turning on the fetal monitor, Jennifer says, "Let's hear this person." When she locates the baby's heart, a loud, insistent beat fills the small office. Sharon smiles through her coughing as Jennifer says admiringly, "A nice thriving child. Do you have a feel for who this child is?" She asks, "Do you have dreams?" Sharon is feeling too lousy herself to attend to Jennifer's soulful questions about her baby. "I'm so hot," she complains. "I'm burning up." "Those are hormones," explains Jennifer sympathetically. "They are like hot flashes. . . kind of like what you experience during the first three months of pregnancy. You'll also feel nauseous."

Jennifer puts on rubber gloves, covers them with cream, and does a vaginal exam. "Sorry I'm poking you so much. This is the head where I'm touching," she reports. "You know what?" she says with surprise. "I think you are a lot more ready to labor than I thought!" This sounds encouraging to Sharon. "Oh good, Friday is my birthday. I wish my baby would come on my birthday! Will you induce it?" she asks, already knowing the answer. "No," says Jennifer firmly. "No way." "A very nice exam," says Jennifer in conclusion. "I think you're doing great."

I watch three more examinations of women in their latter stages of pregnancy. The rituals with each are the same—preliminary questions about how the mother is feeling, how the pregnancy is going, how the family is coping, how the plans are proceeding for the labor and delivery; followed by taking their blood pressures, measuring and feeling their bellies, and listening to the babies' heartbeats—but each encounter feels very different. Despite the routines, each mother uses the time differently and Jennifer responds with full attention, following the mother's lead and giving as much time as she seems to need. With each mother, Jennifer makes immediate contact by facing them directly (her desk behind her), looking into their eyes, and stroking their arms as they talk.

Mariba Oshanti is a large dark-brown-skinned woman dressed in jeans, a sweatshirt, sneakers, and a bright green baseball hat worn backwards. Jennifer looks at her chart, discovers that she is moving, and asks her several questions about her new place, an apartment that she applied for more than four years ago with more space for her new husband, her seven-year-old son, and the baby on the way. Mariba's older child was born in a hospital, so this is her first experience at the Childbearing Center. When she mentions that she nursed her boy for two years, Jennifer exclaims enthusiastically, "Good for you. You get the prize." After checking her chart for weight, calculating the duration of the pregnancy, and taking her blood pressure, Jennifer listens intently as Mariba complains about "short stabs" she has been feeling in her belly that make her double over when she walks. "Do you know what that is? Has anyone ever told you?" asks Jennifer. "The sharp pains are actually caused by spasms that occur when the ligaments and muscles stretch. They are not of any danger to you or your baby. They just feel lousy. But you must keep walking." Mariba seems to be comforted by the explanation, though she finds it "harder and harder" to exercise her body that has grown from 200 to 225 pounds during the pregnancy.

A big smile spreads over her face as she digs in her pocket and proudly displays a fuzzy picture from a recent sonogram of her baby. "I've never seen anything like it. She is sucking her thumb." The mother knows the baby is a girl because she has had an amniocentesis, a procedure recommended to her because of sickle cell that "runs in my family" and a genetic illness carried by her husband. Mariba stumbles through an explanation of the threats to the fetus, the procedures she has endured, the worries it has caused them, and the good prognosis. "She didn't get any of it. What a relief. We decided to name her Aneesa, which means 'joy bring,' because we were so happy after all of our worry!" Jennifer congratulates her on her knowledge ("See what you've learned!") and on the good news and the beautiful name.

Jennifer seems to feel confident that this mother is "taking charge" of her pregnancy, but she expresses some concern about Mariba's needing to get involved with anticipating the baby's arrival and homecoming. When Mariba admits that she has not been going to any of the classes offered at the Center, Jennifer urges her to attend. "This is your first baby with this partner and it has been a bunch of years since the last one. It will give you a space to have this baby ... The classes are kind of nice and fun. They will help you feel ready to have this baby." Mariba nods in response to Jennifer's gentle prodding as she climbs onto the examining table. Jennifer is admiring as she measures and feels her belly. "Your skin is so beautiful. Look how nicely it has stretched!" "Well, I use lots of baby oil," says Mariba proudly. "Actually," explains Jennifer, "it is hereditary ... so you'll pass this along to your daughter." After all the anxiety caused by the possibility of her baby's having genetic defects, Mariba beams at the news of the wonderful inheritance awaiting her daughter. One day Aneesa will have her mother's smooth skin.

Brenda, a small and energetic redhead dressed in crisp light blue shorts and top, is the only white mother I see in the clinic all day. In her arms she is carrying a blond, blue-eyed two-year-old who is clinging to her mom for dear life. A four-year-old, dressed in an outfit identical to her sister's, trails a few paces behind. Before Brenda sits down, she begins her story. "We just spent a week in camp," she says dramatically. Then the punch line: "At Montefiore Hospital." Still standing and holding the child, she recounts a harrowing tale about the sudden illness that consumed her younger child and caused terror in her heart. But most of her story focuses not on the nature of the illness, or the threats to her child's safety, but instead on the unkind and crude medical treatment they received. Her voice rises when she tells about the ways they "tried to separate" her from her baby and did not want her to "know what was going on." "When they told me I couldn't breastfeed, I said that we might as well pack up and go home. The pediatrician was an arrogant jerk who couldn't even look at me when he talked to me. He didn't know what he was doing either. He changed her medication three times . . . And, of course, they don't want you to see what's going on or ask them a lot of questions. When they saw me in the oxygen tent with her, they went crazy!" Jennifer listens to Brenda's outrage and frustration, occasionally asking a question or admiring her assertiveness. When Brenda complains that her husband—a fireman used to handling emergencies and putting out fires—"refused to accept responsibility" and did everything to avoid a confrontation with the doctors ("When he came to the hospital, he always wanted to go down to the cafeteria and eat."), Jennifer explains sympathetically that denial may be her husband's way of coping. "You are the kind of person who wants to talk about it, deal with it directly, and get as much information as possible . . . His way may be to grow very silent and turn inward."

Having tried to offer a view sympathetic to both Brenda and her husband, Jennifer turns all of her attention to Brenda. "*You're* the one growing the next baby," she says firmly. "Did you make more milk in the hospital? Have you been able to sleep?" Brenda points to her two-year-old, who is now whimpering softly and still clinging. "*She* has been my priority. I hardly even remember that I am pregnant." Jennifer nods her head in understanding and empathy, but presses her point about self-preservation. "When you are in a crisis, everything goes to replenish the crisis. But then you need to replenish *yourself.*"

The four-year-old fights for a place on Brenda's already occupied lap, causing her younger sister to kick and scream. In an effort to pacify them Jennifer offers both girls band-aids, and the four-year-old marches out of the room tearing open the wrapper and leaving a trail of paper in her wake. The two-year-old ignores Jennifer's offering and nuzzles back into her mother's chest, almost as if she is struggling to displace the baby growing inside. Soon it is time for the examination and Brenda runs out into the hall in search of her older daughter. "Hurry, hurry . . . or you'll miss it!" she calls excitedly. Soon the four-year-old is at the door, and has climbed up on a chair next to the examining table. Brenda has taken her shorts off and is lying on the table with her arm cradling the two-year-old, who is stretched out next to her. Both of the girls' eyes grow very big as they await the ritual that they have come to expect and enjoy. They pat their mother's belly gently as Jennifer measures and feels Brenda's stomach. "Let's hear this baby," says Jennifer to all three of them. With the amplified sound of the baby's heartbeat, the four-year-old covers her ears and her sister crows with delight. Jennifer asks the girls, "Is he saying 'hi' to you?" Then to the mother she says, "This baby's going to have a lot of stories to tell!" When the trio is about to leave, Jennifer offers her support and admiration. "You are such a great spirit," she says to Brenda, who is now managing to balance two children on her lap. "You're a very special mom." Then Jennifer returns to the story that Brenda entered with. "I'm so sorry you have to go through this. It is so very frightening when it comes to our kids getting sick."

Gina, a Puerto Rican woman, is twenty-two years old and very pregnant with her sixth child. Her first five children—all boys—are romping in the playroom. The younger ones look eager and curious; the older ones are already precociously independent and sullen. They poke their faces into the examining room from time to time and are shooed out by their mom, who needs every bit of Jennifer's attention for herself. Gina is wearing a bright magenta sweater with rhinestones glittering in a heart shape across her breast. Her light brown skin has a gray cast; she looks weary and despondent. She has missed almost all of her prenatal appointments and will, therefore, not be able to deliver her baby at the Center. "How *are* you?" says Jennifer. "I've been worried about you." The rest of their conversation is in Spanish. Gina points to her belly and warns, "After this one I want an operation." Her eyes are red and swollen; from time to time they fill with tears. Jennifer tells me later that her partner is a much older man who is either absent or abusive, and that it is very hard to know how to help or when to intervene. She offers empathy and support, but it feels almost useless. "This is a very heroic woman here," Jennifer says to me in English that Gina fully understands. "But there are too many weights on her . . . too much for one *girl*." I do not know whether Jennifer has referred to her as "girl" on purpose, but sitting there exhausted and hanging her head, Gina seems like a child overwhelmed with responsibility, unable to rescue herself or protect herself from abuse. She pulls herself out of the chair with great difficulty and goes out in the hall to check on the boys, who are scrambling with each other trying to be first at the water bubbler. Her voice is menacing as she tells them to behave and issues a warning. They fall silent and into line. Returning to the room, Gina climbs onto the examining room table to listen to the heart of her sixth child.

Family Building

In helping a woman anticipate birthing, Jennifer urges her to design her own rituals. When the woman is about thirty weeks pregnant, Jennifer begins to ask her about her "birth plan." Usually the woman stares blankly back at her, wondering what she means. Jennifer begins to lay out some of the choices, the ways in which the mother might create a setting and an event that bears her imprint. She tells her, for instance, that she can bring whomever she wants to the birth. "We welcome the woman's family however she defines it," says Jennifer. "Everyone has a role in welcoming the baby." She also suggests that she might want to bring along pictures of family members who might not be able to be present; special music that she might want to play; a favorite nightgown, a comfortable pillow; or special herbal baths. And she urges the woman to talk to family elders about cultural practices or rituals that might help the mother and baby feel embraced by the history and roots of their community. Again, Jennifer rehearses the familiar words to the mother. "This is *your* experience. It should be connected to you and your family's culture. There is a lot of family building in the birth."

When Jennifer helps families anticipate the birthing, she is always concerned about "finding a role for the men." Her stance toward men is steadfastly empathic and inclusive. As a matter of fact, throughout the woman's pregnancy, she makes every effort to include the father in the process and make him feel comfortable enough to ask questions and express his concerns. "We see a lot of men," says Jennifer. "After talking to the woman, I always take the time to talk directly to the man. I let him know, for instance, that he can talk about sex here, or any other troubling things that he is struggling with. And he often returns with questions, concerns, complaints. 'I can't lie on top of her . . . She doesn't like sex any more.' Sometimes he comes in alone to talk about these things. I try to give him information without judgment."

During the birth, Jennifer finds ways of including the father. He may be the one to cut the cord or the first one to bathe the baby. She realizes that even when men become a part of the "family building" at birth, they inevitably do not feel that they are at the center of the process. "There is always this interweaving of men, in and out," muses Jennifer. "But at the *heart* is the woman. Men are *essential* but they are not the heart of it." She tells the story of a birth that took place the day before, when Rodney, a man from Jamaica, was witnessing the birth of his first son. Rodney's mother, a tiny, domineering woman, stood on the edges of the birthing circle offering counsel and support, and watching *her* baby become a father. "Rodney is a very big, strong man, and he was very much a presence during the birth," Jennifer recalls. "This was his wife, Casey's, first baby, and it was a very long and difficult labor." During the twenty-four hours in which Casey labored, Rodney tried to find a way to help and give solace, and he worked to discover a posture and a voice that was not *his* mother's. Throughout the long night of labor, Jennifer listened as Rodney talked about his apprehensions, his confusions, and his excitement; first reticently, then with fervor and passion; his voice rising in a duet with his wife's moans and wails. Time and again Jennifer and Rodney found themselves returning to a discussion about "the role of the man," and she found herself telling him that "it's a crime against men that they have been excluded from births, and it has hurt their parenting." Jennifer looks off into the distance and seems to be speaking to no one in particular: "Men still have an unexplored path."

Fighting for Change

Jennifer's own husband, Haywood Burns, was killed in an automobile accident in 1996. Dean of the Law School at the City University of New York, and a well-known and highly regarded political activist, he had traveled to Cape Town to attend an international convention of progressive lawyers, one of several trips he had made to South Africa in support of the liberation struggle. On his way to a restaurant for dinner with a couple of colleagues, the car was hit broadside by a speeding truck, and Haywood died several hours later in the hospital. Jennifer and Haywood had been married for ten years and they shared five children between them (three from Jennifer's former union and two from Haywood's two previous marriages). Since his death, Jennifer has been trying to heal and knit her life back together. He is everywhere: in her dreams, in her memories, in her conversations, in her stories, and in the pictures and mementos that decorate her office.

As part of her effort to recover, Jennifer surrounded herself with friends and family to commemorate the one-year anniversary of Haywood's death in a ritual of prayer, chanting, and remembrance. She transformed Haywood's study into a meditation room that served as the quiet oasis for the Buddhist ceremony. Such carefully planned rituals have given her some measure of solace and helped her move forward. Her work is part of this effort. As she helps mothers give birth to their babies, she absorbs the hope, strength, and promise of a new life, and is able to release some of the grief of her loss.

When Jennifer decided to become a nurse-midwife—working to empower women in the South Bronx—she drew on her own family legacy of passionate engagement in political activism, a fierce work ethic, and commitment to service. When she speaks about helping young mothers discover "the fullness of their power," Jennifer is expressing themes that have run through her life; themes that are both personal and political, inspired by both her emotions and her intellect. Jennifer's emphasis on roots and rituals in her work with families is built on her recognition of the ways these have shaped her own life.

Jennifer is the child of strong, involved parents. Her mother, despite a harsh childhood, including the loss of her own mother when she was five, "was able to become a nurturer herself . . . a wonderful, whole, devoted mother." Her father, Bernard, was the third of eight children in a hard-pressed family of Russian and Hungarian parents. As a young man, Bernard left home, trying to escape the poverty and his father's cruelty, and worked his way through college and most of law school. Jennifer is unsure of why he never actually completed law school, but she is certain that it left him with an emptiness that could be filled only if one of his daughters chose to be a lawyer. His ambition was realized with the graduation of his first-born—and namesake—Bernardine, from the University of Chicago Law School twenty-five years later. In his work as a credit manager, Bernard, according to Jennifer, "was very well respected by his clients, and he worked incredibly hard, passing on to my sister and me a passion and fanaticism about working." His first wife, who was Swedish, died in childbirth along with her baby, a piece of family lore that remained secret from Jennifer until she somehow discovered it when she was about twelve. She is still puzzled by the silence and the missing pieces of the story, which haunt her as she works to create safe settings for birthing and rituals that would be open and celebratory. Jennifer's own mother, Dorothy, "had very hard births," says Jennifer heavily, in a way that seems to express her wish that her mother might have had births that were as empowering and as exhilarating as the ones that she witnesses. After the births of her two daughters, "My father decided that she should not endure any more pain, that there would be no more children."

The roles within Jennifer's family were traditionally defined; her father was the breadwinner, her mother the homemaker. "My father believed in two things," says Jennifer. "First, he believed in hard work—honest, principled, industrious. Second, he loved learning and loved reading. My favorite memory of my father was being read to by him while I sat in his lap. This was the only time he would let me get physically close. I remember the feel of his flannel shirt against my cheek, the smell of his pipe. This was a big thing to him that we should *love* reading."

Like so many couples of that generation, where the gender roles appeared to be traditionally assigned, the "real power" did not rest with Bernard. "Actually, my mom ran the house and made all of the decisions even though she let my father believe that *he* was the boss." From Jennifer's child's-eye view, Dorothy seemed to relish both her underground power in the family and her overt role as enthusiastic and skilled homemaker. "My mother *loved* being a mother. She loved cooking, baking, sewing the family clothes, creating rituals, and celebrating events." Her sphere of nurturance and intimacy extended beyond her own family. She had a devoted circle of women friends whom she saw almost every day, and whose friendships were deeply sustaining. The women were at the center of the families' social circle. The men to whom they were related were not particularly close to one another, but they managed to get along.

In her work with young mothers, Jennifer seems to want to honor the maternal generosity and underground power that she saw in her mother and the collective strength of the "circle of women" who surrounded her. As a midwife, however, she wants to make the woman's power open and explicit, and she wants the babies' fathers to escape the stereotypic male role and feel included and "essential"; able to feel, and express, the passion of parenting.

"For me," says Jennifer, savoring the memory, "the best thing in the world was to spend a day with my mother." "From these early experiences," she explains, "I lived by the measure of how much I could help someone else. Some of this impulse survives today in my choice of vocation and in the way I often overdo it."

At the same time, Jennifer felt her father's dreams for her.

"Having only daughters, my father believed that we could do anything. He was very ambitious for both of us, and status was very important to him. I was determined to win my father's love, so I went on a path to be smart and I became very successful at school. I was always the top person in my class," she says without an ounce of pridefulness in her voice. If anything, I hear a bit of sadness for having felt such a desperate need to please, such a deep yearning to measure up to her father's expectations in order to win his affection. "There was no institution that I attended," she says flatly, "where I didn't become the valedictorian, and that includes White Fish Bay High School, the University of Chicago, and Columbia."

As Jennifer moved through these high school successes, she was also experiencing an increasing sense of alienation from the conservative and narrow suburban scene. "By the end of high school, I felt so estranged from it all," she muses. "What do you mean 'estranged'?" I ask, wondering how someone who had experienced such success, reward, and achievement might begin to feel like a stranger. "I was wanting to be *found*," she replies. "I would carry Karl Marx's *Communist Manifesto* around the halls of the school because everyone hated it. One of my best friends—who was also the co-valedictorian of my class and went on to Yale—and I joined an integrated book club in downtown Milwaukee. We would go into the city together each week."

All this changed when Jennifer followed her older sister, Bernardine, to the University of Chicago. Suddenly she was caught up "in a time when change seemed limitless; where freedom and dignity for all seemed possible and worth fighting for. It was a time of great drama, learning, experimentation, and politics . . . lots of excesses, as well . . . lots of drugs that held no appeal to me . . . and lots of experimentation around sexuality . . . lots of people didn't make it . . . The second night I was at the University of Chicago, I joined a picket line protesting the return of football to the U. of C. and I never looked back." The seductive pull of politics and radical protest swallowed up both Dohrn sisters and created a chasm between them and their family. Jennifer had not visited home for twenty-five years when she returned with her black husband to a high school reunion, and to her classmates' "silent worries" that Haywood might not be welcome at the country club where the reunion was being held.

By the time Jennifer graduated from college, she was deeply involved in the movement, in demonstrating and organizing, in living the life of political struggle, much of it "underground." Jennifer sketches these years quickly, giving me a sense of her passion and her commitment, but leaving out places, people, and events. She is still fiercely loyal and protective of the memories and of her partners in the struggle.

The Babies Kept Me Going

By the early 1970s Jennifer had moved to New York City, taken a real job, and met Mickey, the man who would become her "partner in the struggle" and the father of her children. Mickey and Jennifer had three babies—a boy and two girls—and life changed dramatically for Jennifer. Although dedication to the political life continued for both of them, "maternal falling in love changes all of that," says Jennifer as she recalls the sudden shift in her priorities and the grief and isolation she felt when Mickey turned his back on parenting their children and loving her.

Just as she was realizing that she would have to raise her children alone, she was also witnessing the deterioration of the political family that she had grown to love and depend upon. "It was a cataclysmically challenging time," remembers Jennifer starkly. "The political community that had surrounded me and inspired me blew up—an explosion that came from both inside and out. These were my closest friends in life. They will be my friends forever. We believed in the dream of dismantling the government and building a new order . . . and then it was all looking so rotten and so questionable." Jennifer's face is creased with pain, but she also wants to remind me of the essential "rightness" of what they were doing and her continued devotion to the values for which they were fighting.

"Maybe we didn't have the right strategies and tools, but we did have the passion and commitment that I still feel and believe in . . . These are the same values I bring to midwifery, the same passion I now bring to empowering women in my work today."

"The three babies kept me going," says Jennifer thankfully. "With the children I couldn't allow myself to get so far out there. They drew me back to everyday reality. I had to *do* their lives. I was breast-feeding the youngest, getting them up in the morning, getting them off to day care." She was trying to bring some coherence and order to her life on the run; to find a safe place in the midst of persistent fear and danger. "My relationship with the children's father was in disarray. I had no money. The people who were living in my apartment and helping with the children moved out suddenly. There would be death threats, and we would have to put our stuff in garbage bags and move in the middle of the night . . . and I had these three little people to feed and care for and love."

When Jennifer works with mothers in the South Bronx—often raising their children alone, in a world still "foul with horrors"—she feels deeply identified with their anguish *and* their fortitude. "I've been there," she says simply. She recognizes the danger and chaos in their lives, but she also believes in their power to overcome and in their capacity to protect and raise their children. Her optimism has a basis in reality. The women are not strangers, they are sisters in the struggle.

When Jennifer was at her lowest point, she began to envision a different life. "I did the Bernard Dohrn thing," she says with a combination of victory and resignation in her voice. "I went to work and went back to school. I raised my three kids." She pauses. "I was leading a path that seemed to have different manifestations from my parents, but I was actually expressing the same values."

"I always saw having babies as a sign of hope," says Jennifer, referring to her own experience of birthing and mothering three children, and her continuing joy in witnessing births as a midwife. When her first child was born, Jennifer delivered him in the hospital. "It was a reasonably good experience with a nice and good doctor," recalls Jennifer, "but I knew that it would be different and a more intimate experience to have my babies at home." So "surrounded by a large circle of friends," she had her second and third children at home. The home deliveries—assisted by a midwife—felt so "right" to Jennifer. "It was so wonderful to have a baby in a peaceful, comfortable, and supportive environment circled by people you loved."

A major attraction of midwifery was that it allowed Jennifer to develop and use "concrete skills." After spending her young adult years organizing, demonstrating, and fighting for human rights, Jennifer wanted to continue the struggle, but also to develop a set of skills and tools that were focused and specific, that allowed her to offer something tangible and positive to the community. "The political culture I was in supported the belief that we should welcome babies into the community."

She knew immediately that midwifery was her "calling," that it was "total, joyful, and embracing." Soon after her own children were born, she began giving childbirth classes in her living room. As her devotion and determination grew, she joined a women's collective, worked under the supervision of a gynecologist, and began assisting in home births. Jennifer loved the work. "When I decided on, and became involved in midwifery, there was no looking back," she says about the sense of mission that consumed her. She struggles to find a way to describe "the amazing fit" that she felt doing the work. "It was like putting on your favorite jewelry," she says, fingering the long, dangling earrings that fall to her shoulders. "You put it on and it feels and looks beautiful."

Jennifer switches to the present tense in order to convey the ways in which she continues to grow and develop in her work. "I am being challenged intellectually, politically, and emotionally." Her work makes her feel deeply grateful, "honored and humbled," and puts all other things in perspective. "Whatever sadness, worry, pain, or grief you bring here, you can go through a labor and everything stops. Time stands still. I am constantly being reminded of what is important."

Time stands still for the families as well. For the miraculous moment of birth on that "high harvest day," they are transported away from the hopelessness, powerlessness, and despair of their lives to an oasis of joy, "where nothing else is important to you." Jennifer describes the transformation. "No matter how brutalized and dumped on these families are, in the moment of birth they feel powerful. The birthing reinforces in the woman how strong she is. She feels reaffirmed. It gives her the strength to confront other battles in her life."

Jennifer also recognizes, however, that part of the experience lies not just in the intensity, but also in the vulnerability of the moment. Although most babies come out whole and healthy, there is always the possibility that mother or child will be in danger, that things will turn out badly. Jennifer feels the twin possibilities of hope and disaster in the birthing. "Death is always lurking. Not every baby comes out perfect." Jennifer is clear about the seriousness of her role. "I am the watch keeper, the guide. I am there to create a boundary of safety. It is an awesome responsibility."

A Vulnerable Time

In order to understand how Jennifer handles these two possibilities, of life and death, hope and despair, I attend several births at the Center. "In every language, it is called 'work,'" says Jennifer. The first labor I witness has already been going on when I arrive early in the morning. At nineteen, Sonia is a petite woman with olive skin and light brown hair pulled back into a ponytail. With a tiny rounded belly and lean limbs, she looks fragile and even younger than her years. Her high voice sounds like a child's wail as she screams out in pain with each contraction. "Mommy, Mommy! I can't take it any more!" Sonia's mother is weepy with worry and weariness. She covers her face with her hands and lets the tears flow. She can't stand to see her daughter in so much anguish, she explains in Spanish, and she is terrified for her safety. Sonia is her firstborn, and she remembers that *her* birth was also long and painful. The birth of her second child—a boy—was quick and easy.

Like most mothers, she would rather be fighting the pain herself than watching her child endure it. She hovers over Sonia, wiping her brow with a damp cloth, caressing her cheeks, whispering soothing words to her, and urging her to sip the ginger tea, a tradition imported from her home in Santo Domingo that she hopes will help reduce the pain.

The ginger tea is the only sign I see of the family's rituals and roots. Although, as Sonia anticipated the birth, the midwives had encouraged her to bring whatever, and whomever, she wanted to the birthing, anything that would make her feel comfortable and celebratory, mother and daughter arrived the night before with only the coats on their backs.

Sonia is wearing a light green hospital johnny over a gray sports bra that she refuses to take off. The bra hides a terrible scar on her right breast, probably the result of being burned badly several years ago. Even in the midst of the worst contractions, she reaches to pull the johnny over her bra, trying to keep the most vulnerable place on her body covered up. Jennifer reads about the scar in her charts, sees Sonia's discomfort with being exposed, feels her tightness and fear throughout the labor, and wonders whether the scar was the result of some early abuse.

Oscar, Sonia's eighteen-year-old boyfriend and father of the baby, hovers silently around the edge of the action seeming a little lost. He has just arrived on the scene, and has not yet found a role for himself. He, too, looks like a kid dressed in sweatpants and sneakers, lost in his big oversized designer jacket. At one point, the sound of a telephone ringing cuts through a momentary silence, and Oscar takes a cellular phone out of his pocket and goes out in the hall to answer it, relieved to have a reason to exit. Jennifer must notice Oscar hanging back, feeling awkward, and looking for something to do. When he returns, she hands him an orange drink with a straw and says, "Oscar, you're in charge of this fluid situation." With that slight directive, Oscar finds his way into the circle of action, takes a spot next to Sonia, kisses the top of her head, and puts the straw up to her lips.

Over the next several hours, I watch Oscar grow right before my eyes. He moves from the edges to the center, from the bearer of liquids to the expectant father, from witness to participant. He is lying next to Sonia on the bed, cradling her head in his arms, massaging her belly, helping her in and out of the Jacuzzi bathtub, encouraging her to push and breathe, offering praise, reassurance, and kisses. Jennifer, ever watchful, reaches out to him with questions and reassurance. When, after helping Sonia through a long and tortuous contraction, Oscar shakes his head and winces with exhaustion, Jennifer says softly, "You never thought it would be like this . . . Making babies is easier, right?" Oscar looks away but nods his assent. "How many children does your mom have?" Jennifer asks, trying to sustain the thin connection. "Two. I'm the youngest," Oscar responds. She tries again. "Oscar, do you think it's a boy too? Everyone else seems to think so." Oscar nods yes. Later Jennifer asks, "Where did you two meet?" "School" is his one-word answer.

As the hours pass, and Oscar becomes more deeply involved, he saves all his energy and intimacy for Sonia. There is no communication with anyone else. He hugs her close and kisses the tears from her eyes; he lies next to her and loops his leg over her thigh to help her hold her legs wide; he constantly rubs her arms and pets her cheeks. As I watch their bodies, they seem to grow into one. Jennifer must see the same merging forms, as she says to Oscar admiringly, "Oscar, your body is going to be imprinted on her . . . Beautiful, you make such a good team." Then she speaks words that I have heard before: "You can imagine how much men missed when they didn't see childbirth. How would you ever know what this was like? There is no way to describe it . . . And it is *so* important that you are here." Jennifer's tone is soothing, supportive, and respectful. She manages to sound wise and experienced, without sounding patronizing. Her voice offers them her strength even as she assures them that they have the power, and the responsibility, to do the birthing.

As I watch Jennifer and listen to her talk with the family, I see the careful and strategic way that she works to empower them. With each move, she delivers a subtle message; one that encourages, supports, and challenges them to do the loving work of birthing, but also one that offers them her expertise and reassurance. For example, she often leaves the room—when she knows they are safe, but when *they* think they need her presence—in order to persuade them that they have the skills, strength, and resources to do it themselves. Or she stands way back from the bed or even crouches in the corner, allowing her to watch and witness the labor, but creating a space and distance for the family to do the work. She is constantly asking Sonia for reports on her status: how she is feeling, the state of her progress, and what she needs and wants to do. "Tell me what you're feeling," says Jennifer gently. "It hurts!" Sonia snaps back. "Can you be a bit more specific?" Jennifer presses. "No!" Sonia cries out.

This balancing act—of close involvement and strategic detachment—is particularly difficult with Sonia and her family because Jennifer does not know them. Although they have come to the Childbearing Center throughout the pregnancy, Jennifer has never seen them in the clinic, so she is at some disadvantage in not knowing their history, the cast of characters, the nature of their relationships, their places of vulnerability and sources of strength. I watch Jennifer get acquainted quickly. She learns, for instance, that Sonia is reluctant and apprehensive, and that her reticence gets expressed in cycles of dependency and resistance, in refusing to take initiative. So at first Jennifer is more directive and protective than usual, and spends a good deal of energy offering soft assurances and vigorous encouragement. She learns that Sonia "hates" to have vaginal exams, so she keeps them to a safe minimum, helps her anticipate when she will need to do them, and examines her gingerly and gently. Each time she does the vaginal exam, she first lets Sonia listen to the baby's heartbeat, holding the microphone on her lower abdomen. The strong steady beat fills the room. "Hello baby," croons Jennifer. "This baby is wonderful!" Then, with her rubber gloves on, she steadies her right hand on Sonia's knee and enters with her left. "Real gentle now," she says as Sonia screams and arches her back. "Open your legs . . . let it relax . . . stay with me here."

The hours pass without much progress. Sonia stretches out in the Jacuzzi, screaming. She lies on her side with a pillow between her legs, screaming. She squats beside the bed with her head on a pillow, screaming. She stands with great difficulty, and takes tiny steps, screaming. Before each move, Jennifer approaches the bed, sprawls on the edge of it, reaches out to touch Sonia, and speaks words of encouragement. "It'll be much better if you can change your position . . . Each thing seems big, but you're doing it." And with each position change, Sonia's mother echoes Jennifer's directions in Spanish, cheers her on, and presses cool, wet clothes on her cheeks and brow. Oscar follows by Sonia's side, finding a position that always allows them to stay close.

At one point, Jennifer goes to the birthing room next door, where a seventeen-year-old woman, who has just delivered a healthy eight-pound, seven-ounce boy during the night, is chatting away happily with a large circle of family and friends. There are three toddlers in strollers (two of them birthed at the Center), an elderly great-grandmother, grandmother, and mother, and several friends "skipping school." It feels like a party as we walk in, far from the difficult drama next door. There is pulsating Latin music, platters of food, and loud conversation, all in Spanish. After taking a turn holding and admiring the new baby, Jennifer asks if she can carry him next door to show Sonia. She hopes that this beautiful sight will help Sonia to feel encouraged and hopeful. But Sonia barely opens her eyes to look at the baby when Jennifer brings him in. "I still can't stand it," she squeals.

As the hours pass, Jennifer carefully watches, waits, and monitors the progress. She is alert to Sonia's state of mind, to the productivity of the labor, to the frequency and length of the contractions, to the dilation of the cervix, to the position, movement, and heartbeat of the baby, and to the energy and optimism of the family "team." She watches the clock and calculates the next move. At one point she asks one of Sonia's friends who has arrived on the scene to give Sonia some honey for increased energy and to stimulate her nipples in order to strengthen the contractions. Later on, Jennifer decides to break the water. She can see that Sonia is "beginning to lose it," and she wants to "move the process along" before she begins to give up. "I'd like to break your water," she says to Sonia. "It won't hurt, you'll just feel pressure. But I have to break it when you're feeling the most pain . . . so you'll have to work with me, all right?" At another point, Jennifer decides to give her a mild medication. She shoots the needle in Sonia's buttock and hopes that the medication will relieve the pain, but not slow the labor. "This will not make the pain go away," Jennifer warns. "It will just make it a little easier so that you can rest in between . . . and Mama can too. It should be working in a second. Close your eyes and get some rest."

By early afternoon, there *is* noticeable progress, and things look much more promising. The contractions come more frequently and last longer, and Sonia grows with them. She whines and screams less, and breathes and pushes more. She listens to Jennifer's suggestions and tries to follow them with all her might. When the time seems close, Jennifer does another vaginal exam, and hopes to pull the baby out. "Nice and loose," she says. "It's getting there. A little push on the baby . . . more, more, more." Sonia pushes and grunts, pushes and grunts. They are beginning to work together, a synchrony of movement. Little Sonia is beginning to look like a woman. As the momentum builds, Jennifer stops her with an explanation. "Let me explain for one second. When you push, I want you to hold it. Take a deep breath, hands under your legs, push way into your bottom. It's a very strange feeling . . . You're doing wonderfully." After intervals of rest, changes of position, and more contractions, Jennifer tries again. So close.

By three o'clock, Jennifer shows signs of weariness and concern. She had expected this baby to arrive a couple of hours ago; she can feel that the baby's position makes it hard for Sonia to push it out; and she can see that the labor has become unproductive and too difficult to sustain. Just as Sonia screams, "I can't stand it any more! . . . I want a C-section. I want this thing out. Now!," Jennifer moves to the next step. She decides to call in one of her colleagues for a consultation. Deborah, an experienced midwife—who has worked at the Center for only two years, but spent several years delivering babies in the mountains of El Salvador—arrives, does another vaginal exam, and feels the same things that Jennifer felt. "Mommy! Mommy!" bellows Sonia. "I want to go to the hospital! I can't take it any more!"

Deborah and Jennifer leave the room, and a sad silence settles over all of us. This is a defeat, and we all know it. Just as I have felt my body tightening and pushing as I watched Sonia's contractions, now I feel the sting of deep disappointment and the tears coming down my face. Sonia's mother falls across the bed and buries her head in the blanket. Oscar closes his eyes and hugs Sonia close. Sonia lets out a long, shrill cry that seems to last forever. I have watched the choreography and emotion of this event; the resistant little girl who turned into a determined woman; the sullen boy who became a nourishing mate; the protective mother who watched her children grow close and take responsibility. I now know what Jennifer means when she speaks about the growth and empowerment that accompanies labor; but I also know what she means when she talks about the possibility of danger, the "awesome responsibility."

Jennifer returns with the news, and it is not surprising. She delivers it first in Spanish, then English. It sounds devastating and relieving in both languages. First, she wants them to know that the baby is *fine*. The problem is with the position of the baby. Despite all the "beautiful and hard laboring," the cervix hasn't changed in the last hour and a half, and the baby has not moved. She fears that Sonia is getting too tired, and that the baby will also become stressed if it is pushed around much more. "So you must go to the hospital," says Jennifer with a matter-of-fact tone that barely hides her own weariness and sadness. "They will be able to give you the medicine that will help the contractions and push this baby out." But everyone is thinking what she does not say. If the medications don't work, the baby will have to be delivered by cesarean section.

Within minutes, Jennifer has called Bronx Lebanon Hospital, spoken to the attending physician on the obstetrics unit, and arranged for an ambulance to carry Sonia to the hospital. The ambulance arrives almost immediately. Two male attendants (one of whom knows Jennifer because she was the midwife for his baby daughter's birth a year ago) carry Sonia out on a stretcher, and Jennifer rides along with the family to the hospital. She returns a couple of hours later—having gotten Sonia settled in her room, consoled and reassured the family, spoken with the obstetrician and the nurses, and filled out all of the hospital transfer forms—looking dejected and totally spent. Even though she has been through this before, transfers of women to the hospital are unusual (15 percent of the birthings at the Center are not successfully completed there), and they always leave her feeling depleted. We sit in the staff room together and give in to our disappointment.

"This was a hard one," sighs Jennifer, " a very hard one . . . But I know we made the right move. It is always hard to release them to the hospital." As she talks, I realize why she is feeling particular anguish "releasing" Sonia to the hospital's care. "As soon as we arrived at the hospital, Sonia's mother totally lost it. She started screaming and yelling; a loud, Latin fury . . . Then she passed out." The mother who had shown so much strength and stamina could no longer sustain herself or be there for her daughter. Then Jennifer describes the "worst part." "They made Sonia take off that gray sports bra. She tried to refuse but they made her . . . and she felt so exposed, so violated. The whole time she was here, we allowed her to keep it on. It was like she was holding on to the last remnant of her dignity."

After a while, Jennifer pulls herself out of her slump, and sits up tall in her chair. Her face is a mixture of resolve and determination as she reframes the event so that we will not linger on the sadness. "It is good to have these experiences from time to time," she muses. "They are painful and difficult, but they are also humbling. They remind us that *nature* is the powerful force. We are not in total control." Somehow, Jennifer's recognition of, and respect for, the limits of her power—*and* the limits of her capacity to empower Sonia—allow her to feel the hope, strength, and reverence that she needs for the next labor.

Boundaries

The "boundary" that Jennifer creates for the safety of the mother and baby is also an essential *line* that she draws for her own balance and self-protection. I ask her how she manages to sustain herself in the face of the suffering that she sees in the families she serves. "It is always a question of how to respect their pain without taking it in. If you just take in pain, you become the pain. You become paralyzed and powerless. So I give them the space, my full attention, and I listen. I acknowledge that I hear them even though I don't always have solutions. Sometimes that is all I can do."

Even though Jennifer's sense of "professionalism" and her need for self-protection help her establish "boundaries," she admits that the boundaries are negotiable, reflecting the nature of the relationship that she develops with each person. They are defined, as well, by *Jennifer's* vulnerability and needs. In order to explain the mutuality that is central to both boundaries and relationships, Jennifer recalls her neediest moments after Haywood's death when she was feeling excruciating pain and loss. "I was facing my husband's death and grieving. I thought that I couldn't burden the women with my anguish. But I soon realized that I am a *person*, and I began to follow my intuitions, which meant that I was able to share my grief with some of them, quite naturally, spontaneously, and meaningfully. This is possible because you have a *relationship*. And they were able to give back understanding and solace."

Jennifer is reminded of the collision of two life and death stories. Soon after Haywood died, Jennifer was the midwife for Tasha, a woman whose partner had been killed before she even knew that she was pregnant. "Tasha knew that my husband had just been killed, so she knew that I would be there for her," says Jennifer, recalling the intimacy brought on by their shared grief. The baby was big, the labor long, and the delivery intense and difficult. In the passion of the moment, the ghosts of the deceased arrived in the birthing room. Jennifer's voice still sounds haunted. "In the midst of it all, we began to feel the presence of Tasha's deceased partner.

He was there with us in witness and love, hovering. Then I began to feel Haywood's presence, soothing and supportive. We were all there . . . and I was so tense with the incredible responsibility. It turned out to be a fabulous birth."

Even though the work of midwifery is intensely relational and requires that Jennifer respond to "the whole person—bringing the physical, emotional, and spiritual into a balanced harmony," the "professional" boundaries that Jennifer draws have become clearer as she has matured in her work. When I ask her how she manages to recover her strength and sustain herself while responding so fully and also setting firm boundaries, her response is tentative, as if she is beginning to explore new territory. First, she refers to the shift in her survival strategies brought on by Haywood's death. "People who work in the caring professions have to have a support system," she begins. "My support system has had to change since Haywood's death. Haywood always said that he was married to a firefighter. When he was alive, as soon as the baby was born, I'd leave the room, take off my rubber gloves, and call him to tell him that the baby and mother were safe. That was part of the ritual that we worked out between us, and it helped to sustain me."

Since Haywood's death, Jennifer has come to rely more heavily on a wonderful circle of women friends. She has also become more deeply immersed in the practice of meditation. Every morning she meditates in the stillness of her newly created room on the third floor of her home, where she lets the sun bathe her face, looks out at the treetops, and gains strength. This "centering" helps to anchor her before her intense workday. It also reminds her of the limits of her power and responsibility. "Like all meaningful relationships," she muses, "the relationships I have in my work as a midwife are defined by compassionate caring. But more and more I've come to believe that I can *listen*, but people are responsible for their own lives."

Jennifer's recognition of the limits of her responsibility came with the awakening of her own spirituality. "I respect passages, rituals, and how people see their own religious and cultural beliefs . . .

how they deal with birth and death." This side of Jennifer was not easily expressed in her political work or community organizing. "Midwifery allows this part of me to find form and flourish."

Studying and practicing Buddhism has helped to balance the frenzy and chaos of Jennifer's life, provided an arena for self-exploration, and brought solace and healing. I can hardly believe it when this woman—whose face expresses a peacefulness, and whose eyes seem to be clear and calm—admits that she suffered from violent migraine headaches all her life. When, in 1990, the piercing pain of the migraines got to be unbearable, she thought that she might have a brain tumor, and—with terror in her heart—took herself to a neurosurgeon. She smiles at the memory of the doctor's rare angle of vision and his healing insight. "I think he must have been a closet Buddhist. He said instead of looking at the migraines as 'the enemy,' that I should think of them as a kind of 'gift,' a finely tuned mechanism that helps my body tell when it has taken in too much pain." If she would think of the migraines in that way, he thought, they would help her in her work. "He said that I should give my utmost . . . problem-solving, empathizing, listening . . . but then I should take a deep breath when the woman leaves . . . let it out and let it go. The problems must go out the door with her."

The neurosurgeon's counsel not only helped Jennifer see her migraines as useful warnings, but also helped her find ways to limit the depth of her involvement while still remaining fully engaged. "I have begun a process of learning the extent of my own limitations. This is wonderfully healthy. You can give to others in a very full way and still have integrity about your own self. I think this balance is especially hard for people working on the front line." Jennifer admits that, even with the help of medication and limit setting, the migraines occasionally reappear. Her forehead creases, her eyes squeeze into slits as she says, "We all have ways that our bodies express our psychic pain."

Another reason that Jennifer must draw boundaries and set limits has to do with protecting the Center for the benefit of the whole community. For instance, by law, the clinic is prohibited from birthing a child when there has been no history of prenatal care. There are medical dangers in taking on a birth without having an ongoing relationship with the mother, and knowledge of a mother's history. To do so would threaten the work of the Center. Defining such limits for the protection of an institution may seem to conflict, however, with responding compassionately to the needs of an individual. "Ever since we opened our doors, we have worried about what we'd do if a woman addicted to crack showed up at our door. For eight years this never happened."

One morning, however, the situation she feared became real. "The woman on crack is standing there at the door, and I immediately want to call 911 to get her transferred to the hospital. But Nancy, the other midwife, takes her into the birthing room and we begin a big argument about whether she should stay or go. Nancy's pulling her pants down; I'm pulling them back up. We're locked in this struggle—down then up, down then up. Ultimately, of course, the woman wins. She pushes, the water breaks, she begins birthing the baby. We have no choice but to participate. And out comes a perfectly healthy baby." After the birth, however, Jennifer insists that the mother and baby be taken by an ambulance to the nearest hospital. She insists, not because she is worried about the fate of the mother or the health of the baby, but because she wants to protect the Center as a community resource; she doesn't want to threaten their ability to give service to the "community of women." Jennifer's voice expresses no ambivalence on this point. The boundaries are clear. "I'm saying to the woman, 'You can't stay here because it is not safe. We don't know you.' And I'm saying to myself, 'This is for the safety of the community. As professionals, we'll complete our protocol, but then you must go.'"

Jennifer knows that she has done the right thing for the woman and for the community, but she admits to contrary impulses that made her want to take this woman in and save her. She shakes her head wearily. "People get to me. Yes, I won't let her get to me in a way that would endanger the work in the community. But if I get too mechanical, I will have lost it. I must never shut down because

I've heard too much pain." She thinks over her ten years of creating and growing the Center, of serving, nursing, and empowering the community of women, and she recognizes that experience and maturity have helped her draw clearer boundaries, both personal and institutional. But she also realizes—and hopes—that her instincts for compassion and care will never diminish. "We are always vulnerable and we *should* be vulnerable to individual women."

Birth

The time is drawing close. It is 9:50 in the evening, and Nadia has been at the Childbearing Center since 4:00 in the afternoon, when she arrived nauseous, exhausted, and ready to deliver her second child. Her cervix is 8 cm. dilated and she is lying still in the bed, her head supported by several large pillows, arms outstretched to either side, her legs bent at the knees and spread wide. She is making short and deep rhythmic grunting sounds. The Center has an eerie nighttime emptiness. The janitor is mopping up the hallway floors, and lights are out in the reception area and clinic offices. The birthing room, filled with intense light, feels strangely quiet and airless. Nadia, at twenty-three, looks pale and drained, but amazingly strong. Her long black hair is pulled back in a ponytail. Her gray eyes, which seem to take in everything around her, are the only signs of expression on her preoccupied face. From beneath the white sheets and blankets, I see her toenails peeking out. They are painted bright orange.

Tony, Nadia's partner, is sitting in the big leather chair in the corner, his legs stretched out, his feet resting on the hassock, and earphones on his head. He is listening to a "Christian station" with the volume turned up so loud that I can hear the cadence of the sermon—in Spanish—several feet away. A year older than Nadia, he is brown-skinned, lean, and handsome, dressed in shorts, a red shirt, and sneakers. Both Nadia and Tony are from Honduras, having arrived in New York with their families several years ago. They had, in fact, known each other when they were in school in

Honduras, but they met again years later in the South Bronx and "hooked up." Tony's English, full of Bronx slang, is better than Nadia's, but both still feel most comfortable speaking Spanish. Tony arrived at the Center an hour ago, three hours into Nadia's labor and five hours after she walked in the door alone. His earphones keep him from hearing her steady grunting; his eyes never look over at her in the bed.

Jennifer, dressed in hospital blues, is being assisted by Shelly, a large, gentle black woman who seems to know the routine and Jennifer's rhythms so well that there is little need for conversation between them. Jennifer puts the fetal monitor on Nadia's abdomen, and the baby's heart sounds cut through the quiet. "Good baby," croons Jennifer. Then, speaking Spanish, she checks with Nadia on the pressure and the contractions, asks her to breathe deeply, and does a vaginal exam. "Beautiful, Nadia, beautiful," Jennifer exclaims in English. She can feel the baby's head covered with "lots of hair."

Now Jennifer looks over at Tony, who is still underneath his headphones. He is biting his nails, then cracking his knuckles, tense and anxious. When she catches his eye, she motions to him. "Tony, come to the bed," she says, trying to force some contact with Nadia. He takes off his earphones, rises slowly, and perches himself awkwardly on the edge of the bed. At first he doesn't touch Nadia, but with encouragement from Jennifer, he finally slides his hand over the sheet and holds her wrist. Still no eye contact. Nadia continues her grunting, her body still, her eyes focused straight ahead.

The next time Jennifer does the vaginal exam, she breaks the bag of waters and announces that the fluid is "nice and clear." "That is what we want," she explains. For the first time, Tony speaks, asking whether the baby will be coming soon. Jennifer reassures him that everything is going smoothly, the baby is on the way, and that Nadia is doing an "amazing job." As if on cue, Shelly helps Jennifer on with her long white plastic coat, changes the pads on the bed, which have become bloodied, and rolls up the cart of sterilized instruments. At 10:05 P.M., Jennifer peels off a layer of bloodied gloves and exposes another clean pair underneath. "Beautiful baby you have here," she says as she checks the baby's heartbeat again. Now there is a crescendo in the noises Nadia is making, higher and shriller, but still contained. The rhythm of her labor sounds are in duet with Jennifer's soothing, calm reassurance. *"Suavé, suavé . . . Bien, bien . . . Perfecto."* Her words seem to sing a lullaby.

Then turning to Tony, she asks, "Are you okay?" "Yeah, I'm okay," he responds, shrugging his shoulders, but looking worried. Jennifer works to draw him in with an instruction. "You could be helpful with holding her legs." He responds to the letter (but not the spirit) of the instruction, grabs Nadia's knee and holds her left leg open, but doesn't let his body touch hers. Now with Shelly on Nadia's other side, both of her legs are being held back, and Jennifer bends down and cups both of her hands around the opening. Through the circle of her hands, I can see the top of the baby's head. "Beautiful. *Perfecto*. Look at that beautiful head . . . Nadia, you're so strong," Jennifer exclaims.

Time stands still. The next moves feel to me like pure grace. Nadia is now pushing hard. Tony and Shelly hold tightly to her legs. Jennifer helps the baby's head move through Nadia's vaginal opening, and lets us know what is happening. "The baby's turning its head to get out more easily . . . moving and maneuvering its way out . . . working with us." She continues to sing her support, *"Bien, bien, bien . . .* So good." Still holding Nadia's leg open, Shelly puts the fetal monitor on Nadia's abdomen one last time. *"Mas, mas . . . Respira,"* Jennifer urges, and Nadia discovers even more power within her. Hard, painful, sustained pushing. No wincing, no whining, no resistance. "Beautiful. *Perfecto*," croons Jennifer. One last push—at 10:16 P.M.—and Jennifer announces, "Here it comes!" First the head, next—in one smooth, graceful movement—the baby's shoulders turn and slip past the opening; finally the whole perfect body arrives wriggling with life.

"A boy! A boy!" screams Tony as Jennifer puts the wet baby—the umbilical cord still joining them—up on his mother's chest. Then we hear the blessed baby cries, a whispered whimper followed by welcome wailing. A smile spreads across Nadia's face as she clutches her son to her breast. "I'm so tired," she says with relief, letting herself let go for the first time. "A boy!" exclaims Tony again, his eyes on fire. Jennifer puts a blanket over the baby and kisses Mama. "What a wonderful woman you are. I'm so proud of you! Nadia, you are *amazing*. So strong and *dignified*." "Thank you," says Nadia shyly. Jennifer tries again: "Tony, give her a kiss. Nadia *deserves* a kiss." Dutifully, Tony reaches down and kisses her once on the cheek. Both of them blush. Then the new parents look down and fill their eyes with their new child.

Finally, Jennifer gives Tony a job that he clearly relishes. Following her direction, he puts on rubber gloves and carefully cuts the cord. "Your papa is cutting you free!" Jennifer exclaims to the baby as the first tears roll down Papa's face. He quickly wipes them away, but remains transfixed as Jennifer takes the baby off his mother's chest, wraps him in a clean blanket, and puts him in his father's arms. A few moments later—as Jennifer massages Nadia's abdomen to help the last contractions release the placenta—Tony is standing several feet away with his back to the activity, smiling at his son, who is resting peacefully in his arms. "How's the baby?" asks Jennifer after a while. "Beautiful," says Tony softly. "I think you may never see those men of yours again," jokes Jennifer to Nadia. "They're totally in love."

I walk over toward the father and son. For a brief moment, Tony takes his eyes off the baby and looks up at me. (Actually, he seems to look *through* me.) His voice is dreamy and the tears return. "Wow! She was so strong, so powerful. I've never seen anything like this... Nadia was so good." His words ring with admiration. He has witnessed the force and passion of his woman. He now knows—in a way he may not have understood before—that his son has an amazing mother.

CHAPTER TWO

Healing

I say more: the just man justices;
     Keeps grace: that keeps all his goings graces;
Acts in God's eye what in God's eye he is—
     Christ. For Christ plays in ten thousand places,
Lovely in limbs, and lovely in eyes not his
     To see Father through the features of men's faces.

—Gerard Manley Hopkins,
  "As Kingfishers Catch Fire,
  Dragonflies Draw Flame"

R espect is not something one can imitate, but something one must embody. While we might say that a person has a disposition to act with respect, it is only in the individual acts of respect that the quality becomes actual. "Respect" as an integral aspect of life, both personal and social, is maintained by the respectful acts of individuals. Both individually and collectively, we are entrusted with the responsibility of preserving respect. When Hopkins says the "just man justices," the unfamiliarity of "justices" as a verb attracts our attention, while to say the "respectful man respects" may seem deceptively obvious. Some lives, however, remind us that respect is a verb.

Johnye Ballenger is in action, a woman on the move. Even when she is still, her face is in motion; grinning, frowning, scowling, exclaiming. Her talk is punctuated by laughter and shrieks as she pokes fun at herself and at the humor and absurdity in the world she inhabits. Her high energy is infectious, fueling the drama that she creates around her. Johnye's round face is framed by short brown curly hair. In her flat, no-nonsense shoes, she stands tall even though she is probably only five feet four inches. Everything about her—her smooth, light-brown skin, her physicality, and her dancing temperament—makes her seem younger than her forty-eight years.

It is through her acts, her gestures, and her energy that Dr. Johnye Ballenger, a pediatrician, communicates respect for her young patients and their families. She practices respect through practicing medicine. Her respect is embedded in action, not in after-the-fact interpretation or analysis. As a matter of fact, Johnye seems a little impatient with all the *talk* about respect that our conversations seem to demand, or the elaborate discussion that is inevitably part of the clinical teaching and mentoring that she does with her pediatric residents. As with many clinicians or activists her actions are more nuanced and complex than her talk; and she seems to worry that too much scrutiny might, in fact, distort her purpose, disturb her timing, or interfere with her pace. The best place to see Johnye Ballenger in action is at the South End Health Center in Boston, where one afternoon a week she delivers respectful care to her patients, who are mostly brown, black, and poor.

Acts of Care

It is April third, two days after a huge April Fool's snowstorm. The snow is melting in the 60-degree sunny day, making rivers of muddy water in the streets. I dodge the snowdrifts and the water currents, and make my way over to the South End Health Center. The street is quiet today, a sharp contrast to the hustle and bustle that greets me inside the Health Center. The waiting room is crowded but welcoming, with bright colors and lots of light. Mothers and children are perched on chairs waiting for their appointments or being called into examining rooms with huge numbers written on the doors. Nurses and technicians in white coats, and doctors mostly in street clothes, are moving around calmly and efficiently. "Good people work here and many have been around for a long time," says Johnye later, when she is describing the unusual commitment, care, and intimacy found in the Center.

Across the room, I spot Johnye waving and beckoning me in her direction. Inez, the nurse with whom she works, sizes me up with a smile. "Have you taken your stimulants today? Are you wearing your running shoes?" She knows that following Johnye Ballenger's tracks will require energy and speed.

In the Center, Johnye works with children and families in an environment that is not as precious or as privileged as that of her private practice across the river—and worlds apart—in Cambridge. The South End Health Center is a community health center and Johnye sees as many patients as can be crowded into her afternoon schedule. At least eighty-five percent of the families who walk through the doors are Latino and the rest are black, white, or Asian. All five families that I observe with Johnye are Puerto Rican; more than half (including mothers and children) do not speak any English. Johnye admits that her Spanish—all of which she has learned either on the job or listening to Spanish language tapes—is "bad" (*"muy malo"*) but she communicates very well and with a lot of flourish. Her mobile face, her expressive hands, and her unself-conscious attitude serve her well, and are clearly appreciated by the patients. After an appointment with a non-English-speaking mother who has brought along her daughter to translate, Johnye comments on the way their common struggle with each other's language seems to be a great equalizer. "I can speak bad Spanish . . . She can speak bad English . . . and somehow we are even."

Dr. Ballenger's first patient is a lovely ten-year-old light-brown-skinned girl with green eyes whose name is Rosa Martinez. She has come complaining of a painful throat that has kept her up the whole night and that hurts even when she is "just sipping a Sprite." She is accompanied by her mother—a lean, elegant woman dressed in black; her five-year-old brother Juan, who is very large and outgoing for his age and manages to capture most of the doctor's attention; and an eight-month-old baby sister, who sits attentively and happily on her mother's lap. The family has traveled all the way from Revere for this appointment, a forty-five-minute trip on the train and the bus. Although Rosa is the only child with an ailment, the visit—like all the others I witness that afternoon—is a family affair, and Johnye manages to give every family member some attention.

"How may I help today?" begins Johnye. Mrs. Martinez, who speaks fluid English, describes Rosa's symptoms, allowing her daughter to add the details. "Did you take her temperature at home?" asks Johnye as she puts a thermometer in the girl's mouth and gently strokes her cheeks. "Is anyone else at home sick?" "I have cavities," announces Juan in a big, look-at-me voice. Johnye's attention shifts as she turns toward Juan and inquires with a voice volume that matches his, "Who told you so?" She leaps up quickly and gets the flashlight. "Open your mouth. Let me look at you." In fact, she does find a gaping cavity, and warns Juan's mother that he will need to be taken to the dentistry clinic. "How many times do you brush your teeth each day?" asks Johnye. "Five times a day," says Juan holding up five stubby fingers. "Does he brush his teeth five times a day, Mother?" the doctor asks skeptically, raising her eyebrows. "Well," admits Mrs. Martinez, "he brushes about two or three times. He's pretty good about it." "Excellent!" beams the doctor. Then turning toward Rosa again, she takes the thermometer out of her mouth. "You don't have a fever, darling. Open, please, say 'ah,'" says Johnye to Rosa as she sticks a tongue depressor in her mouth. "It hurts too much," replies Rosa opening her mouth only slightly, then widening it after gentle urging and encouragement. Johnye finds a "real swelling" that will require heavy doses of antibiotics.

Watching Johnye attend to this family is like watching a juggler balancing many balls. She is amazingly adept at shifting her attention, concentrating fully, and going with the flow. At the health center, where she almost always sees a mother and several children when only one child is actually coming for her attention, Johnye seems to see her role as responding to all members of the family. Whether it is cooing at the baby sister and admiring her soft brown eyes, or offering empathic support to the mother who has been up all night with a sick child, or responding to brother Juan when he shows her an injury on his hand. "Would you like a band-aid for that?" asks Johnye, looking for one in her desk. When she pulls an "ordinary" one out of her drawer, Juan asks, "Do you have a Power Ranger one?" "Not here but I'll check with the nurses outside," she promises. And true to her promise, before the family leaves the building Johnye has searched several examining rooms and tracked down the coveted band-aids. Johnye seems to know that illness is a family affair; that if one member of the family is sick, the others will be affected and may feel even more needy for the doctor's attention and care.

Each time Johnye shifts her attention, she looks directly into the eyes of the child or adult to whom she is speaking. If the child is gazing at the floor or otherwise distracted, she insists—firmly but gently—that she look at her and that she respond. Occasionally, Johnye will hold the child's face between both of her hands in an effort to grab her attention. She will tip her chin back so that their eyes can meet. Johnye also insists that her young patients be polite and deferential; several times I hear her direct the children to say "please" or "thank you" to their mothers. She waits for the appropriate response, and then follows with words of praise for their good manners. Her insistence on civility—the good old-fashioned kind—never feels overly stern, but it does feel didactic. She is clearly trying to teach respect in these interactions, and she does it with both earnestness and humor.

As soon as Johnye discovers the severity of the swelling in Rosa's throat, she asks Mrs. Martinez to come back the next day for a reexamination and another intravenous dose of the antibiotic. "It really is quite swollen," she explains. "I would feel much more comfortable with her getting a dose directly rather than just taking it by mouth." (She chooses her words carefully in order to avoid giving Rosa—and her ever attentive brother Juan—a graphic description of the scary intravenous "needle" that she is prescribing.) But before she completes her thought, Johnye is interrupting herself and asking the mother where she lives. When the mother replies "Revere," Johnye exclaims, "Oh, Lord! Well you can't come all this way tomorrow. What is the hospital ER which might be closest to you?" (The Martinezes used to live in the South End close to the health center but they have recently moved to Revere.) The doctor and mother settle on trying to get Rosa seen the next day at the emergency room at the Floating Hospital for a followup. For the first time Rosa perks up, laughs, and asks, "The Floating Hospital, does it go swimming?" Johnye is already dialing the telephone to arrange an appointment for the following day. While she is put on hold, she begins to explain to Rosa why the hospital is called the Floating Hospital. She weaves a fabulous story that she ends up telling to the hospital operator as well. "I'm here explaining to my young friend why your hospital is called the Floating Hospital," says Johnye before finishing her elaborate explanation and asking to be connected to the physician in charge of the emergency room.

For the next ten minutes she is on the phone, first trying to track down the right hospital unit, then trying to speak to the right person, then endeavoring to convince the attending physician that she should see Rosa and give her the appropriate medicine in the appropriate way. Of course, I can hear only Johnye's half of the conversation, but I am amazed by how much time this transaction takes and by how much energy, strategy, patience, and charm Johnye has to use to get this relatively simple procedure accomplished. I sit there thinking to myself how difficult it would be for almost any parent—no matter how assertive or savvy—to negotiate this appointment successfully for her child, without Johnye as a guide and advocate.

After holding . . . and holding . . . finally someone picks up the phone in the ER at the Floating Hospital. "I'm holding to speak to Dr. Granger," says Johnye patiently. When Dr. Granger comes on the line, Johnye begins what she hopes will be a short exchange. "I have a ten-year-old girl here." Her language switches to medical terminology as she describes her diagnosis of the child's ailment and what she thinks the treatment might be. Then she gets to the point. "You see, the family lives in Revere and I would like to make them not have to travel all the way back to the South End tomorrow if you might be able to see them. I think it is going to need attention. It may get worse before it gets better." Dr. Granger seems to have lots of questions and maybe some resistance, because Johnye is forced to repeat her appeal several times, offer a defense for her diagnosis, and be lavish in her appreciation of the doctor's help. "No, it's not dramatic . . . it is just beginning . . . yes, a healthy host . . . yes, amoxicillin . . . no, she's not allergic to anything . . . yes, that would be fine. Does that make sense to you? . . . You know I'm trying to save the family from traveling all that distance. They had a tough night last night. Yes, she has two other children. You know she has been shlepping three young children through all this snow."

The conversation goes on and on. Johnye's advocacy is steady, her tone conciliatory, but underneath I imagine that she is feeling angry and frustrated. "Why should this be so hard?" she exclaims out loud to no one in particular after she hangs up the phone and wipes the sweat from her brow. Her voice rises in exasperation as she says to Mrs. Martinez in mock humor, "I don't know that I like that ER person . . . She just doesn't seem to want to *get* it. But we've now spoken to her and accomplished something, I hope." Now she is punching the air. "Bang! Bang! Bang! How many times can you say it?" laughs Johnye, describing the exasperating dialogue. Mrs. Martinez smiles shyly, appreciating Johnye's persistent, strong advocacy, and her surprising playfulness.

The scene is quintessential Dr. Ballenger. With almost every appointment I observe, I watch her pave the way for her patient to get further care. She is an activist as she picks up the phone in the midst of the appointment and makes contact with the doctor to whom she is referring her patient. She is a strategist and a charmer as she dodges her way through the barriers that the bureaucracy places in her path. She is conciliatory and deferential as she tries to negotiate with her physician colleagues for their help, attention, and resources. Then, like Jennifer Dohrn, she works to empower her patients as she tries to prepare them for what they can expect to encounter and cheers them on. "You're strong. I believe in you. I know that you can tell them what you need," she encourages Mrs. Martinez.

After each appointment, Johnye moves to the next examining room, where the next family is waiting with their ailment and their story. She always begins by introducing herself, getting the name of the patient, and then asking, "How may I help you today?" Waiting in the next room is the mother of a family of three who has brought along her ten-year-old daughter to translate. The eight-year-old boy perched on the examining table is complaining of a terrible earache. Johnye looks in the right ear and sees a clear channel, but notices a blockage in the left one. "Did you put anything in your ear?" she asks José. "No Q-tips, *por favor.*" She leaves the office briefly to fetch a pair of tweezers. While she is gone the mother and sister grill José in Spanish about what he might have put in his ear, and the truth comes out. When Johnye returns, the sister tells her the story. "He said that when we were all sleeping he went into the bathroom, took a Q-tip, and cleaned out his ear." The sister's voice is filled with drama and urgency. "He did it without permission!" she exclaims as her mother nods in vigorous assent. "Okay," says Johnye, "that's fine. Just lie down on the table so I can get a better look at it." The sister's voice cuts in again, "He did it without permission!" Johnye is holding the boy's head steady and peering and poking in the left ear. Finally, very carefully with her tweezers she goes in, retrieves a large wad of cotton, and holds it up for all of our inspection. "Oh, my God!" screams his mother in the first words of English she has spoken during the appointment. "And he did it without permission!" repeats the older sister for the third time. "Don't do that again," says Johnye firmly and quietly. "Do you feel any more pain in the ear?" "No," José responds, leaping off the examining table and looking very much relieved. We are all smiling as the family departs, all feeling the satisfaction of the simple, relatively painless procedure that has made everything better. As Johnye scribbles on the medical chart ("foreign body left ear canal") she exclaims to me, "These are the easy ones . . . all done with a pair of tweezers. But it makes *me* feel so good."

In a conversation several days later I ask Johnye to talk about the blur of activity I saw at the Health Center. She begins by reminding me that a pediatrician's work is always with families, not just with the child who is ill. So as she attends to the sick child, she says to the sibling, "Yes darling, I see you too," or she communicates to the mother that she understands how hard it is to cope when you haven't been able to get a decent night's sleep, or she plants a kiss on the chubby cheeks of the baby sitting in her mother's arms. "I want to convey to them that I appreciate their coming and I'm glad that they are there."

Oftentimes during a family's visit, Johnye becomes the teacher. "Civility and manners" are very important to her, and she can't stand to hear children being disrespectful to their parents. "I can't help it. I hear voices in my head from home," she explains as a way of describing her "passion" about "teaching manners" to kids. At the same time, she recognizes that she must be circumspect in front of the parents; that they might feel embarrassed by her intervention. "It is a very delicate process. I must be very gentle and courteous in my admonitions when I correct their behavior because parents know this is something that they should be doing. So I say to the children, very solicitously, 'Darling, would you please take your shoes off the chair. Do you do that at home?' I am aware of modeling a kind of behavior to the children *and* to their parents." Johnye believes that respect breeds respect.

Advocacy

Johnye takes very seriously her role as patient advocate, a job that takes an enormous amount of her time and energy, but one that she sees as crucial for the practice of good medicine. She also knows that she is a very skilled advocate, a role that suits her temperament and values. "I know medical systems," crows Johnye, warming to the idea of talking about the "aggressive" and "playful" part of her nature. "I can call any hospital or clinic and be absolutely charming, disarmingly so . . . I say sweetly, firmly, 'Hello, I'm Dr. Ballenger. I have a patient that I'd like you to see.'" If Johnye meets resistance or inertia, she is prepared to change her tone and become more assertive or manipulative, but she never allows herself to lose her civility. "You see, institutions are fiefdoms, and people protect them with their lives. But this is a place where I feel confident. I feel I can get almost anything done. A couple of times I've come up empty but that is very rare."

I am curious about Johnye's stamina and persistence in the face of reluctant colleagues and guarded institutions. "How do you keep going?" I ask. "I decide that it is a *game*," she responds immediately. "I'm *playful*. I love strategizing. And remember, I'm not trying to change the whole system. I'm trying to solve this discrete problem and I'm very pragmatic. I am working to figure out who is the best person, what are the best resources, and how can I give my patients access to them."

Johnye Ballenger uses her discipline and industry in the service of her clients. Like Jennifer Dohrn, she sees herself as servant and helper, using skills, charm, strategy, and influence, as well as knowledge of the institution, to advocate for her patients. Both must cut through the routines and hierarchies of the medical establishment. They work against the grain of the bureaucracy. Dr. Ballenger works from the *inside* on behalf of her patients. She clears a path for them through the maze of clinics, appointments, and referrals. When she meets resistance from colleagues, she rises to each challenge as a game to be won. Amidst the frustration and occasional setbacks, Johnye has fun and anticipates success. Her moves can be strategic, nimble, aggressive, or deferential; tart or sweet. Rather than challenging the entire medical system, she sees her activities as limited to getting reasonable care for her patients. If she can count a number of successes by day's end, she feels she has done a decent day's work and lived up to the admonitions of the "voices from home."

Like Johnye, Jennifer uses her intellect, her heart, and her activism to advocate for her patients, but her efforts are focused *outside* the system. The field of midwifery itself stands as a bold challenge to the traditional medical establishment: a clear alternative to a system that midwives view as hierarchical, routinized, often uncaring, and technologically intrusive. Jennifer's work in the South Bronx also stands as a challenge to certain aspects of modern midwifery, a field that has been limited almost exclusively to serving highly educated, relatively affluent populations.

Each day Jennifer, like Johnye, sees women and gives them her full attention and care. Advocacy is paired with empowerment. While she will not threaten the safety and care of the "community of women" by serving those at risk, and will insist that they deliver in the hospital, mostly her actions are designed to avoid the contaminations and humiliations of the hospital, and her work is focused on helping women discover the resources within themselves that will make them knowledgeable and discerning advocates for themselves. Working from the inside and the outside, then, Johnye and Jennifer show their respect for patients through active and determined advocacy that empowers women to seek the care they need.

Johnye and I revisit the long and tortured encounter that she had with the attending physician at the Floating Hospital whom she had called on behalf of the Martinez family. The details of the conversation are still vivid in Johnye's mind even though she must have had dozens of similar encounters since then. She sticks her chest out and screws her face up as if she is about to do battle again. "Somehow this attending physician could not seem to understand the needs of this child and this family. I wanted to use a general medical term to describe what was happening with Rosa—'parenteral therapy,' meaning outside the gut—because I didn't want to say 'injection' in front of the child, who was listening to every word I was saying like a hawk. I realized that the swelling and infection could go either way but that it would probably get worse. But the doctor was not hearing me. I gave her the name of a good drug that I thought might work . . . perhaps it was too big a gun . . . but she was being resistant and unresponsive like she just didn't want to be bothered." I remind Johnye that despite the ER doctor's reluctance, she got what she wanted. Johnye lets out a victory howl, even though it is very clear that she is used to winning.

Finally, I ask her whether the Floating Hospital doctor, an internist who treats adults, might have been "looking down" on Dr. Ballenger, the pediatrician; whether she might have been engaging in the hierarchical behavior that is often part of collegial encounters in medicine. Johnye stretches very tall in her chair and her voice is strong and forceful. "I don't *allow* for there to be hierarchy! I have more experience; I'm older; I'm more skilled." She is punching the air with her fists. Then she leans forward and says with mock seriousness, "If I may use a four-letter word . . . Damn it! I've worked too hard; I've come too far. I'll be a slave to no one. You *can't* disrespect me!" Now she is dead serious. The "ancestors" seem to be speaking and there is no laughter in the air.

Legacy of Action

Away from the action of the clinic, I meet Johnye in her study, a "calm oasis" in her apartment, which is filled with beautifully framed family photographs. We spend several minutes looking at two of the photos, pictures that Johnye feels "symbolize attitudes of respect." The first is a very formal photo of black men and women in Tuskegee, Alabama, dressed in fancy finery, the men in black suits, the women in long, cotton and lace white dresses. Two of them are her husband Bill's maternal grandparents and they are joined by their friends for a photo at their annual picnic. Johnye points to the elegant gathering and says, "These folks demand respect. Their clothes speak loudly of their dignity, their poise, their stature in the community. There is no way you could look at this collection of people without feeling respect for them. The external signs are there."

Johnye then shows me a picture of her maternal grandmother surrounded by her neighbors out in the country. This group is also gathered in a semicircle for the picture, but their clothes are simple and functional. They are poor, rural folks. Johnye's grandmother is stern faced and scowling, and she has a quilt draped over her front "in order to hide the fact that she has not dressed up for the occasion." The quilt looks just like those that are piled up in Johnye's living room. Johnye looks at the face of her grandmother and says she must have been "very embarrassed" at not having the right clothes on for the occasion. "Someone must have forgotten to tell her that they would be taking pictures," says her granddaughter protectively. "But you can still see that these are proud people with a lot of self-respect. You don't see it in the dress so much . . . it is not external. But you do see it in their posture, their demeanor." Even the draped quilt covering her grandmother is a sign of her wish to be presentable and poised in the eye of the camera. Both of these ancestral photographs seem to speak about the origins of Johnye's self-respect, her refusal to let *anyone* disrespect her, and underscore her fierce advocacy for "folks like them" with whom she works.

In anticipation of my visit, Johnye has covered the dining room table with more photos and memorabilia, precious remnants of her roots. There is a document from 1882, yellowed by age, and so fragile that Johnye almost tears it when she opens it up to read to me. Written in elaborate calligraphy, the text commemorates her great-grandfather's participation in the Civil War, indicating that he should receive a modest remuneration for his services. There is a copper pot, dented with age, that Johnye tells me has been passed down through her family from slavery times. Over the decades it has been used for many purposes; for boiling potatoes, for hauling coal and water, and for taking slop to the pigs. Now it is the home for a yucca plant. There are numerous photographs of her aunt Irma, who was a pediatric public health nurse, in whose footsteps Johnye followed. She is sitting in her starched nurse's uniform on the steps of the Red Cross Hospital in Louisville, Kentucky, where she worked, and the place where Johnye was born in 1949. And there is a picture of the sixth-grade class at St. Elizabeth's, the Catholic school Johnye attended. The children—all white except for Johnye—are sitting at their desks with Coke bottles in their hands, looking scrubbed and attentive.

"I think back to my childhood in Louisville, Kentucky. Children had to respect their elders. Adults always had a handle to their names. You always said 'Yes, ma'am, Aunt Irma' or 'Aunt Ursel' . . . You never called them by their first names." The "handles" were always matched to the name. For instance, Johnye's mother Anna was the youngest of eight children and five sisters, but her sisters were not all called Aunt. As a matter of fact, Johnye's aunt for whom she was named was always called "Mamma Johnye," and her older sister was "Mamma Jessie," even though the other two sisters were called "Aunt Irma" and "Aunt Ursel." Johnye reels off the names of extended family and neighborhood folks whom she saw daily. The names come tripping off her tongue, lovingly spoken as if she saw them yesterday.

Johnye tells the stories of the civility demanded by her parents' generation with great humor but her message is dead serious.

It is a legacy I share and I nod my head in full understanding. As she speaks about the "handles" attached to all the black folks' names in Kentucky, I remember my own father's stories from rural Mississippi of parents who named their children "Dean" or "Mister" or "President" so they would never suffer the disrespect of being called by their first names. And I recall my mother's story of humiliation when she was called "Margaret" by her first employer in Jackson, Mississippi, making my father feel so impotent and angry that all he could do was weep.

Closer to home and to the present, I think of too many of my white graduate students at Harvard who somehow feel perfectly comfortable calling me by my first name, but feel reluctant to refer to my white male colleagues—even those junior to me—in the same way. And I think about how my black students almost always refer to me as "Professor Lawrence-Lightfoot" even when I have known them a long time and urge them to be less formal. The title indicates their respect for me, but also their own feelings of self-respect, that part of them that gets mirrored in my eyes. And besides, if their mothers or grandmothers heard them call me by my first name, they would be embarrassed; they would think that they had not raised their children right. So I completely understand when one of them says to me (in response to my request that he call me Sara after we have worked together for years), "I'm sorry, that is not in my repertoire, Professor Lawrence-Lightfoot."

These private daily encounters with white and black students are punctuated by public moments—too numerous to recall—when the humiliation of being called by my first name seems to demand an explicit response; when I feel I must react to the assault not only for my own self-protection, but also in order to teach a lesson on respectful behavior. I regard these public encounters as "teachable moments." I make a *choice* to respond to them; a choice that I know will both help to shield me and render me more vulnerable.

A few years ago I was asked to speak at a conference at the University of Chicago, a meeting for social scientists and their graduate students about race, class, gender, and school achievement.

The other speaker was Professor James Coleman, a distinguished sociologist, a white man several years my senior who was well known and highly regarded for his large-scale statistical studies on educational achievement. Both of us came to the conference well prepared and eager to convey our work to fellow scholars. The language of the occasion was full of the current rhetoric of our disciplines; focused, serious, sometimes esoteric and opaque. I say all this to indicate that there was nothing playful or casual about either of our presentations. Neither of us said anything that suggested informality or frivolity.

When we had finished speaking, the moderator opened the floor for questions, and several hands shot up in the air. The first to speak was a middle-aged white man who identified himself as an advanced graduate student finishing his training at another prestigious university. He began, "I would like to address my question to both Professor Coleman and Sara . . . " I could feel my heart racing, then my mind go blank. In fact, I could not even hear his question after he delivered the opening phrase. I sat there having a conversation with myself, feeling the same rage that my parents must have felt sixty years earlier in Jackson, Mississippi. How can this be? How can this guy call him "Professor" and me "Sara"? And he has no clue about what he has done, how he has injured me. I'm not even sure that the others in the audience have heard what he just said; whether they've recognized the asymmetry, the assault. Somehow, I must have indicated to Jim Coleman (we were friends and colleagues) that I wanted to respond first. He must have seen the panic in my eyes and my shivering body. I heard my voice say very slowly, very clearly, "Because of the strange way you addressed both of us, 'Professor Coleman and Sara,' I am not able to respond to your question. As a matter of fact," I say, leaning into the microphone, holding on to it for dear life, "I couldn't even hear your question." The room was absolutely still. I was not sure that there were any people out there who had any idea how I was feeling, any idea that I was on fire. But my voice must have conveyed my pain, even if the cause was obscure to them. "Would you please repeat your question?" I asked the man, who had by now slid halfway down his seat, and whose face revealed a mixture of pain *and* defiance. "And this time, would you ask it in a way that I will be able to hear it." Like those of Johnye Ballenger, my ancestors were speaking, reminding me of my responsibility to teach this lesson of respect; reminding me that I deserved to be respected.

Johnye Ballenger speaks of the "respect demanded" as a "legacy of slavery." "Growing up in the South, black people gave each other the respect that white folks denied them," she explains. "Within our communities we could at least respect each other. And for young people, it was important that they learned respect for elders in order that they would not one day slip and offend white folks." Johnye is laughing again, remembering a man, who was married to her cousin Tommye Dixon, who found a very clever way of outmaneuvering the white folks. When black folks would walk down the street in the South, they would always have to get off the sidewalk when a white person approached. At these moments, Tommye Dixon's uncle would with great style and deference tip his hat to the white person approaching and say in the most syrupy voice, "Good morning, white folk." Invariably, the person would be flustered by what they perceived to be a strangely mixed message. "But they couldn't say anything!" exclaims Johnye. "They couldn't say, 'Don't call us white folks.'" So black folks, living the legacy of slavery, found ingenious ways of following the decorum of black-white hierarchies without relinquishing all their self-respect.

Johnye rehearses these rules of civility, deeply imprinted in her childhood, when she works with the children in her practice. It is in her private office in Cambridge, where her patients are more likely to be from privileged, well-educated families, that Dr. Ballenger usually feels the need to teach "the appropriate respectful attitude." She tells me of a scene in her office the day before when she was seeing an eleven-year-old boy and his mother. Robbie, a boy suffering from "pervasive developmental delay," has a "quirky personality," "does not respond to questions clearly," and is often "silly, giddy, and overanxious." To most people who see him, his behavior appears inappropriate and puzzling; he is hard to read. Yet, he is always eager to visit Dr. Ballenger. He seems to love her full attention, her directness, and her fearlessness. Yesterday when he came in, he had one thing on his mind: he wanted to find out his doctor's first name. He could hardly wait to ask her, so he blurted out the question as soon as he walked through the door.

Much to his surprise and annoyance, Dr. Ballenger refused to tell him. "I had just returned from the South—the home of civility and poise," Johnye intones with a southern drawl, "where I had been visiting premed students in some of the historically black colleges, trying to get them to think about applying to Harvard. None of these young people to whom I was talking had presumed to call me by my first name." She speaks with mock amazement in her voice, but she is only half kidding. "So I said no to Robbie . . . and I told him that I didn't think that it was polite for children to call adults by their first names." Robbie countered immediately, saying that he was, in fact, used to knowing adults' first names; that in school the teachers let the kids refer to them by their first names. That was all well and good, perhaps, for the teachers in his school, responded the doctor; however, she had a very different view. She would not reveal her first name. He was to call her "Dr. Ballenger." Robbie persisted; first playfully, then insistently, then angrily. His mother, embarrassed by her son's aggressiveness, tried to get him to stop. But finally after some banter and some cajoling, the doctor's voice firmly and clearly drew the line, and Robbie stopped his pleading and dutifully acquiesced. Even Robbie, who sometimes has a hard time interpreting other people's intentions, understood that Dr. Ballenger was serious.

"I want to respectfully teach him about respect. You play, you banter, you align yourself with children . . . then you set the rules of the game." Although the conversation shifts depending on the age, stage, and maturity of the child, Johnye always manages to do two things at once. First, she "listens to the children and tries to empathize with where they are coming from"; then she "gives her opinion." She always envisions herself as sitting "with" the patient, "looking out together at the world." "We sit on the same side," she says as she plops down for a moment beside me on the couch so that we are sharing the same perspective. "I am aligning myself with the child . . . not being frightened, not being too judgmental . . . and I am trying, as well, to model behavior, set an example . . . to say 'do as I do, not as I say' . . . " Her approach is one of alignment, fearlessness, and truth telling. The "rules of the game" have been handed down through the generations, moving from rural Kentucky to Cambridge, Massachusetts, shaping the doctor's clear and purposeful actions.

In Johnye's family, education was seen as the only vehicle out of poverty, the only protection from the most terrible ravages of oppression. "Education could keep you from having to do the most menial work," says Johnye, "and it would make you less vulnerable to disrespectful situations." So each of her mother Anna's siblings in turn escaped the poverty and parochialism of Corydon and moved to Louisville, the nearest big city, in order to attend school. Aunt Irma first left to go to nursing school, graduating in 1915 with her diploma. Mama Johnye and Anna followed and went on to become elementary school teachers. After arriving in Louisville, Anna first finished high school, then went on to normal school, and finally attended the University of Louisville. "She was an excellent teacher," declares her daughter. "She had a tremendous respect for education and for the authority that she brought to the classroom. She insisted upon order and decorum in the classroom." Johnye feels that all three of these sisters' work with children "subconsciously" influenced her decision to become a pediatrician.

The only Gibson sister who did not pursue an education was the oldest, Aunt Ursel. Johnye describes her as a "Mae West type"; the one with the "big ego"; "the pretty baby whom everyone doted on and spoiled"; and "someone who was also a bit of a tomboy." "She had three husbands," laughs Johnye, "and I remember as a child asking her what happened to them . . . and she said nonchalantly, 'They're buried here, there, and yonder.'"

Aunt Ursel's early exit from school is an old family legend that captures her temperament and style, and dramatizes the way she dared to defy the rules of respect and etiquette that every other Negro child in the county dutifully followed. It seems that when the Gibson sisters were growing up in Corydon they went to a small one-room rural schoolhouse. One day Ursel's younger sister Johnye was hungry and she asked the teacher very politely whether she could get something to eat. The teacher would not allow it and Ursel leapt to her sister's defense. She rose up out of her seat, put her hands on her hips in a gesture of outright defiance, and then did the unspeakable. She called the teacher by her first name. "Lula Belle, I won't be back," she said, taking her sister Johnye by the hand to get her something to eat. She stormed out of the school, never to return. For most of her life thereafter she worked as a domestic.

Johnye's mother had converted to Catholicism as a young woman, and she raised her only daughter with the fierce commitment often typical of converts. After spending a few days in first grade at the public school—where Johnye remembers sleeping on the rug surrounded by blocks—her mother sent her to one of the two black Catholic schools in Louisville.

From the very beginning, Johnye loved school and felt comfortable there. Her memories are "sweet." "I went to first grade when I was five years old. Sister Mary Emma was my teacher and she was a very kind woman with beautiful penmanship. When I would get tired during the day, I would put my thumb in my mouth, get up on my desk, twirl my hair, and cool out." When it was time for her to choose her confirmation name, she chose "Mary Magdalene," and her full name became "Johnye Irma Inez Mary Magdalene Ballenger." She speaks each one of her names dramatically and asks me why I think she chose the name. "Because," she says swinging her head back and forth, and looking exactly like the seven-year-old who chose the name, "Mary Magdalene had long hair. She used it to wipe the feet of Jesus."

Johnye may not have "bought" the literal landscape of Catholicism or the milk white European religious images, but she has clearly been deeply affected by the spiritual symbolism of

God's grace and the notion of "Christ in everyone." Her actions show that she "sees Father in men's faces." Nowhere is the religious imagery and interpretation more pronounced than in her work with adolescents. Johnye is one of those rare adults who really seems to enjoy the company of adolescents; who loves their "energy," their "wit," and their adventurousness, even as she empathizes with their struggles and their confusions, and tolerates their narcissism.

There is a lot of adolescent behavior, however, that she finds rude and repellent, and they often do things that she would never choose to do. "But with all of that—the unruliness, the crudeness, the self-destruction—I will still respect them," says Johnye forcefully. Particularly with adolescents, Johnye tries very hard to look past the strange behaviors, the eccentric attitudes, the tough facade, and "respond to the core." As she tries to move beyond the surface, religious images stored up from the Catholicism deeply ingrained in her childhood shine out. Her hands make arcs in the air, and her voice grows soft and tentative as she tries to give form to the spiritual symbolism. "There is Christ, the deity in all of us, and I try to address the divinity in everyone. I always have in the back of my mind, the depth of my soul, the search for that part of the person that transcends the outer body."

Johnye's comments about building respectful relationships with adolescents strike me as refreshing. Most of her professional colleagues would tend to use psychological labels and developmental interpretations to describe their views of teenage angst and rebellion. Instead of the explanations that I am used to hearing—about adolescent needs to battle parental authority in order to claim their autonomy and identity, for example—Johnye seems to focus on the need to look beyond the facade and see their souls (not their psyches). She expresses her determination to listen to them carefully, see the world as they see it, and then express her opinion clearly and honestly.

Johnye's religious allusions are accompanied by a clear-eyed pragmatism. She is worried about the way too many adolescents behave disrespectfully; "the way they talk back to teachers," for example, "swearing, screaming abusively, getting up in their faces." She worries that too many teenagers "especially in the inner cities," do not know how to respond productively to correction or criticism from teachers, and become wild and explosive "when they feel dissed." "Ultimately, some of them respond by killing somebody in retaliation." Johnye is clutching her chest, thinking of the horrors and violence that hang in wait when there are "disrespectful encounters."

Johnye thinks that young people need to "learn *not* to respond." "They need to be able to look at the other person who is being disrespectful and say "you *poor* soul. Look at the way you must have been treated if you have the need to speak to me this way." Johnye offers a funny example, but one that seems to convey a rule that she lives by. "I don't respond to snappy dogs. When they come up to me barking and yelping and trying to scare me away, I say, 'Stop that nonsense!' Or if I'm being more generous, I might exclaim, 'What a voice! What a big, barking voice!' . . . You see, what that dog is really saying is 'See me over here. Listen to me. Pay attention.'" As I listen to Johnye's admonitions and advice to adolescents, I hear her asking *them* to find a way of being respectful to those who might challenge them, annoy them, even hurt them. She hopes that if adolescents feel seen and listened to, if they feel that adults see God's grace in them, that they will begin to offer the same kind of "deep respectful attention" to others.

Johnye's experience with Catholicism continued at St. Elizabeth's, the formerly all-white neighborhood Catholic school where she transferred in the third grade and became the only black child in her school. She remembers the move to the new school as "working out all right" because of the enormous support she got from home. "I was utterly secure at home," says Johnye. "I was well protected and sheltered. I never expected harm. After all, my primary source of learning was not the school but my family." Not only did her family provide a loving home base, her mother had also managed to create a deal with the school that made it feel like a safe environment to enter. Johnye does not know who initiated the arrangement or how it was communicated to her but she does recall its substance. "I knew that if I felt badly or felt threatened that I had permission to leave and talk to the priest about what was going on. Whatever I was doing I could stop and go to him. This was a very big deal. I knew I could walk from a painful, disrespectful situation and go to a higher authority. I always had recourse." Johnye's voice is strong and clear as she recalls this special arrangement that allowed her to feel protected in the midst of an "utterly white" environment that she alone had "integrated"; that allowed her recourse to the highest authorities.

Only once does Johnye remember having to call on this special privilege, and the memory is fairly dim. She seems to recall that some child called her a "hurtful" name, something like "Farina or Buckwheat from Spanky and His Gang," a comic character dressed in rags and black face, "sort of black Sambo-ish." Before she could even feel the full sting of the assault, Johnye was on her way to the rectory to speak to the priest in charge. He listened to her story and told her that the name-calling was "bad, sinful, and a naughty thing to do." Johnye can't remember whether the naughty child was ever punished; probably not. She does recall that after the brief attention from the higher authority, she "felt just fine."

The nuns at school were bigger-than-life figures for whom Johnye felt great reverence and awe. She speaks about their powerful embrace. "I remember the nuns wearing big black dresses and long, long rosaries. I always imagined the rosaries were like a lasso. They would twirl it, toss it out, and lasso you into it. They commanded enormous respect because it was always assumed that they lived a much harder life than the rest of us . . . a life of chastity and poverty. Each day the nuns at St. Elizabeth's would require that their pupils write "Soli Deo Gloria" meaning "All for the Glory of God" at the top of their papers. Johnye muses, "Somehow this allowed you to put yourself second. You could lose yourself in it. It was somehow quite *freeing*. You see, you were not doing this for yourself, you were not doing this to impress, you were doing this all for the glory of God."

Healing Service

Boston City Hospital (BCH) was the only place that Johnye applied to do her pediatric residency. Although most of her professors and friends in medical school thought that her decision to "put all her eggs in one basket" and to devote herself entirely to a public city hospital was "a little strange and very foolish," Johnye relished the chance to work with poor folks and people of color, and do the kind of medicine for which she had trained so hard. Her journey to medicine had been long and circuitous, full of starts and stops, questioning and resolve; winding her way through four colleges (finally graduating from Brown University) and exploring several majors (finally majoring in biology); experimenting with various kinds of work, adventures in the arts, and life in the Big Apple; and surviving a failed marriage. By the time she arrived at BCH, she was in her thirties. She felt that she had earned her stripes and was raring to go.

Her voice is full of energy as she describes her yearnings and ambitions as a newly minted doctor. "I was very happy at BCH. I wanted to give respectful care to patients who didn't always get it. I also knew that I could model that kind of care to other health professionals, including doctors. Actually, what I really wanted to do," she says with emphasis, as if she has landed on the core, motivating ideal, "was give the care that I would want if I were the patient." That was Johnye's high standard, and she wanted to meet it with patients in a big, underfunded city hospital. Though high, she always thought of the standard as totally reachable, as part of the code of professionalism, as deeply rooted in the ethical stance that should define all doctor-patient relationships. Johnye shrugs her shoulders and says, "Actually, I was about doing what comes *naturally* .. . the fundamental values and teachings from my childhood ... doing what you know, what you've seen, what you ought to do. But you see at BCH it was considered something special, rare, and unusual." An edge of cynicism creeps into her voice. "Because to be rude and to be disregarding is the way it tends to be in these institutions."

As I hear Johnye speak about the ways in which all of this

came so "naturally" to her, and about how the lack of civility of some of her colleagues was endlessly upsetting to her, I picture her origins in Louisville. I hear the "handles" that children had to attach to all the names of the adults in the family and the neighborhood as a way of showing respect and deference. I see the ways in which blacks learned elaborate codes of behavior that allowed them to be deferential and nonthreatening in the presence of white people while still maintaining their sense of dignity. And I understand why some of the lack of decorum and respect that Johnye experienced between doctors and patients at BCH must have felt harsh and crude to her ears. I also see why she made a conscious choice not only to work against the grain of the institutional rudeness, but also—in her own work with children and families—to model civility and care.

"I got a bit of a reputation for being able to talk with families even if they were considered by others to be very difficult, even frightening, to deal with," says Johnye proudly. She leans toward me, looks me straight in the eyes, and pretends that I am a mother who has come to her with a sick child feeling anxious and desperate. Her voice is comforting, reassuring. "What you and I both want is the best thing for your child. I know you must be very worried, but I am going to try and help you and we will work together." She thinks back on the fear she saw in that mother's eyes and the way she clutched her baby so tightly to her breast. "I saw poor people who had very little, who had been beaten down, oppressed, and disrespected all of their lives. They came to the clinic with their most precious prize, their child . . . and they were afraid that the hospital might be trying to sever the tie and take their child away from them. That would be the last straw! Their outrage spilled out all over the place."

Johnye understood the mothers' desperation and would often speak to them directly about their fears, sometimes letting them know when their outrageous antics were making matters worse. But mostly she saw herself as a kind of "mediator" and "translator," one who could decode the behaviors and feelings for her fellow professionals, a kind of "griot" sitting on the boundaries, engaged in acts of dialogue and interpretation. "I was able," says Johnye thoughtfully, "to sort of mediate the explosions of affect and anger that tended to be read as threatening and inappropriate by the professionals."

Johnye repeats herself: "All the parents were doing was fighting for their child and fighting to keep their child, fighting not to sever the connection, break the bond." Then she says something so simple and straightforward that it sounds revolutionary. "I have *never* met a parent who was mean, evil, or didn't care about her child. Maybe they don't parent very well, but they do love their kids . . . all of them do . . . and I've known lots of parents as young as thirteen and as old as in their fifties . . . and they generally do the best they can do with the resources they have."

If you are one who believes that all parents love their children, then it follows that there must be some way that they express that love, something they do that is positive and caring. Johnye "always begins with the positive" as she searches for the strengths in families that she might be able to identify and build on. This allows her to bring up the "areas that might be difficult and threatening." Again, she returns to the power of her roots, "doing what comes naturally." She is able to see the love that all mothers have for their children because she was so "utterly loved" by her mother and extended family. Johnye whispers to herself, almost as if she is naming a newly discovered revelation, "All of this is reflecting experiences of my childhood."

As she speaks about the search for strengths and gifts, Johnye returns to a spiritual theme in her work. "As a child, I had a very fixed picture of God, the pictures on holy cards, Renaissance images of Jesus, blond, blue-eyed angels and archangels." But over time, these pictures have become less clear even though the faith— "the belief in, and respect for, a higher spiritual being"—has continued to be strong and embracing. "We could say that there are a gazillion faces of God all around us, in every person, that should cause us to be respectful of each person. You know, you will never know when you will meet up with Christ . . . You could look into the face of a beggar, a teacher, a young child, and see Christ." Now Johnye is getting carried away. She gestures as if delivering an impassioned sermon. "Maybe you will meet Christ in a policeman, a used car salesman, or Governor Wallace in his heyday!" She dead-pans. "It is hard to picture it."

Seriousness returns and Johnye is speaking about the "power of the spirit" that surrounds her and works through her as she min-isters to children and their families. "I know that I am not in control of everything that happens. I must do my best, of course, always . . . but I know that I am not alone in the work of healing." Although she is always aware of the presence of God, she remembers feeling it most acutely when she worked on the Newborn Intensive Care Unit (NICU) at BCH. "You see," she begins with a shudder, "they never called you to the delivery room unless they expected trouble or death. They would call you to the delivery because they knew that the baby would need immediate emergency help in order to make the transition after birth. There are always warning signs . . . some-thing wrong with tracing the mother's contractions, or the baby's heart rate, or the mother coming in intoxicated, or decreased fetal movement . . . all clear signs of vulnerability and trouble." Johnye lists the various danger signs and says, smiling, "Of course, they never call you when the birth is going wonderfully or when everyone is having a mystical, heavenly experience." Her voice is urgent again. "It is an extremely stressful time. The baby may be born too soon—it takes forty weeks to make a baby and the baby decides to come out of the oven at twenty-six or twenty-seven weeks, before it is fully done—and there is no heart rate and it is your job to resuscitate him. The timing is crucial, everything has to happen all at once. Does the baby have a pulse? Is there an airway? Can you get a line? You need to get the tube down the trachea—not the esophagus—and get the fluids going through the IV. . . all with this very tiny crea-ture. Your heart is racing; your fingers working. It is all a blur."

During these moments, Johnye would often find herself pray-ing, "asking God in my Catholic sense to make me an instrument of healing." She is looking down at her outstretched palms, rehearsing the words of her beseeching prayer. "Use my hands, O Lord, I sur-render to you. I will use all that I know . . . all my abilities, skills, and practice, but I surrender to you." As she so often does, Johnye breaks the spell with a big hearty laugh. (She seems to use laughter to cut through the heaviness of the moment, not wanting to sustain the seriousness or the sadness for very long.) "I never asked God to make me an instrument of technical expertise . . . maybe I should have."

"*Primum est non nocere,*" she recites three times. "I always try to do my best. I hate to make mistakes because the consequences can be very grave . . . and people do not want to hear apologies. In fact, they expect the physician to be perfect." Johnye knows that it is impossible to be "perfect," but she does believe that she must "always give her best" and that her best has always been "good enough." Only one time does she remember having failed in the blur of activity in the NICU. Somehow she was not able to move quickly enough in getting the tube down the baby's trachea and the baby had seizures. "Later on," she says, trying to piece the "almost for-gotten" story together, "there was evidence of brain hemorrhag-ing." Even though the early seizures may not have been connected to the brain damage, Johnye still feels "haunted by" the memory. "Maybe, maybe," she says as her voice drifts off, "I did some harm."

The respectful service offered by both Johnye and Jennifer Dohrn to the families in their practices could be seen as a mission. For both of them, work with individual patients is motivated and shaped by a desire to be agents of change in the community. Their professional ethic is guided by a commitment to work for justice and equality, among those who are disenfranchised and under-served. Johnye practices medicine "intimately and respectfully," seeing her work both in a spiritual perspective and as part of a larger public action devoted to dismantling discrimination and injustice.

After more than a decade of living and breathing radical activism, Jennifer wanted to move beyond revolution and rhetoric to acts of care. Like Johnye, she found in midwifery the opportunity to express the spiritual dimensions of her being. As a practicing Buddhist, Jennifer might resist the Christian images and metaphors that are rooted in Johnye's practice, but she confesses her "deep spirituality." She, too, moves beyond the surface "to the core"; she searches for the resilience in her patients and offers them her strength. In Gerard Manley Hopkins's words, she "justices" in the community she serves. For both Johnye and Jennifer, then, the arcs of action spread out from the center. Skilled professionals, they seek through pediatrics and midwifery to "act in God's eyes."

Respect in Practice

Respect is a primary theme in Johnye Ballenger's teaching. At Boston Children's Hospital she works with pediatric residents; modeling, mentoring, and instructing them in the routines of medicine and the rituals of civility. She often worries about the residents' preoccupation with technique, technology, and scientific rigor. These are all vital to skillful practice, but they are not enough. She also worries about the young doctors' tendency to focus on the symptoms and forget the child; to see the pathology and be blind to the health and resilience. She knows that their tour through medical school has probably exaggerated their paternalism, their elitism, and their dogma; impulses contrary to developing respectful relationships with their patients. Before they become full-fledged attending physicians, before they begin to train others, Dr. Ballenger has one last chance to capture their attention, offer alternative perspectives, introduce a little humanism, and sing Aretha's anthem on behalf of the children and families in their care. She tries to do this respectfully and strategically; recognizing how stretched and overworked the residents are; how often *they* feel disrespected by the doctors above them on the hospital hierarchy; and how ambitious they are to hone and exhibit their doctor skills. One afternoon a week, Johnye attends the seminar for pediatric residents, where she sits on the edges of the group, listens attentively, deftly questions, and occasionally offers her "two cents."

The conference room where the residents gather for their weekly sessions, to meet informally, eat on the run, pile their stuff, and feed data into computers that line the room's edge, is windowless, cramped, and much too hot. A large rectangular table dominates the space surrounded by scattered chairs and random desks shoved into the corners. The bright fluorescent lights make a dull humming noise that mixes with the soft whir of the heating system making its own internal adjustments. But none of these conditions—which cause me to feel uncomfortable and claustrophobic—seem to affect the movements and rhythm of the pediatric residents who slowly fill the room. As they chomp on their lunches, review patient records, work at the computer stations, share information about families, gossip about their lives, or just sit still for a moment, they seem much too consumed by the pace and strenuousness of their work to take in their environment.

About twenty residents gather, their faces and colors a mix of cultures and backgrounds. About half are women, with six white males, six white females, a black man and two black women, an East Indian man, a Japanese man, and a Korean woman. About to leave for four weeks of intensive language training in Guatemala, the Korean woman dominates the main conversation with stories about her efforts to speak her beginning Spanish with patients in the emergency room. She is a colorful and lively raconteur who makes frequent references both to her allegiance to the Asian population and to her commitment to communicating more effectively across cultural and language boundaries. Her stories seem to land on the ears of a half-interested audience, either too weary or too distracted to respond. As more and more people enter the room and enter into conversations of two or three, the space seems to grow smaller and the noise level rises.

A voice cuts through the din, bringing the meeting to order. A second-year resident seated at the head of the conference table hands out a detailed outline to his colleagues and begins his presentation on seizures. With a very dry delivery, he begins by examining some of the historical origins of the ways medicine has perceived and responded to seizures in children. "The war between religion and science has been at the root of views of seizure," he says provocatively. But this historical exploration is tantalizingly brief, as the presenter (a medical doctor and a historian of science) moves quickly into a discussion of the "science" and sticks closely to the points raised in the written outline. His voice becomes a dull monotone as he dissects the physiological, metabolic, and neurological roots, and describes the various syndromes, the appropriate strategies in the physical examination, the relevant laboratory data, and the problems and puzzles related to diagnosis.

Dr. Ballenger slips into the room around 1:45 P.M., fifteen minutes after the start of the seminar; she stands on the edge of the room leaning up against a desk. A black woman resident leaves the room and returns with a chair for her to sit on. Johnye listens intently, following the outline on the handout and occasionally asking for a clarification. The presentation begins to feel monochromatic and lifeless, devoid of examples or illustrations from clinical practice. Once in a while one of the doctors offers an example from his or her experience in the emergency room in an effort to connect the material to the clinical work that they are engaged in each day. The talk is accompanied by people eating communal food brought in from other parts of the hospital, sipping sodas and waters, and occasionally nodding off. The atmosphere feels dreary, the people weary.

Johnye Ballenger intervenes only twice, both times in an effort to bring in the realities of clinical work and the perspective of the patient. Her points are gentle but sharp, brief but probing. The first time she raises a question is in response to an aside made by the speaker in the context of a larger point about the history of science. He begins, "The delightful thing about seizures is . . . " I feel myself take in a deep breath just as Johnye holds up her finger in protest. "Delightful for whom?" she inquires. "What?" says the speaker as if he hasn't even noticed what he said. Johnye repeats herself and he gets it this time. "For the historian," he says as if his comment was completely self-evident. He extends the thought. "For the medical historian . . . in an effort to catch the imagination, catch the memory." Johnye and I seem to be the only ones in the room that startle at the word "delightful" in reference to seizure. The rest of the doctors either don't hear it or they have already become too jaded, too locked into a perspective that sees the patient as a specimen, or as a tiny remnant of data on the historical record.

When the speaker has finished his formal presentation, having taken up nearly all of the allotted time for the seminar, Johnye squeezes a question in before the group disbands. Her voice is gentle but urgent. "What language do you use to talk to parents and their children about seizures?" The question cuts through the heavy air like a refreshing breeze, but the speaker seems to feel slightly defensive and dismissive in response. Johnye touches on a central issue for practicing pediatricians. How do you communicate what you know, especially when the news is difficult to hear, the illness is difficult to diagnose, and when the disease is shrouded with negative and confusing mythology? She softens her question with praise. "Your talk was wonderful . . . but primary care people need to be thinking about their relationships to patients." Then she directs their attention to the "real" work they have ahead of them. "We don't have time to pursue this today because the charts have accumulated on the door and we have patients." But it is clear that her comment has sparked both interest and concern. As people are rising from the table, a young white woman says, "The cultural issues are so important here . . . This past summer I worked on a Navajo reservation and the people there believed that seizures were a sign that there had been incest in the family." But there is no time to take this up even though a few of the women murmur, "Wow, that's frightening."

Later on, Johnye expresses her frustration with the way the time was used. She complains about the "scientific" focus that neglected clinical practice and human relationships. She complains about the presentation, which was dull and didactic and did not allow the space for questions or dialogue. She complains about the "arrogance" of these young doctors, their lack of humility and curiosity. And she complains about the "lack of respect" that they show one another—the eating, the nodding off, the inattention shown the speaker—that is reflected in the ways that these young doctors treat their patients. "We do to each other what we ultimately do to our patients," she says firmly.

Later, as we talk about this gap in medical education, Johnye tells me of an experience she had on an "ordinary" morning when she was in her second year of medical school at Howard University. She remembers "the moment" when she suddenly understood "the essence of respect." Like many such epiphanies, it was but one moment, in one of "ten thousand places." Paradoxically for Johnye—the activist, the doer—in that moment, she discovered that respect was expressed through *doing very little* when there is little to do. For the first time she saw clearly that respect can also be carried through "a certain stillness," simply by being present, attentive, and loving.

Trying to get a sense of what to expect in the third-year clinical rotation, Johnye accompanied one of the senior residents on his rounds. It was early morning when she and the resident approached the bedside of an elderly black woman. Even though the patient looked fairly comfortable to Johnye, the resident told her—out of earshot of the woman—that she had "agonal breathing and would probably die by evening time." Johnye had never heard the term "agonal" before; neither could she see anything in the woman's status or demeanor that would seem to indicate that she was about to die. Later she learned that "agonal" meant "terminal."

In contrast to the resident's blunt and clinical diagnosis was the lovely way he treated the dying woman. "He asked her gently and caringly how she felt; he held the glass of water so that she could slowly sip it through the straw; he asked her if she needed to have her pillows adjusted. He just tried to make her feel comfortable." Johnye took this all in, greatly moved by his tenderness. "This will always be seared in my mind. This young doctor's care was so respectful, so very human. He couldn't have done more for her if he had been her son."

In telling this story, Johnye captures a theme that seems to define her medical practice. It is one that I hear her refer to over and over again. She admits the crucial importance of science, technology, and technique in the practice of medicine. But she never feels as if that is enough. Good practice also requires that doctors enter into "relationships" with their patients, that they actually "see" them. Good practice requires that doctors be respectful, tender, and gracious. "Gracious," she almost sings it, "that's a wonderful word and it really applies here." The resident at Howard could not give the woman any medicine or perform any procedure that would prolong her life or reduce her pain. He could, however, offer her tenderness, the sweet attention of a son.

CHAPTER THREE

Dialogue

I have spread my dreams under your feet
Tread softly because you tread on my dreams.

—William Butler Yeats,
"He Wishes for the
Cloths of Heaven"

Making oneself vulnerable is an act of trust and respect, as is receiving and honoring the vulnerability of another. Such an offering of oneself aligns with Martin Buber's idea that a person who says "You" does not "have" something, but "stands in relation." Dreams, when "offered," do not become the possession of the other. They represent the trust and respect that forges a connection. Yeats's offering of dreams shows the power of trust and respect, as a generative force, in relationships. He also conveys the risk: how will it be received?

Kay Cottle, a teacher of middle and high school students, sees the mutual trust that is so crucial to teaching and learning. Her students begin to learn how to question, listen, and receive, when they feel safe enough to begin to take risks and to make themselves vulnerable to one another; when their ideas are offered as "dreams," not to be possessed by anyone, but as a way to explore and connect. Five days a week, Kay tries to provoke dialogue, encourage risk taking, and sustain the trust in her classes at Weston High, an affluent, suburban school with a fine academic reputation west of Boston. Although Kay enjoys these students and is inspired by teaching in this privileged environment, her career—which spans over thirty years—has been an eclectic mix of suburban and urban, rich and poor, and white and black schools. In all these settings, she has earned a reputation as an inspiring and creative teacher whose intellectual prowess, eclectic repertoire, and passion make her a force to be reckoned with. "She definitely disturbs the inertia," says one of her colleagues with obvious admiration in his voice. In this school system, filled with an experienced and aging faculty, which "tends to rest on its laurels," Kay combines team playing with stretching the rules, realistic goals with idealism, and comforting rituals with risk taking.

On my first visit to Weston High School, I am swept up in what one student tells me is the traditional "High Holy Day of Halloween," a celebration of costumes, masks, and mirth. Several of the teachers are dressed in elaborate costumes: a delicate Little Bo Peep; a sexy hooker in a sleek black dress with an exaggerated, padded bottom; a frumpy, friendly clown. As I sit down to wait for Kay in the school's reception area, the principal—in a doctor's white jacket with a stethoscope around his neck—leans over me solicitously, says he hopes I'm not in too much pain, and asks me to wait patiently for the next appointment.

I am surprised when Kay arrives *without* a costume (and so is everyone else who sees her). She explains to all who ask that she doesn't want to distract the middle-schoolers (her sixth-grade classes), who are not allowed to wear costumes and who can't seem to focus on their work when the teachers come to class in disguise. Last year, when she was not teaching in the middle school, Kay wore a costume that folks are still talking about. She was a fortune-teller decked out in a burgundy and purple silk robe, a black long-haired wig covered by an ornate gold and silver turban. Her face was covered with heavy, glittering makeup; her dark eyes reading the occult messages from a large shimmering glass ball. This year—for the benefit of the sixth-graders—she decided to play it straight and she seems to miss the chance for theater and mischief.

Kay Cottle moves quickly and gracefully, leading me through the halls, waving and speaking to students. In her late fifties, with a full head of curly red-brown hair, and an intense, direct gaze, she is full of an energy and finesse that allow her to do several things at once: talk to students, rewind a film from the class that has just concluded, move the desks and chairs into a new shape for the next class, and tell me about the curriculum. As the newest member of an aging history department, she teaches five courses (requiring four different preparations) to sixth-graders (in the middle school), freshmen, and seniors. Her day requires quick shifts of focus, from world history to U.S. history to social science, from eleven- and twelve-year-olds to seventeen- and eighteen-year-olds. She admits to the difficulties of juggling these many demands, but she clearly enjoys the variety and changes in pace.

Kay's high energy and pace remind me of Johnye Ballenger charging about at the South End Health Center. Both the doctor and the teacher seem to be able to respond to a dizzying array of demands, shifting focus constantly as if they had several pairs of eyes, always in motion. But when the action stops, when they need to pause and focus, there is a stillness and an attentiveness that are immediate and disarming. It is in that moment of channeled energy that I sense the respect being carried. The combination of high energy and watchful witness seems to make their focused attention both convincing and magnetic to those who receive it.

Nurturing Inquiry

Kay opens her honors freshman world history course by referring to an assembly program she had organized the day before. A guest speaker from the Hemlock Society had come to talk about physician-assisted suicide (death has been a theme that has threaded its way through many of their readings and assignments *and* it is also something that seems very much on the minds of her ninth-graders). Standing, Kay asks her students for any reactions they might be having the day after the talk (any new "stirrings or concerns"), and praises them for their excellent questions and comments to the speaker the day before. The students—many of whom are decked out in costumes (a poison ivy, a Frankenstein, a mermaid, a sailor)—do not have any further reflections and Kay, sounding slightly disappointed, comments, "Actually, it was not as controversial as I thought it would be . . . Once the speaker described all of their thinking and planning, the reasoning seemed careful and pretty sound."

The event—that turned out to be not so controversial—is quintessential Kay Cottle. She uncovers a theme in the course and offers another angle on it, pushing the debate into new realms. She invites a speaker from the "real world" and helps students make the connections between their classroom learning and current concerns. Not only is Kay's reaching out to resources and people outside the school emblematic of her approach, the "hot" topics are also her specialty, the ones that cause ripples and debate. She gathers resources and pursues speakers—all on her own initiative, using her own networks and connections, and often proceeding without seeking the administration's counsel or approval.

In an affluent school system with a reputation for excellence, Kay knows that teachers and administrators can easily begin to feel satisfied with the status quo. They may start to resist change as they adopt the habits and routines that have worked so well for so long. She also knows that if she *asks* for permission to do the offbeat and provocative things she wants to do, the superintendent or principal may balk, a reluctance often based on fear of litigation. If she goes ahead and does what she thinks is "intellectually and spiritually enriching" for the students—stretching their minds, raising hard questions—she believes that it will usually work out. Kay sometimes risks reprimand (as when she invited the folks from Planned Parenthood to speak and they brought along condoms to distribute to the students), but she is willing to tolerate the occasional slap on her wrist in order to teach in a way that she believes is challenging and productive for students.

Her ambitious schemes can cause even some of her most sympathetic colleagues to shake their heads in disbelief. For her sixth-grade class in U.S. history, where the curriculum focuses on patterns of migration and living spaces, she wrote a proposal for a small grant of one thousand dollars to build a yurt on the school property. She received the grant from a local curriculum enrichment fund and has begun gathering information about how to proceed, consulting the library, the Internet, architect and builder friends, and the school's carpentry teacher. It turns out that the construction of a yurt is no small feat and requires a great deal of skill, planning, and materials, but Kay has already swept people up in her high-energy wake and gotten promises of help and support. Wendall, her good friend and the other history teacher who teaches the same curriculum, leafs through a pamphlet that Kay has found on nomadic Muslims and lets out a sigh of exhaustion. While he seems to love the idea of building the yurt and clearly admires Kay's ingenuity and dedication, he worries about the energy and time that the building project will require. He makes a motion with his hands that says "let's slow down," as he gently pleads, "Kay, let's think realistically about all that will need doing in the next month."

Kay brings this same intensity to her work in the classroom. Her curriculum is spiced with myriad approaches and mixed media that urge students to confront ideas from a variety of perspectives and appeal to a number of senses. In her world history class, there are sixteen students whose desks and chairs are gathered into a rectangular shape. The students are in the midst of reading *The Mists of Avalon,* an eight-hundred-page book about the legend of King Arthur told through the lives of the women who wielded power from behind the throne. These "honors" students have had to pass a placement exam that stresses "critical thinking" and be highly recommended by their eighth-grade teachers in order to earn a seat in the class. They strike me as extremely focused and well-prepared academically, with a collective sense of intellectual prowess and status. They have brought posters that they have made, illuminating the themes and symbols of magic that they have discovered in the book. Some are simple sketches, others elaborately painted; some bear concise written explanations, others have magazine cutouts pasted on; some are large and colorful, others are small and monochromatic. After brief opening comments, Kay asks her students to describe their exhibits and each in turn offers an explanation. The students are relatively quiet as their peers speak, but they do not seem to be very attentive to each other. Kay, on the other hand, is totally engrossed, catching every word, praising students for their efforts, questioning them about some detail or nuance. She sits attentively, leaning into their words, eyes connecting with theirs, nodding approval, expressing reassurance, eliciting reflection.

Kay's focused attention is revealed in her subtle responses, and her probing questioning, which asks them to articulate their thinking process. "How did you arrive at these choices?" she asks each student in different ways. To Raji, an East Indian student who has included a drawing of a stringed instrument, Kay inquires, "How is the music magic?" "Well," he responds tentatively, "it is not like rational or anything . . . it's more about feelings, getting emotional." "Yes," exclaims Kay, "you can certainly get swept away by music . . . It can transport you to another realm, spiritual and magical." To Maya, a tall black girl who stands and offers a very elaborate explanation of every detail of her drawing, Kay asks about what is missing. "Why did you choose not to include the sword?" "I didn't want to emphasize the violence," Maya replies with certainty, "and I didn't want to try to tell too many stories at once . . . If I put too many symbols in, it would be hard for everyone to know what I thought was most important." Kay elaborates, "One of the things Maya shows us here is that stories are as much shaped by what the writer or artist chooses to leave out—the empty spaces, the silences—as by what she chooses to talk about and reveal." Kay's students seem to be used to her style of questioning, which invites reflection, introspection, and criticism. They know that in Mrs. Cottle's class there are no right or wrong answers, only opportunities to deepen the dialogue.

After each presentation, Kay amplifies the ideas and honors the student's contribution. Dave is the first to present his poster, a modest and literal effort that displays the various modes of magic found in the book. He interprets each piece of the diagram, each explanation sounding discrete and disconnected from the other ones. "This is a picture of clouds before a storm . . . sorta like the mist in the book . . . This is a cymbal . . . kinda like a big and sharp sound of music, kinda scary . . . you know, like mysterious." When he is finished, Kay draws it all together; connecting the pieces, raising the thematic issue, and giving Dave credit for the good ideas. She sums up: "Dave is raising the critical issue about how people can bring about natural change."

As each student presents his or her work, Kay stresses the connections among them, weaving together the pieces, pointing to the convergences. But she also reveals her own motivation for having them do the exercise. She wants them to see the connections between what the book describes as magic and what we today might call insight and intuition. "Does anyone have examples of someone who has intuitive powers? . . . who acts in a way that is not wholly logical or rational?" Later on she asks, "Do your coaches of your sports teams ever tell you to *visualize* scoring a goal? Do they stress the power of positive thinking . . . anticipate success and play toward that? Does that seem to work for you?"

Throughout the class, Kay stays focused on the inquiry, resisting the typical teenage distractions. "Mrs. Cottle, may I go to the bathroom?" asks Maya as soon as she has finished her presentation. Kay barely nods her assent, not letting the request interrupt the flow of the dialogue. Later, a few students begin to pass around Frankenstein's white rat—an amazingly real-looking stuffed rodent—dangling it by its tail and waving it in front of each other's faces. Kay notices the whispering and commotion. She first chooses to ignore it, then tries to quell it by silently staring at the student holding the rat and shaking her head back and forth. When that doesn't work, she says in a stage whisper, "Shall we just pass it back to Adam?" and the rat is returned to Frankenstein's pocket. No time is wasted as Kay quietly but firmly insists that her students sustain their attention and join in the dialogue.

Central to Kay's teaching is variety, offering and honoring diverse ways of perceiving and knowing something. At the close of the class, Kay plays a CD of monks singing Gregorian chants from the fifteenth century. She wants them to experience the sensations, the feeling of the music that conveys the "mysticism" of the time, and she wants them to experience—in yet another realm—"magic" inherent in all kinds of human experience.

In every class she teaches, Kay works to create a place for the "meeting" of minds and hearts; for communication—in all its myriad forms and guises. She claims that whether she is teaching sixth-graders or twelfth-graders, honors courses or heterogeneous classes, she always hopes for the same result: that her students will begin to experience the excitement of inquiry, the adventure of learning, and that they will begin to take responsibility for their own work. Her respect for her students makes her hate rote learning and work against empty rituals and classroom routines. She works for student involvement and engagement, by provoking debate, challenging assumptions, and pushing the boundaries of learning.

Legacy of Trust

Kay Cottle feels the imprint of home in the way she crafts relationships with her students and "grows" respect in the classroom. Like Johnye Ballenger, who hears the voices of her ancestors as she practices medicine and "justices" in the community, Kay is also conscious of the ways she rehearses and reinterprets the lessons of her childhood in her teaching. But unlike Johnye, whose respectful relationships echo with voices going back generations, in the shadow of slavery, Kay locates the origins of respect in her immediate family, in the dialogue and differences among them.

Her mother, Eloise Michelson, a portrait artist, had captured the faces and spirits of three generations of children in St. Louis. Her clients liked not only her artistry, but also her sensitive and perceptive way with their children. Kay remembers how her mother would take several rolls of photographs of the children, and then go down to her darkroom in the basement to develop them. "I loved to watch her," recalls Kay. "It was like magic, mysterious and wonderful." Eloise would show the array of photos to the parents and ask them to choose the photograph of their child that they liked the best. Their choices were often surprising. Instead of the prettiest or most likable image, they would often choose the one that conveyed the child's character or temperament, or perhaps those qualities that they wanted to see developed more fully. Kay would watch her mother help families navigate these sensitive and important choices. "She would always listen very carefully to them; she was always deeply respectful and very generous," says Kay. The relationships allowed her to create portraits that were "not merely decorative . . . My mother wanted to honor the preciousness and uniqueness of each person."

Kay learned equally powerful lessons from her father, Eddie, who was a civil engineer and contractor. "Although they were different in every way and had different crafts, I was very much influenced by the ways each of them interacted with their clients," remembers Kay. "I saw all of this and I grew to recognize the value and beauty of the process." Eddie was a man of few words who rarely felt the need to elaborate or embellish. But this did not mean that he had any difficulty communicating. In fact, Kay remembers admiring the spareness of his language and the ways he dealt with everyone with great civility and fairness. "When he would be working with an architect, and they would have different views of the project, my father was wonderful in the way he would help the person see the problem, and find a way of solving it together. He had a way of mediating and communicating ideas without being dictatorial or authoritarian."

The lessons that seem to have informed Kay's teaching the most flow from intimate moments she spent with her father when they would go fishing, hiking, or camping together. Kay still savors these moments. As the second daughter in the family, and as someone who loved vigorous physical activity and the out-of-doors, Kay assumed the role most often taken by the son in a family. "We did things the sons would do." She remembers, for example, going to football games with her dad, learning how to chop wood by his side, being instructed in fly fishing, and going for trout fishing expeditions in Colorado. They were always so comfortable together, an alliance and intimacy that was rarely spoken about, but one that had a deep impact on Kay. "He was such a wonderful teacher . . . so patient and so skilled in choosing such few words of advice. I remember how he helped me retrieve and untangle the line. There was almost complete silence in that moment . . . just patience and gentleness." But it was not just Eddie's skillful and spare teaching that Kay loved, it was also his wonderful spirit of adventure that seemed to enhance the simplest of experiences. "He helped me learn to trust my instincts in the woods or swimming in the ocean."

Kay believes that her dad's appreciation of physical pursuits, his teaching that was always embedded in shared experience, and his vigorous "manliness" have all had a profound imprint on her own teaching. It has made her, for instance, eager to support the learning of her students that goes on beyond the walls of the classroom, and helped her realize the importance of physical pursuits to the development of the whole child. She tells me about a recent evening when she attended the basketball game of one of her favorite female students. "I was yelling and screaming and cheering her on and she was so surprised I came and so appreciative . . . but it was bringing *me* such pleasure and I was so comfortable just being there." These shared experiences always remind Kay of her father.

Being the "son" of Eddie Michelson "made me more receptive, and respectful of, the qualities in male and female students." She has no trouble, for instance, appreciating and decoding the more restrained, unexpressive side of many of her male students whose talk in class tends to be spare and unadorned. Neither does she recoil from the boisterous, male bravado and humor that often seem to be the counterpoint to their masked silence. Unlike many female teachers, she finds these characteristic male behaviors neither unattractive nor puzzling. That part of her that has "absorbed" the manliness of her father finds her boy students familiar and comfortable to be around. It also makes her resist the gender caricatures that have dominated so much of the "feminist discourse." She thinks that it is wrong to read male reticence as a deficit, to label it as their problem with communicating, building relationships, or expressing emotion. Having watched the passion underneath her father's reserve and the deep connections he made with folks that didn't require paragraphs of talk, Kay understands how such stereotypes might disadvantage boys and limit the legitimacy of their style in classrooms. She understands that dialogue includes talk *and* silence.

Kay's teaching also embraces Eloise's "more expressive side," the way she liked to communicate with words and pictures to capture experience. She uses Eloise's colorful language, grand gestures, storytelling, and emotionality in her teaching as well. These different styles and tastes no doubt related to the ways in which Eddie and Eloise were brought up, as boy and girl; patterns that were reinforced over the years. But Kay knows that sex is not determinative, and that the differences she saw in her parents also reflected their family origins, their characters, their interests, and their temperaments. "My father was a Missouri farm boy. My mother was sophisticated, urbane, articulate."

"Teaching in a heterogeneous classroom makes me always feel like *I'm coming home.* The variety, the differences feel very familiar to me since I was raised by parents who were so distinctly different. First I want to help my students enjoy the differences. I want them to appreciate the incredible variety of feelings and thoughts . . . then I want them to work together to find a common ground."

Forging Connections

Although the great contrasts that Kay saw in her parents seem to have fueled her appreciation for the range and variety among her students, it is her relationship with her older sister that seems to have motivated her to find "common ground." "We were very different," she begins. "There was tension and misunderstanding in our differences. I was always active, adventurous. I am sure that she considered me childish and immature, and I sometimes felt diminished by that." Kay is struggling to be fair, but her voice reveals the still lingering disappointment and the lost moments of intimacy. The differences that led to distance were never articulated, confronted, or resolved. Kay believes that the lack of connection and resolution with her big sister, whom she admired and always wanted to know and be close to, may have been an impulse behind her desire to help her students forge connections. "When you don't fully solve problems that get in the way of a harmonious relationship, you find a way of recreating or rehearsing those in your adult life. There is a desire to play it again."

As Kay remembers these childhood longings to connect with her sister, she describes a moment in class that brought her the "greatest pleasure." "Justin was vigorously making his point, and in the midst of it he made a link to the comment of a girl who had spoken earlier. He said, 'I kind of agree with what Mollie said about mysticism' . . . You see, he was listening carefully enough to her and wanting to incorporate her idea and respecting it enough to use it as a part of his comment." Not only was Justin showing his respect for the contribution of his fellow student, Mollie was beaming with pleasure. "The look on her face was amazing! She had been given credit. She had been validated in that moment."

This "interweaving of ideas" that characterizes respectful interactions does not happen automatically or immediately in the classroom. It evolves and grows over time with modeling and reinforcement by the teacher, and it must be nourished in an environment of trust and openness. Kay refers to the work and patience involved. "Respect has to be earned; it has to grow. Teachers must facilitate that attitude, that opening of minds." As the months go by, the students become more familiar with Kay's values and style, and more comfortable with one another. The conversation "deepens" and the discussion becomes more dynamic and authentic.

She uses an example from her senior social science class, a course that offers the teacher and her students ample opportunity to test out the boundaries of trust and intimacy. In the context of a discussion about substance abuse, Rachel opened up for the first time and revealed to her classmates her former addiction to hard drugs, her struggles to reclaim her life, and her victory at finally "being clean." "It was a moment of enormous trust," recalls Kay. Even though Rachel told her story as a tale of striving and resilience, her classmates worried out loud about the scars that remained and her possible vulnerability in the future when she might face rough and painful moments. "Her peers were able to communicate to her a mature concern, and she was comfortable enough to trust us," says Kay. They warned her about what seemed to be her casual attitude about returning to soft drugs. They worried about how her general tendency toward addiction might show itself in other parts of her life, and might interfere with her success. "At that moment," remembers Kay, "I saw the class as a laboratory for self-understanding and the understanding of others."

Kay wants to make sure that I understand that the journey toward mutual understanding is not necessarily peaceful or comfortable. It is full of minefields. It requires that people be "ready to put themselves out there." The pretense of harmony never leads to the kind of vigorous questioning and "interweaving of ideas" that is the bedrock of respect. "To pretend to understand is a cardinal sin in my classroom," exhorts Kay as if she is describing the worst possible transgression. "If you sit there passively, not learning, not taking advantage of the moment . . . " Her voice drifts off as she remembers her own English teacher in high school. "She helped me learn that agreement and consensus are not always the best thing."

"In high school I was gregarious and outgoing," Kay recalls. "I was uninhibited and quite confident . . . I was seen by my teachers as *very* diligent." A wide smile spreads over her face. "Not *dangerously* talented but diligent." She wasn't the most brilliant student perhaps, but she seems to have been the one who actively engaged the conversation, was not afraid of conflict, and reached for understanding. "I helped to make a class work. I learned the art of asking questions."

Kay then touches on an ingredient of respect that will resonate later in this book. "Real curiosity often gets knocked out of kids during their early schooling and almost disappears by the time they reach high school. I so much want them to enjoy what happens when you raise a significant avenue of inquiry or find a way of formulating a good question. Do you know what I love the most? I love when students say, 'Mrs. Cottle, I think this is off the subject but' . . . And I immediately respond, 'You know that nothing is off the subject in this class!'" Kay practically sings the last line. "The most important things are the endless questions. It's a wonderful sign."

"Questions are my major mode," says Kay. She is constantly asking her students, "How could you make this clearer?" or "How did you make the *choices* you've made?" She admits that her approach is partly fueled by her "rebellion against the autocratic style" of so many teachers. "I will not call on students or single them out or force them to participate," she says. Such an approach can both humiliate students and diminish their power. She would much prefer to create a respectful classroom environment that makes it safe for people to speak their minds, that encourages diverse views, that "questions authority" and "questions the facts of history."

"I don't feel I have to exert a disciplinary attitude," says Kay. Quite the opposite. The respect she enjoys and projects grows out of a symmetry and mutuality all around, "a genuine appreciation of one another." As a matter of fact, it is rarely a conscious concern of Kay's, because the respectful regard among students is usually quite "naturally" expressed. Kay notices it only by its absence, by the "lapses" that symbolize a "major breakdown" in the usual patterns. When a student is "rude or uncivil" or mean to another student, or even when a student sits *"passively"* by and refuses to "buy into the process," she sees a rupture in the respectful relationships. In the former case—of outright rudeness or animosity—she speaks directly and publicly about it. In the latter case of student passivity, the remedy is often more complicated and subtle, and usually private. She will find the student in the cafeteria over lunch (Kay makes it a point to speak privately with *all* of her students at some point during the semester), and speak with him about his reticence, urge his participation, and cheer him on. "The more you give to this enterprise, the more you will get from it" or "We need you! . . . your contribution is valuable to the rest of us." Often this private engagement works to draw out students. They feel *seen*, listened to, and challenged. They begin to feel known.

Kay's style of empowering her students to question authority and participate recalls Jennifer Dohrn's work with young mothers in the South Bronx. Just as Kay challenges her students' passivity and pretense, their mask of understanding and acceptance, so too does Jennifer encourage the women to challenge authority, to question those who give them care—doctors, nurses, or midwives—until they receive the information they need and can understand it fully. She tells them everything that she knows, everything that is written in their charts, so that they will have the knowledge to make informed choices. Ultimately, Jennifer wants them to learn to be discerning and critical so that they will be able to take responsibility for their bodies, their health, and their babies. In the birthing clinic and in the classroom, the midwife and the teacher create safe places for developing trust, by provoking inquiry and by resisting the institutional hierarchies that inhibit a respectful meeting of minds and access to knowledge. "Knowledge is power," says Jennifer, borrowing the rhetoric from her revolutionary days. "I want a level playing field," says Kay to express the symmetry of power that good teaching requires.

Storytelling

Another way in which Kay forges a "meeting" of minds and hearts in her classroom is through stories. One story invites another as the teacher and her students weave more and more human connection. "In lots of ways," says Kay, "teaching *is* storytelling . . . It is the place where lives can meet."

During the discussion of magic and intuition mentioned earlier, Kay offers a story she heard: "I have a horrible story that illustrates that point . . . A friend of ours, about your age, was with his friend up in New Hampshire swimming in a river where there was a big rope vine that swung out over craggy rocks and landed you in the water. His friend took the first leap and crossed over the rocks, landing in the water. But when it came to my friend, he was feeling this big fear . . . He grabbed the vine, *hesitated,* and fell on the rocks. He hurt himself very badly. *His fear and the ensuing hesitation . . . his inability to imagine himself doing it, might have led to the fall."*

Kay's students are riveted by her story; for the first time they seem totally absorbed. One story invites another as they offer up their own mysterious happenings: an elderly great-aunt who predicted her son's fatal car accident; a younger sister who is "an old soul" in the way she seems so "wise" and so "cool" in facing tragedy and coping with emergencies; a sports psychologist who helped a friend confront her performance anxiety and become a top-ranked tennis player. After several students speak, each contribution building on the last one, Kay concludes with an exclamation and a question. "This is fascinating, uncanny, amazing . . . extraordinary perceptions of sensing, resonating, and understanding . . . not cerebral, not literal. It sounds a little like what Howard Gardner means when he refers to interpersonal and intrapersonal intelligence . . . Can we see a distinction between seers and prophets and ordinary people who possess intuitive intelligence?"

Even though Kay recognizes the ways in which stories give shape, texture, and depth to classroom discourse, she also believes that teachers must be strategic and restrained in their storytelling; that stories can become opportunities for narcissistic excursions, for the teacher's catharsis and self-indulgence. So Kay tries to be very conscious about when, how, and for what purpose she might use a story in class. First of all, she tries very hard to let her *students'* stories, illustrations, insights, and experiences dominate the discussion. If their voices and perspectives are productively engaged, she feels it is "wrong" to interrupt the flow or inject her story into the discussion. "I will not jump in," says Kay, "if they are on a roll and doing the work, communicating the ideas, pursuing the questions . . . I do not want to turn it into a Kay Cottle autobiographical exhibition."

Kay is also careful about selecting and shaping stories to match the developmental stages and temperaments of her students. Her sixth-grade classes, for example, could never understand or integrate the kinds of stories that she tells in her ninth-grade advanced placement history class or in her twelfth-grade social science course. With her seniors, she feels most free to tell stories that reveal the personal and emotional dimensions of her life. This is partly due to the nature of the social science curriculum (which examines the works of Freud, Erikson, Gilligan . . . and most recently Goleman's *Emotional Intelligence*), but also to the maturity and sophistication of the seventeen- and eighteen-year-olds.

Kay recalls a dream that she recently told her senior social science class; a dream that she had when she was about thirteen or fourteen years old; a dream that still seems to hold a great deal of meaning for her. In the dream, young Kay's body quite suddenly changed from slim and curvaceous to pregnant looking. Her belly grew huge and she waddled when she walked. Her girlfriends at school teased her mercilessly. They mocked her pregnancy, and they taunted her for losing her virginity. "The evidence was right there in my massive stomach," says Kay, patting her belly and sounding like a defensive teenager. But Kay just knew that she couldn't be pregnant. She had not, and would not have sex with any boy. She was much too young. But her friends' accusations stung her. So one day, in an act of desperation, Kay got a big, sharp butcher knife, and sliced straight down the center of her abdomen. Kay pauses dramatically, "And out popped a huge watermelon."

When Kay told this nightmare to her seniors they apparently howled with relief. They were able to get a glimpse into their teacher's adolescent psyche, and they were first horrified, then relieved, then amused. In reliving this dream with her students, Kay wants to capture their interest by revealing some of the personal struggles of her own adolescence. She suspects that many of her students will feel identified with some of the themes: the taunts and assaults of one-time friends and the pain of being bullied and spurned; the turmoil and confusions around sexuality; the temptations of self-destruction when you are feeling hurt and desperate. She expects that if she confesses some of her own adolescent growing pains, her students will feel as if they can too. They will know that this personal material is legitimate and welcome in her classroom. Kay also hopes that her students will see some of the values embedded in her narrative—loyalty, honesty, and friendship—that were being challenged during her adolescence. She also wants to make herself more accessible, more open, more real to them. "I want them to see me as human, as imperfect, as someone with feet of clay." She says adamantly, "I want to show my respect for them as peers. I want to treat them as friends."

Kay recognizes, of course, that there is some risk in being so personally revelatory. Students may begin to feel threatened by the intimacy or the passion; they may feel that some boundary has been crossed, and retreat from the discourse. Or they may feel that the teacher's voice overwhelms their own; that there is no way that they can match the nuances of her narrative or the depth of her experience. Or they may not be able to trace the connections between the autobiographical excursions and the larger concepts or ideas that the stories illustrate.

Kay also knows within herself the feelings of overexposure; the times when she has left the class with the aching sensation that she has given away too much; or when she suspects that the intimate storytelling might offend the other adults in the school who have a more restricted sense of what is appropriate classroom fare. Taken out of context or taken to the wrong authorities, for instance, her pregnant dream might cause a stir, with disapproving whispers from colleagues, notes of protest from parents, or a warning from an administrator. Kay admits that she might not have told this dream to her class if her principal had been present. But she reverses herself immediately. "Well, yes, I think I would tell it if I needed to press the point of Freud's notion of the unconscious."

But these worries about self-censorship are rare for Kay. Although she never wants to abuse the power of storytelling, and she uses stories with restraint, she rarely second-guesses herself. "I am willing to live with the risk in the service of underscoring an intellectual point or in order to capture the quality of relationships and emotion that will enrich and deepen our dialogue." She spreads her arms in a gesture of embrace. "I want us all to have the universal experience of being human."

Jennifer Dohrn knows the act of faith that Kay describes. During the weeks and months when Jennifer was still feeling the sharp pains of her husband's sudden death, she tried very hard to keep her anguish from spilling over into her work. She did not think that it was fair or wise or "professional" to unburden herself with the expectant mothers. They had enough to deal with in their own lives, and their birthings, she thought, should be moments of joy and optimism. So she wept at home, and surrounded herself with her good women friends who held her close and tried to help soothe her pain. At the Childbearing Center, she tried to be a constant, strong presence. But on the night when she was participating in the birthing of a woman—whose man had been killed before they even knew that she was pregnant with his child—Jennifer felt "called" to make a deeper connection. She decided to tell the woman about their common bond; to reveal the story of her husband's death, to take the leap of faith. She needed to tell the story as much as the woman needed to hear it. Their shared vulnerability created a union of strength, and brought back the ghosts of their men, whose spirits hovered over the successful birth of a perfectly healthy baby.

Kay, too, emphasizes the ways stories create intimate conversations across boundaries. "Telling stories," she says thoughtfully, "is such a fundamental impulse . . . I rarely feel it is too intimate a confidence or too revelatory because I'm actively trying to marry the realms of loving and thinking." Kay means "loving" in two ways: that "students should love one another *and* grow to love thinking . . . They should begin to develop the capacity to find truth." Because "blurring boundaries" is her "philosophical stance," Kay does not feel the tension between head and heart, closeness and distance. She hopes that her students will develop a "passion about the beauty of ideas"; that they will learn to "merge these realms"; that they will "learn to talk from the heart." "Sometimes," she says, "I even think the discussion gets too intellectual; it needs to be disturbed and challenged . . . by humor or passion, or irrationality."

As I listen to Kay, I feel completely identified. In my own teaching of graduate students at Harvard, I have thought about, and used, stories in many of the same ways as Kay does: as counterpoint to abstraction, as an opportunity for improvisation, as a way to develop greater symmetry with my students, and as a way to encourage the "meeting of minds and hearts." For example, each fall I teach a large lecture course in the "Sociology of Education," a course for master's and doctoral students that uses sociological perspectives and frameworks to examine educational institutions, processes, and relationships. For many of my students, who are confronting sociological rhetoric and theory for the first time, the language and ideas seem opaque and difficult, very removed from the practice of education in which they have been engaged. Throughout the course, from the very first lecture, I use stories—selectively and strategically—as a way of grounding the abstractions, as a way of illustrating the concepts, and as a way of reducing the fear.

But I also use stories—as Kay does—to create deeper connections with my students, to reveal the universal human themes that we share, and to bridge the realms of thinking and feeling. As the one hundred and fifty students sitting in the lecture hall hear *my* stories—of awkwardness and confusion during my own adolescence, of struggles, humiliations, and tender moments with my teenage daughter, of learning a new computer program at age fifty under the tutelage of my thirteen-year-old son, each story embroidered into narratives that illustrate central ideas in the course—they begin to see themselves reflected in my experiences, and they respond with feeling *and* insight, passion *and* analysis. In these moments of personal revelation they also experience my vulnerability, my trust, and my respect. As one young woman said to me after the recent finale of the course—where I told a few stories and also closed by singing the haunting spiritual "Balm in Gilead"—"I feel so honored by what you gave us . . . so respected that you let us into your life." A middle-aged man echoed a response I hear all the time: "Even though there were more than a hundred of us in this course, I felt as if I was the only one there. You were talking *directly* to me . . . and *only* to me." The respect is carried in the discussion, in the stories, in lives meeting. I, as teacher, offer them my "dreams," and I ask them to "tread softly."

My sister Paula, an educator, artist, and priest, also uses stories to nourish the I-thou connections. In a piece titled "The Miracle of Bread Dough Rising" she recalls a morning in her kindergarten class when the five-year-olds found "common ground" with their forty-year-old teacher. Like Kay's high school seniors, Paula's young students felt the respect carried in their teacher's revelations, in her vulnerability, and in their common humanity.

A child comes to school on Monday morning, comes to our circle of five-year-olds with the news that he has fallen off his two-wheeler. He shows us his Band-Aids of courage. Hands spring into the air. Everyone has a story to tell. Some are about two-wheelers, others are about falls and scrapes, some are about car accidents, still others seem to be unrelated to the original story told, but I am sure by the child's urgency to tell it, now at this moment, that it is related in some way.

It has touched my store of memories, too, and I tell the children my story.

It was my time, my turn to learn to ride a two-wheeler. A rite of passage, a milestone. I'd inherited my sister's sixteen-inch two-wheeler and had wobbled up and down the driveway with my father trotting alongside, hand steadying the frame. (By the third child in the family, nobody remembered where the training wheels had disappeared to.) Dad's voice encouraged me to "keep pedaling, keep pedaling, keep pedaling." Soon I knew he had let go because "keep pedaling, keep pedaling, keep pedaling" faded into the distance. All I could hear was the "clank, clank" of the pedal hitting the chain guard as I breathlessly wobbled along, eventually and harmlessly careening toward the side of the driveway and a soft landing somewhere between the blackberry bushes and the poison ivy. Triumph! Applause from way down the road somewhere. You did it!

Some days later, I am with my mother at the top of Skyview hill. I head down the hill first, pedaling, pedaling toward the intersection at the bottom where I intend to turn left toward home. Just then, the sound of Walter Haines's old Chevy appearing out from behind Andy Pless's hedges just where I planned to turn, and my mother's voice, from the top of the hill, yelling "brakes!!!" How do I do "brakes?" I don't remember brakes. I don't think we covered brakes. I just keep pedaling, keep pedaling straight into the woods in front of me, into the trees, slow motion flip over the handlebars, momentarily suspended in midair, finally landing in the sticker bushes. Then there is my mother's firm hand lifting me back on my bike. Side by side, we pedal home, where my mother cleans my bruises and gives me paints to paint a picture of my treacherous flight.

The children in the classroom circle thirty-five years later have not moved a muscle. They are listening intently to every image, every familiarity as the teacher tells this story of her own. She was five once too. She had fears. She has fears. She was afraid and she was comforted. After circle time, the children work at the easels painting pictures of their treacherous flights.

Risk and Faith

Although Kay's experiences with her students at Weston High have been almost uniformly and mutually respectful, in her three decades of teaching she has not always been as fortunate. Respect, after all, grows best in an environment where *teachers* feel supported and nourished in their work; where the school culture allows a focus on teaching and learning; and where teachers feel able to foster trust, questioning, and risk. In Weston High Kay has enjoyed, and made optimal use of, those conditions. But she can recall incidents—though not many—where her efforts at forging respectful relationships with her students were not successful. Kay remembers, for example, an incident when she was a twenty-five-year-old teacher working in a public high school in Oakland. Although she found the work difficult—the meager resources, the lack of collegial support, the bureaucratic inertia, the chronic distrust between the school and the community—Kay loved working with her students. She loved their energy, their responsiveness, their hunger for a better life. Like many devoted, eager, young teachers who seem to have unlimited energy, Kay became "totally involved" with her students, spending time with them on weekends, taking them to cultural events in San Francisco, and filling her nighttime dreams with them. She believed that her success with them was dependent on first building a genuine rapport, on knowing them as individuals, and on their having a sense that *she* was knowable. If she was asking them to take the "risk" of committing themselves to the "educational enterprise," then she also had to "risk" opening herself up to them.

One January morning, Jamal, one of her favorite students, strolled into her small class of juniors and seniors. He had his hand in his pocket and a scowl on his face as he slowly swaggered up to the front of the room. This was his usual style—slow and cocky—so Kay thought nothing of it until he was suddenly "up in her face" and she looked down to see that he had pulled a knife from his pocket and was flashing it in front of her eyes. Kay's response was one of surprise. After all this was Jamal, her beloved student. He was one of her most "enthusiastic learners." They had become friends. They trusted one another. Her voice still seems to reflect her astonishment. "I was puzzled, not afraid. It was a tantalizing act, but I didn't feel he was threatening me." Her response was quiet and measured as she took her eyes off the knife and looked him directly in his eyes. "You know that is illegal," she said to him. "You had better put that away." Then she said the words that described the real source of her injury and the words that apparently spoke directly to Jamal: "That is *not* showing respect!" Jamal turned on his heels and headed back to his seat; the knife disappeared back in his pocket, and nothing more was said about it.

As Kay relives the story, both Jamal's behavior and her response still seem to baffle her. She cannot remember—maybe she never knew or tried to find out—why he brought the knife to school, why he decided to wave it in her face, or what his explanation was when they talked about it later. She muses, "Maybe it was just a bold act of defiance . . . maybe my classroom was the only place where he felt safe enough to do it . . . maybe he was just testing me . . . letting me know some of the dangers that go with trusting someone so much." But there are no ready answers, no solid memories, and Kay keeps returning to the "biggest disappointment of all." "It was just so disrespectful."

Jamal's story does not seem to be simply a chronicle of a single treacherous event, or the story of the dangers awaiting a young, idealistic teacher working in a neighborhood where poverty and racism conspire to limit educational opportunity for students. For Kay, it seems to stand as a kind of cautionary tale full of important lessons about the risks and tensions that go with building respectful relationships with high school students *anywhere*. "Teaching is loaded with risk. Good teachers are comfortable with this. And adolescents often define themselves by testing, by flirting with danger, by pushing up against the rules and defying the laws of gravity. To be in sync with that, as a teacher, you sometimes have to take a leap of faith . . . and you must often make the decision to leap in a millisecond. Timing is everything. There is always the possibility that it will not work out . . . Of course, you would never knowingly take a risk that would hurt a student. No, the risks usually come from a different place. Risks are about the *teacher* seeming too open, too candid, too childlike to students . . . so that it looks out of character with what students think that teachers should be doing. You are—quite simply—risking their respect."

CHAPTER FOUR

Curiosity

The instructor said,

> Go home and write
> a page tonight.
> And let that page come out of you—
> Then, it will be true.

I wonder if it's that simple?
I am twenty-two, colored, born in Winston-Salem.
I went to school there, then Durham, then here
to this college on the hill above Harlem.
I am the only colored student in my class.
The steps from the hill lead down into Harlem,
through a park, then I cross St. Nicholas,
Eighth Avenue, Seventh, and I come to the Y,
the Harlem Branch Y, where I take the elevator
up to my room, sit down, and write this page:

It's not easy to know what is true for you or me
at twenty-two, my age. But I guess I'm what
I feel and see and hear, Harlem, I hear you:

hear you, hear me—we two—you, me, talk on this page.
(I hear New York, too.) Me—who?

> —Langston Hughes,
> "Theme for English B"

The City College instructor in Langston Hughes's poem "Theme for English B" honors his students by asking them to write a page that emerges out of their own experience, that tells him who they are. His assignment is respectful but also puzzling. The narrator suspects that the story that needs telling is far more complex and nuanced than his teacher makes it sound. When he begins to think about his own life—his origins and the distance he's traveled, the structure and geography of his days, the whiteness of City College and the blackness of Harlem—he sees how very difficult it is to know "what is true" for him.

Hughes's poem is full of questions: questions about the origins, shape, dimensions, and expression of the young man's identity. The verse is fueled by curiosity. Who are you? Who am I? How are we different? How are we the same? What are the feelings and experiences that we both share? Each question invites another and offers the opportunity of going deeper and discovering more. Each question hopes for understanding and is an offering of respect.

When photographer Dawoud Bey talks about his art, he points to the "development of a relationship" with his subjects at the center of his work. If most of us think of photographers with a camera held up in front of their faces, using their equipment as mask or barrier, hiding out while they expose others, then Dawoud Bey stands in defiant contrast. He believes that photographers must enter into relationships with their "subjects" that are mutual and symmetric, where both photographer and subject are unmasked, making way for trust and dialogue. If most of us think of the photographer's work as predatory, capturing people in their most vulnerable and exposed moments, then Dawoud surprises us by making himself vulnerable and "conspicuous." He is interested in documenting and amplifying those qualities in his subjects that are "resolutely human": the universal themes of fear, pain, and joy, the quest for an identity, and the dynamic movements of emotion. Unlike the darting opportunism of many photojournalists, Dawoud's slow, patient, deliberate work puts the photographer and his subject in open, intense communication. Like the teacher in Hughes's poem, Dawoud "lets the page come out" of his subject. His photography is more about discovery, more about finding out what is "true" for each person through listening to his or her stories, than it is about presenting a likable portrayal.

When we meet, Dawoud Bey is in his second residency at Phillips Andover, a prestigious preparatory school about forty minutes north of Boston, where as a Visiting Artist at the Addison Gallery he is teaching, lecturing, and taking photographs. When he visited Andover in the same role five years ago, he stayed for several months and built relationships with students and faculty. This time he has squeezed his visit into four weeks, interrupted by teaching duties at Rutgers University, where he is a professor in the art department, lecturing across the country at museums, galleries, and universities, and weekends with his wife and son, who live in New Haven. Although his life is packed and his schedule crowded, he never seems rushed or frantic. At forty-three, Dawoud is a handsome, large man with an ample girth that he carries gracefully on his five-foot ten-inch frame. His erect posture and long gait make him seem much taller than he is. His light brown face is partially covered by a beard that he strokes when he is concentrating. His dark eyes, which dominate his face, are luminous and intense as they study a photograph or peer directly into the eyes of another person. When he is talking to people, he stands close, reading their eyes and their lips, and maneuvering himself into a position to see their full faces. Even with a hearing aid— lodged in his right ear—Dawoud is still hard of hearing.

The Color of Curiosity

When Dawoud traces the beginning of his interest in photography, he always goes back to his first trip to New York's Metropolitan Museum of Art, where he went to see an exhibit called "Harlem on My Mind." The year was 1969, he was fifteen years old, and he was curious. He was intrigued by reports that he had read in the newspaper about the big controversy that was swirling around the photographic exhibit. He had seen television coverage of picketers parading out in front of the museum, challenging the ethics and authenticity of the show. African-American artists, politicians, and intellectuals were critical of the show because—except for the work of James Van Der Zee—there were no black artists featured prominently.

On the other side, he had heard of Jewish folks who felt that they had been maligned in an essay written for the show's catalogue by a young African-American graduate student at City College, who claimed that the Jewish shop owners in Harlem were draining valuable resources from the community. "She was chosen," guesses Dawoud, "not for her expertise on art or her politics, but because they thought that she would add some local flavor to the dialogue." There was also a third stream in the controversy that was harder for fifteen-year-old Dawoud to unravel. It focused on a piece written by the white curator of the exhibit, whose voice seemed to be both empathic and patronizing as he sought to describe the roots of oppression, poverty, and violence in Harlem. Dawoud recalls the mixed message: "He was reveling in the strength of the art, but at the same time, denigrating the life of the community. He was saying something like 'from my position of privilege, I know that I could leave Harlem, but what about the people who have no escape.' He was assuming that life in Harlem was so miserable and so distasteful that anyone who had the choice and the resources would get out as soon as they possibly could."

Before he went to the exhibit, Dawoud remembers being fascinated by the political upheaval, not particularly curious about the photography. "I was not so much interested in seeing the pictures as I was in seeing the *action*. I was going to see what was going on . . . I was drawn to the *politics*. My sense of social engagement started in junior high," recalls Dawoud. "I remember seeing pictures of poor people camping out in the mud in D.C., and feeling that I had to do something." The next day he went to school and began collecting money for the Poor People's Campaign, a vigil he kept going for several weeks, and a commitment that he made without interest or support from other students. "There was no sense of group dynamic about this. I was all alone."

Just as he had been drawn to the tents in the D.C. mud, so he was attracted to the drama that surrounded "Harlem on My Mind," and he decided he *had* to go. He seems to remember that his parents did not express much interest in attending the exhibit; maybe he didn't even tell them about it. In any case, for the first time in his life he found himself taking the subway all alone from his home in Queens to the middle of Manhattan. "I come from a middle-class black tradition," he explains, "where if I wanted to go some place, I'd mention it to my father and he'd say 'get in the car and let's go.'" So Dawoud headed off by himself to the Met, with no idea of where he was going, with "great curiosity," and "huge anticipation" in his heart. It took him a while to get there because he made several mistakes along the way as he navigated the underground system. "I kept passing the 81st Street stop," laughs Dawoud. "You see I was on the Eighth Avenue express train that goes from 59th Street to 125th Street. In order to get to 82nd—where the Met is—you have to get off at 59th, take the local and walk across the park. But I didn't know that and I didn't dare ask anyone." Thirty years later, his face shows all the confusion, eagerness, and anxiety that he must have felt that day. "Finally," he says, "I think I just got off at 59th walked the twenty blocks north, and somehow found my way across Central Park."

"When I arrived at the Met, there were no picket signs, no demonstrations, no noise. . . and the controversy just disappeared, all the politics just dropped away." He couldn't even think of politics as he stared up, awestruck, at the grand edifice before him. "It is such a physically imposing, awesome place, and it was over-whelming to me." Except for a couple of school trips during elementary school, Dawoud had never been inside a museum, and the scale and grandeur of *this* one seemed especially daunting. He opened the heavy brass doors and walked inside to a cavernous lobby filled with people who seemed to know exactly where they were going and what they were doing. "Once I got inside the doors," recalls Dawoud, "I had no idea where to go and I was too intimidated to ask anyone. I was too nervous to approach the guards or the people behind the information desk, so I just started roaming the museum."

Before long he came to the Egyptian Hall, and the magnificence made him pause and stay a while. "This was before they put the pieces behind glass," remembers Dawoud, "so you could walk right up to these things and actually get real close and touch them." From there he just "kept roaming, not knowing how to ask someone." Finally, he walked up a wide set of marble stairs that led to a big banner announcing the exhibit. He could not have imagined a more inspiring and seductive first experience. His eyes grow very large, as if he is seeing it all again for the first time. "This was an over-the-top presentation," he begins. "Everything was very large, very dramatic. Some of the photographs were hanging from the ceiling. Just as you entered, there was a huge print of James Van Der Zee blown up to mural size. It was bigger than life. I'll never forget the impact of that photo of Adam Clayton Powell Sr., standing on the church steps with kids surrounding him. I was mesmerized. It had tremendous power." As Dawoud recalls the scale of this "over-the-top" show, he is struck by a surprising realization. "Come to think of it," he says thoughtfully, "my work has grown to that size. Maybe that is somehow related to that early experience."

Dawoud spent about three hours wandering around the exhibit, circling back to James Van Der Zee's work for refueling. His mouth must have been hanging open the whole time as he took in a scene that filled him with excitement; not just the pictures, the whole scene. It seems to be hard for Dawoud to find superlatives that will do his memories justice. "These photos were totally extra-ordinary to me . . . and seeing the *people* looking at them was just as amazing. For a long time I kept looking at the people looking at the photos. I had never seen such a display, and I was profoundly moved." Besides being "mesmerized" by the beauty and drama of the work, Dawoud also began to recognize the unique legacy expressed through the photographs. "I realized for the first time that there was no other way that we could have a similar *physical* experience that people had twenty, thirty, forty years ago except through the medium of photography . . . This is the experience of Miss Alice Brown, who lived in Harlem in 1924. It was all so real, so immediate."

Dawoud came away from the show feeling as if he had a "real sense of the community," as if he had "walked the streets of Harlem," as if everything there "had come alive" for him for the first time. Although he had deep connections to Harlem—his parents had lived there for years and they often went back to visit family and friends—he had never explored it, and had never been so com-pletely drawn there. "You see," he smiles, "as a kid my view was lim-ited to looking at Harlem through the car window. My father would park the car in front of my aunt's house. We'd get out right there and climb the steps to her apartment, where we would stay for the rest of the afternoon." "Harlem on My Mind" felt real, colorful, alive, next to the narrow landscape Dawoud saw on his family visits.

"Did you take your camera to the museum?" I ask, remem-bering that he had inherited his godfather's camera the year before. For a moment Dawoud's face goes blank. Then his eyes light up and he says with great certainty that he *did*, in fact, have his cam-era with him that day. He can't actually remember wearing it around his neck, and he certainly can't recall taking any pictures with it, but he does still have one negative of a photo he took that day of the "Harlem on My Mind" banner. "I would not have remembered," he smiles, "except that I know I have the negative." His smile expands into a wide grin. "Actually, I really wasn't sure how to operate the thing. I'm surprised it came out okay."

Curiosity and Intimacy

Now almost thirty years later, I approach the darkened studio in the Addison Gallery and hear Dawoud's voice carefully forming words that take a while for my ears to disentangle. Once I get used to the hollow, muffled sound of his voice, I enjoy the clarity of his insights. He is showing slides of his work to a class of twelve Phillips Andover students, tracing the evolution of his craft and perspective over the last twenty-five years. The students are sitting in chairs scattered around the studio. Dawoud perches backwards on his seat, resting his broad forearms on the curved back of the chair. Occasionally, in midsentence, he slowly rises from his chair, approaches the screen, and points to a detail on which he wants the students to focus. His explanations are clear and unadorned. There is nothing in his choice of words or tone that smacks of arrogance or mystification. He talks to these adolescents as if he expects them to understand, as if communicating with colleagues.

The first slides in the series are not of his own photographs. Dawoud takes his students back to the photographs of James Van Der Zee that greeted him on his first trip to the Met, and he has no trouble creating the excitement of the moment. To this group of sophisticated, generally well-heeled, casually appreciative students—most of whom must have visited scores of museums in their young lives—Dawoud recounts his "innocence" and his "fascination" when he "followed his curiosity" and dared to enter the imposing edifice of the Met, "all alone and awestruck." He projects Van Der Zee's work on the screen: photographs of proud, strong, elegant black people. Large posed family photos, brides in white dresses with long trains, small children looking like miniature adults, dancing couples at the cotillion, men standing proudly in front of their shiny automobiles. "You see," he says, "Van Der Zee was a photographer for hire whose business it was to make his subjects look good. But in the process of doing that, he had managed to construct an image of Harlem with people who were self-possessed and dignified . . . I looked at his work and began to realize that his photos could serve as a repository of collective memory."

The exhibit was a "turning point." His soft, steady voice barely masks the epiphany. He admits to his students the serendipity of his first encounter with a camera as a way of amplifying his dramatic response to the exhibit. "I started off as a photographer by chance," he recalls. "When I was fourteen years old, my godfather died, and my godmother gave me a camera that had belonged to him. I was just about to leave the house and she said, 'Hold on, I've got something for you.' I didn't particularly want it. I had never seriously looked at photos or cared much about photography. I took the camera to be polite." But after "Harlem on My Mind," Dawoud treasured the old camera and knew exactly what he wanted to do with it. He wanted to learn the tools of photography and he wanted to "construct a set of alternative images of African-Americans."

In a conversation with me after his class, Dawoud underscores this central motivation in his art. "Over the years my work has changed, but what has remained the same is my wanting to make pictures that are *resolutely* human, always about the human experience. In the photographic literature and in media images, we have been misrepresented, stereotyped, and distorted. I felt the need to engage in a dialogue that would stand in opposition to the prevailing cultural images and depictions."

Following the lead of Van Der Zee, Dawoud chose the Harlem streets as his beat and spent five years—from 1975 to 1980—hanging out there. He knew many family members, whom he and his parents visited frequently. But Dawoud chose to photograph people he had never met, people he would encounter on the street. His "hanging out" was methodical. He would select a particular area—usually a ten block square like 125th to 135th Streets, moving from east to west—and he would land there each day with his 35mm camera hanging around his neck. For several days he wouldn't take any pictures; just stand around, approach people, and begin a conversation. Dawoud was "feeling and seeing and hearing" Harlem as Langston Hughes's narrator was in the poem. Sometimes he'd go to the same bus stop for several days in a row and begin to recognize the people who would arrive at the same time each day.

They would also begin to notice him, and eventually they'd strike up a conversation. "This was very hard for me," admits Dawoud. "I was an incredibly shy person by temperament. As a child, I was very reticent, a stutterer, real fearful of reaching out. I think making pictures was the way I began to engage people . . . the way I came out of my shyness. I wanted people to gain a sense of me as a person first and a photographer second."

Almost as an afterthought, Dawoud mentions that his hearing loss may have amplified his "natural reticence." "I'm sure," he says tentatively, "that some of my awkwardness must have come from it being hard for me to hear what people were saying. *They* never seemed to notice or mind much, but I was aware that I was very dependent on my vision. My eyes were doing most of the work."

"How would you actually approach a stranger?" I ask, realizing how difficult it must have been for Dawoud to overcome his reticence, initiate contact, and make other people comfortable. "I was learning and struggling all the time," he says, squinting his eyes as if trying to bring back the feelings of anxiety and discomfort that he must have had to endure "just to get over the hump." "After a while I would be drawn to someone and I would ask them if I could take their photograph. 'Mind if I take a few pictures?' Inevitably, the response would be 'what are you going to do with it?' So I'd tell them, 'If I can find you I'll bring you a print.' I had no formal training. I was improvising, making it up as I went along."

But even as a novice, Dawoud knew that photographs grew out of relationships and that the process had to be reciprocal. "I did not want to make the transitory relationships that are typical of photographers. There is a long predatory history in photography where photographers think of themselves as exempt from the normal codes of social interaction . . . an aggressive kind of stealing of an image. I wanted the relationship to be much more meaningful, more symmetric, more respectful, more reciprocal."

This reciprocity usually emerged out of the sharing of stories. "I was fundamentally involved in listening to people's stories," he says, recalling a funny encounter with a barber he used to know named Dees MacNiel. One day Dees came out of his shop and flagged Dawoud down so he could show him his picture in *Jet Magazine.* "How did you get into *Jet*?" Dawoud asked incredulously. Dees explained that he had been hired to go to the military bases where they had only white barbers who didn't know how to cut "nappy hair." When he was showing them the techniques, the photographer took his picture and the moment was captured in *Jet*. This story would lead to another, and Dawoud would find himself hanging out in the barbershop all afternoon, listening to the gossip, spinning tales, and sometimes taking pictures. "It also involved telling them my story," says Dawoud. "I would often meet people in the community who could tell just by looking at me that I was Ken and Mary's boy . . . they'd always have tales to tell about my family."

Dawoud sees storytelling as an important part of the process of building trust and "growing" respectful relationships. In her classroom, Kay Cottle also uses stories to engage her students' hearts as well as their heads; and to move toward a symmetry, a "common ground" necessary for meaningful communication. She, too, knows that the students' stories will not work their magic unless she also becomes a storyteller, unless she makes herself vulnerable.

Courageously pushing past his reticence, Dawoud forces himself to reach out to the folks in Harlem (not a "natural impulse" for him as it is for Kay) and make a connection. Sometimes he must begin the storytelling in order for people to feel moved to carry on. But once the "ball gets rolling," he finds, as Kay does in her classroom, that one story encourages others. Before you know it the afternoon has slipped into evening, and an atmosphere of reciprocity emerges. The stories are usually inspired by a question, by genuine curiosity about the other person. The curiosity cannot be faked. "People can tell if you are truly interested or if you are just jiving."

Despite his shyness Dawoud thinks part of the reason he was able to learn how to reach out to people was because his father was an amazingly friendly and gregarious man who "had the ability to engage everyone." He could stand on the street all day and enjoy "talking to anybody about anything." Dawoud remembers how his father, Ken, would stop and talk to the man selling hot dogs on the corner. "His curiosity was provoked by anybody . . . He'd ask the guy how long he'd been selling hot dogs, who his supplier was, how much profit he made, and so on . . . endlessly curious." But it was not only that Ken was eager to engage in conversation that amazed his son, it was also his ability to connect with all kinds of people whatever their station or status.

Ken was an electrical engineer by training, and he usually held the position of manager or director in whatever shop he worked. But he never used the power of his position to diminish others or to pull rank. Dawoud remembers visiting his dad at work and "never having the sense that he was the boss." "He had an easy relationship with all the men who worked for him." Dawoud loved his father's curiosity, his gregariousness, and the evenhanded way he dealt with everyone around him. Even though he grew up feeling awkward and shy, so different from his father's ease and cool, he must have absorbed some of this social inheritance. In his early days meeting people and taking pictures in Harlem, a part of his father seemed to grow up in him.

Curiosity and Consent

After working with the 35mm camera for several years, Dawoud decided that he wanted to "slow down" the way he was working in order to "force a more sustained relationship" with the person he was photographing. He switched to taking pictures with a black-and-white 4 by 5 Polaroid camera, a camera that produces both an instant print and a negative, and a camera that required that he set up a tripod every time he would shoot a series of pictures. "With a 35mm camera," he explains, "you can be invisible. You can take ten pictures without people even noticing. I had begun to have ethical problems with using the person as unwitting participant. This was not the kind of person I was. I wanted to work differently. With the 4 by 5 you have to get a *commitment* from the subject. You have to ask someone to stand in front of you, be still, and cooperate. I wanted the act of *consent* . . . I liked working much more self-consciously. I wanted to be involved in a much more *conspicuous* activity."

The idea of "consent" was especially important to Dawoud working in the black community. He not only felt that it was crucial that he "construct a set of alternative images of African-Americans," he also believed that the process of the work needed to express a respect for the dignity of his subjects, that the process needed to be "deeply relational" and "fundamentally human." "I wanted to avoid the hierarchy and voyeurism of traditional photography where the power always rests with the photographer." The process could not be separated from the image. He explains the equation: "If I wanted the pictures to have a more intense quality, then the relationships needed to be more intimate and reciprocal. I needed to build up a series of relationships slowly and patiently."

People around Harlem got used to seeing Dawoud roaming the streets carrying his large camera and tripod, making himself "conspicuous." If he were going to ask people to make a "commitment" to being photographed, "I had to let people see me. I had to put *myself* on display." Dawoud recalls the huge challenge of having to overcome his shyness and "put myself out there." "I think I was the only one there taking pictures in this way . . . very public, very visible." His voice turns serious as he reflects on a goal that he seems to recognize only in retrospect. "In working in this way, I was beginning to have a dialogue with other artists and photographers about the interplay of art, ethics, and relationship building."

At this point, Dawoud and I recognize the connections between his approach to photography and our work together on this book project. As he speaks about the authentic curiosity, the consent required, the mutual commitment, and the equality of power that he needs to develop with his subjects, we hear the echoes of our encounters with one another. He and I have experienced the deepening intimacy that allows for a "truer" image. We, too, have tried to navigate the boundaries between voyeurism and curiosity. We, too, have traded stories in an expression of reciprocity and symmetry. We, too, are reaching for what is "fundamentally human" between us. In our conversations we have—slowly and patiently—tried to make ourselves visible to one another. Dawoud says the words I often hear from other people whose stories I am collecting, and whose lives I am witnessing: "You know, Sara, this feels like therapy." At that moment, I think that some of those people who are photographed by Dawoud must also feel the nourishment, challenge, and insight that therapy encourages.

For me, this work feels deeply familiar. So much of my own research over the past two decades has depended upon making connections with people that allow them to feel safe and trust me; that encourage storytelling, revelations, and reflection; and that honor boundaries and silences. Like Dawoud's, my curiosity has to be genuine and the relationships need to be successfully forged in order for me to capture the richness and depth of experience. The process of building relationships is fraught with possible misunderstandings, overexposure, and intrusiveness. Each encounter requires a vigilant watchfulness as my "subject" and I try to calibrate closeness and distance, warmth and coolness, intensity and calm. When Dawoud speaks of his work as a "conspicuous activity," he knows that the vulnerabilities and empathy go in two directions—from the artist to the subject and back again—even though it is the artist's (and researcher's) job to keep track of the emotional minefields.

While doing the interviews for my book *I've Known Rivers,* I felt the eerie reciprocity; the entanglement of two stories, and our recognition of shared vulnerability. One of the "subjects," Katie Cannon, a professor of theology, helped make this clear to me.

> . . . before moving on, Katie has one final thought inspired by our last interview. I am relieved to hear her say, "I need to slow down," because the pace and intensity of her talk had left *me* feeling breathless and exhausted last time. But Katie is not only referring to the tempo of her talk last time; she is remembering

its pitch; its urgency and energy. She wants to make a distinction between real life and melodrama; between nonfiction and fiction. Referring to a contrast she first heard made by Maya Angelou, Katie observes that fiction is a gentler form more bearable in its expression of pain. Nonfiction, which records people's real lives, can be too harsh, too traumatic for the reader to incorporate. The storyteller must be "careful" not to assault the listener with too much emotion, or else the story will not be heard and received. The listener will put up a shield to protect herself from the barrage of intense feelings. Katie worries that in her last interview she might have been "too raw" and too intense in telling of her experiences, that maybe some of the feelings are "too painful to even name." She ponders about the need to "filter" some of her emotions, dilute some of the pain, and hold back some of the tears in order that I will not feel assaulted or overwhelmed by her narrative. I see her look of concern; I hear her message of identification with the *listener*, and I am moved by her empathy. But, though I too had been "wiped out" by our last interview, I feel fully able to withstand the "raw feelings" and strong enough to hear her "name the pain." I say as much as clearly as I can. Katie smiles, looking thankful and relieved—"Yes, I have no doubt you're sturdy enough to hear this."

In working the streets of Harlem, Dawoud discovered that there could be an important tangible exchange with his subjects that accompanied the mutual acts of consent. With his 4 by 5 Polaroid camera, he was able, within twenty seconds of taking the picture, to hand his subject a print, an immediate symbol of his gratitude and visible evidence of the moment of exchange. "I found," recalls Dawoud, "that possession of the image was a large part of the process." Perhaps the most important sign of the intimacy of these encounters was in Dawoud's request that his subjects look "directly at the camera." "These were not casual shots," explains Dawoud. "They were consciously set up, very posed. There was great power in the gaze returned. Believable but posed." He laughs. "There was a layer of fictive in this work. If someone looked at you that way in real life, you'd probably say, 'Don't stare' or 'What are you lookin' at?'"

After working the streets in this way for about four years, in 1979 Dawoud had his first show at the Studio Museum on 125th Street in the heart of Harlem. Just as he wanted to give folks their own pictures as soon as he made them, so he wanted to give his collection of their images back to them "at home." "It was very important to me that the photos be shown in the community where they were made," he says resolutely. The exhibit, called "Harlem USA," drew a large audience and a lot of acclaim from fellow artists and critics. But what was most satisfying and exciting to Dawoud was that, for many of his subjects, this was the first time that they had ever set foot in a museum. He smiles as he recalls their pleasure at "seeing themselves on the wall" and his joy at witnessing their pleasure. "I knew then that part of creating an empowering relationship between us was to find a way to make subjects the audience for the work."

Direct Engagement

Perhaps the intensity and intimacy of creating this "resolutely human" art began to be difficult to sustain for this man who describes himself as "filled with reticence." For a time, soon after the show at the Studio Museum, he decided to take "formal pictures with no human subject." "I became interested in exploring the physical space around the person. I wanted to focus on the quality and character of the light, the luminosity. I wanted to be more dramatic." He shows the art history class photos from this period, many of them taken far from the streets of Harlem, in Mexico and Puerto Rico. In one photograph from Puerto Rico, called "On the Way to El Yunque," the "human figure is totally absent" as he focuses on the decayed walls and remnants of an old dwelling against a distant landscape. In another, "Four Shirts," Dawoud photographs white dress shirts drying outside, hanging from a tin-roofed house shaded by palm trees. The bright light reflecting off the white shirts contrasts sharply with the dark shadows under the roof and the shade of the tree. For a year and a half Dawoud worked in this way, exploring "problems of structure and composition," enjoying the "play of light and shadow," and resting from the rigors of relationship required in his work with human subjects. During this time, Dawoud could enjoy the pure aesthetic of the process, relish the play of light, and rest that part of himself that always had to be poised for response and engagement.

This retreat from the intensity of "people-work" reminds me of Jennifer Dohrn's frank recognition after years of activist work in the community—both as a revolutionary and as a midwife—that she had to find ways of drawing clearer boundaries and protecting moments of solitude if she was going to sustain herself. In order for her to "be there" for the mothers in the clinic, she had to find a way to nourish herself. Jennifer was drawn to Buddhism because it offered her the chance for spiritual expression and growth, but also because it could become a refuge from the pressures and stress of her work. Each morning she meditates in her prayer room. This interlude of silence, the centering of prayer, allows her to carry on; allows her to offer her strength to the mothers who need her care.

After his sojourn away from "humanity," Dawoud was ready to be drawn back "into the fray." By the early nineties, his work was beginning to be widely known, and was attracting a great deal of interest and praise. He was offered the opportunity of working with a 20 by 24 Polaroid camera, one of five such cameras in the world. His selection—as one of a handful of artists—was a sign of his emerging status in the field, and marked the beginning of a major shift in his work.

With the 20 by 24 camera, his work moved inside the studio, and the context of street life dropped away, but he remained "resolutely focused on describing the human experience." Just as

Van Der Zee's work had been an enormous source of inspiration for his Harlem photographs, so now his even earlier fondness for Rembrandt's portrait painting echoed in his studio work. He speaks of the long "love affair" he has had with Rembrandt, ever since fourth grade, when he did a paper on the life and work of the artist and was "mesmerized" by his use of light. "I wanted to bring that luminous quality to my own work," says Dawoud as he projects a slide of a Rembrandt portrait on the screen for the class to see. After the elegant dark parade of contemporary, urban African-Americans in the streets of Harlem, the Rembrandt painting comes as a surprise. The European man in the painting is carefully posed and aristocratic, adorned in silks and finery, looking out at us with poise and self-confidence, but without the clues of context surrounding him. His gaze is steady and intense.

In the first pictures Dawoud shows us of his studio work, we see many of the same qualities. The individual images dominate the photograph; they feel bigger than life; all context is eliminated; the gaze is direct and unguarded; and most surprising, the work is in vivid color. Mimicking the dramatic light of Rembrandt, Dawoud even uses a brown backdrop and places a single light source angled off to the side. "My use of color had to do with wanting to make an unabashedly lush and romantic rendering of people who seldom receive that kind of attention," says Dawoud. These were not modern versions of the Renaissance aristocrats that Rembrandt painted, but ordinary people bathed in rich and royal hues, and their images shone with a deep beauty. "Quite purposefully," he says, "I was interested in subverting the idea of aristocratic art. I was specifically taking pictures of people who were not privileged and could not afford to commission portraits."

As Dawoud began to explore this new genre, again his work slowed, the relationships deepened, and the quality of the work grew more intense. Working with this huge nontransportable camera required more patience, resilience, and "commitment" on the part of the subject, who endured two- or three-hour sittings. "This not only requires a kind of mental concentration," explains

Dawoud, "it is also intense physical work . . . not like lifting five hundred pounds, but certainly it is physically strenuous."

Not only is the process of taking the pictures more cumbersome and demanding, the pictures that are produced differ from positive/negative photos. They are negativeless, direct-positive, one-of-a-kind of prints; and the absence of negatives and avoidance of any enlargement process make them virtually grain-free. Dawoud tells the class that no other photographic system is capable of producing such rich and nuanced detail, more minute description than you can possibly see with the naked eye.

When Dawoud began working in this medium, he would pin up the individual images on the wall and scrutinize them. He soon discovered that the images looked more interesting when he put them together, that with multiple pieces he was able to evoke the "complex relationship of time and psyche." He began to pair photographs that revealed different aspects of the person's character, capturing, for example, the "private and public self." "One photograph might show the direct engagement, the public posture, while the other would reveal the more private self with an inner-directed gaze." Through these multiple images Dawoud was searching for a fuller, more complex representation of human experience, moving beyond the surface, beyond the posed exterior.

The curiosity deepened and the exploration continued as Dawoud began to experiment with using more than one subject, creating "multiple images of multiple persons," seeking to record the dynamics and quality of relationships among them. Putting three panels of photos side by side, each with some element of relationship revealed—a daughter's hand resting on her mother's shoulder, a piece of a boy's arm wrapped around his girlfriend, a young son leaning into his mother's side—Dawoud was suggesting both the connection and the separation, the boundaries and the intimacy that are part of human relationships. He was moving away from "literal representation" toward work that had more depth and complexity. "In the process, I was creating more possibilities for how to represent time and movement," reminding me of the time required to build intimacy, and the movement that is always central to developing relationships.

Bathed in Full Attention

When Dawoud describes the curiosity and commitment that are part of his work, and the depth and complexity that he strives for, he takes me on a "flashback" to his second-grade teacher at P.S. 123. When he photographs his subjects, and bathes them in light, he wants them to feel "seen" in the way he felt "seen" in Mrs. Jones's classroom. "Mrs. Jones," he recalls, "was profound and extraordinary and very inspiring." "In what way profound?" I ask, somewhat surprised at a word that seems to go beyond most people's recall of second grade. His response is immediate. "She established *real* relationships with every single child in her class. Everything was possible and everyone could do it." Ever since second grade, all Dawoud's other teachers and all his other educational experiences have been measured against Mrs. Jones's "amazing skill and compassion," and they have all come up wanting.

P.S. 123 was the public school in Dawoud's neighborhood, a largely middle-class black community in Jamaica, Queens. Except for a couple of white kids ("whose families had not yet joined the rapid white flight out of the neighborhood"), the school was filled with African-American students and teachers. When Dawoud was promoted to second grade after a benign but unremarkable year in first, he was not assigned to Mrs. Jones's classroom. But Dawoud's mother, Mary, who was a homemaker, an avid PTA parent, and a staunch advocate for her children's education, felt that the second-grade teacher to whom Dawoud was assigned "didn't like teaching and didn't like children." So she marched up to the school and spoke to "someone in charge," and Dawoud was moved to Mrs. Jones's class. Even as a young child Dawoud remembers loving Mrs. Jones's energy, her expansiveness, and her drive. "She was a one-woman dynamo. She was out to save the world, one kid at a time."

"How do you think she saw you as a student?" I ask, wondering if in this classroom, where everyone seemed to "get special atten-tion," Dawoud might be able to describe in what ways he was spe-cial. Dawoud pauses and then says tentatively, "I think she saw me as a bright little boy. I loved to read and I was already devouring books." Then he brightens up remembering how Mrs. Jones—knowing of his passion for reading—also encouraged his artistic development. "Actually, I made my first drum in her class using a tin can, a rubber inner tube, and some of the electric wire that my father always had hanging around. I punctured holes in the rubber and drew the wire through. It probably didn't sound like much, but it was fine with me."

With Dawoud's mention of the drum's "sound," I wonder—as I have many times during our conversations—what it is that Dawoud hears. I also wonder whether he thinks that his hearing loss might be related to his decision to do work that is solely dependent on his vision. He responds to my questions a little vaguely, but with-out defensiveness. It seems to be something he rarely thinks or talks about, certainly not something he would have raised on his own. "I'm not really sure of the origins," he begins tentatively. "I think it was some kind of nerve damage. I'll have to check with my mother on the details." I am surprised that Dawoud has never seriously examined his hearing loss, that it doesn't seem to interest him much, and that the story he is able to piece together is so sketchy. After a long pause, he traces the discovery of his hearing loss back to second grade, a time of many meaningful discoveries. "I think it was actually Mrs. Jones who recognized that I was hard of hearing. I think I began the year sitting in the back row, and she noticed that I was doing a lot of daydreaming . . . so she moved me to the front of the room and noticed that I was completely attentive."

Mrs. Jones must have urged Dawoud's parents to take him to the audiologist, because by third grade he was wearing a hearing aid; the kind that requires a "two-by-two-inch box that you clip on your shirt with a wire running to your ear." The doctor, in fact, dis-covered that he had "a profound hearing loss." "I was literally off the chart of the normal hearing range," recalls Dawoud. "In fact, when

I took the audiology exam, the doctor wondered how I was able to speak so clearly. But I had learned to rely on my eyes. I have very good eyes. My peripheral vision is amazing. It was a matter of over-compensating." In his family and in his neighborhood, Dawoud remembers hardly being aware of his "profound hearing loss" or people's response to it. "It was a non-issue in the neighborhood, and my parents never made an issue of it. I never was put in any special kind of class, or given any extra help with work or chores. I came up feeling pretty *normal*." But when Dawoud went off to school, "it added another layer of difference." "Hearing was less an issue than the color issue in school," he says, comparing the two potential sources of discrimination. "But I do remember not wanting to wear that clip-on box, and worrying that the kids would make fun of me." Dawoud finds the silver lining: "I think this has given me an inherent sensitivity to people who are marginalized."

Although Dawoud relishes the memory of his second-grade year, and recalls "great times" writing poetry, doing spelling bees, making music, and being bathed in his teacher's full attention, what is even more amazing to him is the way his relationship with Mrs. Jones spread to his family and has been sustained through the years. Just as he fell in love with Mrs. Jones, so did his whole family. She inspired their growth and development as well, encouraging them to purse their goals and broaden their horizons. "My parents got to know her through me," recalls Dawoud. "Now my whole family is close to her whole family. She even inspired my father to return to school, to get his master's, and then his Ph.D."

It was probably on Mrs. Jones's advice that Dawoud's parents decided to bus Dawoud and his older brother Ken Jr. to a predominantly white school in a fancier section of Jamaica the following year. Dawoud is not sure that it was Mrs. Jones who instigated the move, but he thinks that she probably recognized the boys' high intelligence and diligence, and their parents' ambitions for them, and thought that the white school—P.S. 131—would provide a more rigorous education. The move was shocking to Dawoud. He understates his sense of "disorientation." "It was a very different kind of experience." Then he says it all in one sentence: "I was not in Mrs. Jones's class any more."

Although as an eight-year-old child he felt that P.S. 131 was a "strange environment," at the time he would not have "characterized the difference as being related to race." He experienced the contrasts in the daily rituals ("Rather than my parents walking me to school, now I was dropped off at the bus stop"), at the same time as he felt an uneasy, unnamed anxiety every time he stepped off the bus and into the school. Now he knows what he didn't know then: that he was experiencing the heightened visibility and distortions of tokenism (there was one other black boy in his class of thirty) and his teachers' inability to accept his shining intelligence. "The teachers at P.S. 131 recognized that I was a bright little boy. I was always reading three to four years above grade level, and I loved to write. But they always had a problem with that. They were always skeptical, disbelieving."

Dawoud remembers an incident in fourth grade when one of the little girls got her lunch stolen, and he looked up to find the teacher singling him out. He saw her cold stare and her accusatory finger waving in his face, and he felt baffled and confused. "I was innocent, I didn't even get the connection. '*Me*?' I stammered. 'Are you talking to *me*?'" asked Dawoud in a sweat. Yes, she meant *him*, and he was to go down to the guidance office immediately. He was the culprit. There was no doubt in her mind. Dawoud rose up from his seat, walked the long march to the door amid the quiet stares of his classmates, and dutifully took himself to the guidance office, where the counselor interpreted his "acting out" as some kind of "mental problem" and gave him some "weird" tests "putting square pegs in round holes." In Dawoud's memory this is one story among many. "I'd get singled out. Much of the time I was in a conflicted state. There were strange things going on, but what do you say? I couldn't name what was happening, and I couldn't find the words or the courage to ask."

The following year, in fifth grade, he remembers that the class was writing a group play about Colonial America, and the play was to be written in verse. Dawoud loved the assignment and he leapt right into the middle of the work. "I *loved* writing poetry. It was a breeze for me. So I started knocking this stuff out." The teacher was gratified by the way her class pulled off the assignment so quickly and with such apparent ease and mature collaboration. She inquired of everyone how they had been so incredibly productive, and the children all pointed to Dawoud, who smiled back shyly. "I remember," says Dawoud with hurt in his eyes, "how her expression changed in that moment. The raised eyebrow, the amazement, the surprise." She must have applauded his inspired work and thanked him for his contribution. But the only thing that Dawoud can remember is her utter bafflement and *his* inner confusion. "The teacher was unable to reconcile my brightness with her stereotype of me. How could this black boy produce this verse? She seemed *tormented* by this. It was always this way in elementary school. At the same moment I'd receive these great commendations, and be sent off to the guidance counselor."

When Dawoud was in junior high school, this unwanted and unfair visibility was replaced by an even more painful invisibility. He heard that tryouts were going on for the school orchestra and that they needed a drummer. Although he did not yet have a drum set, and he had never taken formal lessons, Dawoud had taught himself and was already a proficient and skilled drummer. "It came like second nature to me," he smiles. "I had a very good instinctive feel." A white classmate of Dawoud's, Roy Gold, was also trying out for the orchestra, but it was clear to both of them that Roy was nowhere near as good a drummer as Dawoud. "He just didn't have it," recalls Dawoud dryly. One part of the audition required that they do what is called a "press roll." Dawoud shows me the fast movements with his hands and makes a fluttering, guttural noise with his mouth that sounds exactly like a drum roll. When Dawoud went for the audition, he did a perfect press roll; so good that he kept it up for a long time after the music teacher signaled him to stop just to show the level of his proficiency. Roy, on the other hand, couldn't even get his press roll going. He stuttered a few times and then gave up halfway through in order not to further embarrass himself. "Now, who do you think got to be in the orchestra?" he asks with mock seriousness? "*Roy* did! He couldn't play the drums but he got into the orchestra. I felt terrible but I did nothing about it. I didn't know how to make the noise and complain. I just let it pass."

Dawoud's tales of being overlooked or misunderstood—the ways in which his white teachers were blinded by their prejudice—remind me of the opening passages of Ralph Ellison's classic novel, *Invisible Man*, a book published just before Dawoud was born.

> I am an invisible man. No, I am not a spook like those who haunted Edgar Allan Poe; nor am I one of your Hollywood-movie ectoplasms. I am a man of substance, of flesh and bone, fiber and liquids—and I might even be said to possess a mind. I am invisible, understand, simply because people refuse to see me. Like the bodiless heads you see sometimes in circus sideshows, it is as though I have been surrounded by mirrors of hard, distorting glass. When they approach me they see only my surroundings, themselves, or figments of their imagination—indeed, everything and anything except me.

The plight of Ellison's invisible man echoes through Dawoud's later childhood stories. He suffered what Ellison describes as "the construction of their inner eyes"; and he learned—the hard way—that to exist we must be visible. The contrast between the biased oversight of his white teachers, and the full, empathic attention bestowed by Mrs. Jones, surely influenced Dawoud's approach to his art. His photographs—motivated by curiosity, shaped by a commitment to his subjects, and their consent and participation allow his subjects to express themselves, bathed in respectful attention.

The Value of Their Lives

By the time Dawoud reached high school, the accumulation of "micro-aggressions" had poisoned his spirit and sapped his energy. His memories of his high school years are a "total blank." The seven-year-old, who had blossomed as an ambitious student, an eager poet, and an avid reader in Mrs. Jones's second-grade garden, had all but disappeared. The only remnants of her glowing attention survived in his drum playing. "All I remember about high school," says Dawoud, his voice still heavy with the loss, "is wailing on the drums and jamming with my buddies." He now realizes that his work with adolescents—the main focus of his art for the past few years and his current preoccupation—has been an attempt to redress the invisibility of his own adolescence. "Four years missing from my life . . . dark and shadowy, lost from memory."

Unlike the silence and emptiness of his own teenage years, the experience Dawoud wants young people to have is one of being seen and heard, a chance to voice the chaos and uncertainty inside of them. "Teenagers are always trying to figure out what they're going to become," says Dawoud with a certainty born out of long hours of listening. "They don't have a clue, and there is great confusion and a lot of anguish. So I spend a lot of time talking, hearing their stories, their dilemmas. All the stuff is put on the table. I become a kind of a sounding board."

The trust that develops between Dawoud and his young friends seems to grow out of his clear-eyed acceptance of who they are and where they are coming from. When he began taking photographs of folks in Harlem, Dawoud made a fundamental decision that not only shaped his relationships to his subjects, but also had an impact on his art. "I made a conscious decision," he says with certainty, "that I would be *nonjudgmental* . . . that I would have relationships with people with whom I might not share the same standards or values. After all, the purpose in meeting people is not to change them." The decision was also driven by his belief that "curiosity cannot coexist with a judgmental attitude." The combination of

Dawoud's undiluted attention, deep curiosity, and open-minded-ness makes young people feel seen and respected.

The trust and rapport that Dawoud seeks to develop with his teenage subjects do not come immediately or easily. Just as in Kay Cottle's classroom, where "respect has to be earned," requiring a daily vigilance and calculated "leaps of faith," there is often a period of testing, when the students see whether they can shock him, frighten him, blow his mind. But Dawoud keeps his cool, at the same time as he communicates his empathy. In each school he vis-its, he lets the students know, for example, that he has *chosen* to be with them. "When I'm in schools, they know I'm not a teacher. I have no official capacity; I will not be evaluating them. They know that I don't *have* to be there. I *want* to be there." And he lets them know that their stories don't frighten or disgust him. "Sometimes they'll try me out and talk about some horrendous stuff, some crim-inal activity that they've been involved in, some naughty teenage stuff. They'll tell me about doing drugs or wild fights." Dawoud laughs as he remembers the parade of raucous and outrageous tales he has heard over the years. "So as I'm sitting there, I'm thinking to myself, *I* never did it. Never had any *need* to do it . . . so keep talking." They do keep talking, and he keeps listening. The rela-tionships grow, and the art making commences. "So much goes on *away* from the camera," says Dawoud. "Depending upon the nature of the project, and the time we have together, the relation-ships we grow are more or less deep. But even within the limita-tions of time, I try to connect."

Together the conversations and the photography nourish the self-esteem of the youngsters. "The process is about convincing them of the value of their lives," says Dawoud. "If you engage with them continuously, this leads to the suggestion that they are worth engaging with. I am clearly *not* interested in shaping or molding them into model citizens. I *am* interested in letting them know that I have a tremendous amount of respect for them, and that they have choices." But the relationship stretches further; it moves out from artist and student to a wider audience whose participation and appreciation support the development of the youngsters' self-images. It moves from a private intimate encounter into a public space as the photographs get displayed on the walls of galleries and museums. Dawoud speaks about the transformation that this causes in the subjects who become part of the audience and in the development of new audiences. "When you put their pictures up on the wall in a public arena, others will begin to recognize their value and worth. The kids can see themselves represented in a museum. They have never experienced that before. You know, you always go to a gallery to see someone else. But here they are, and their presence begins to engage a different audience . . . their parents, their friends . . . people who may never have been to a museum before. 'Jimmy's hanging up in the museum. Got to go see this!'"

After arriving at the campus of Phillips Andover, during his first residency there, Dawoud took it one step at a time—moving slowly, listening intently, and making it up as he went along. It was a long time before he took out his small camera to shoot some black-and-white shots, and even longer before he invited some of the students to travel into Boston on the weekend to be photographed in the studios of the Massachusetts College of Art, where the huge Polaroid was housed. As he looked through the lens of the camera and saw his subjects from a different perspective and in a new light, Dawoud often recalled his "pivotal experience" at the Metropolitan Museum of Art when he was about the same age. This work—like looking at himself in the mirror—allowed him to "reconsider who I had been at that age" and offered him the chance "to give kids access to another set of possibilities for their lives."

Dawoud offers his students at Phillips Andover this chance for a "reconsideration" of who they are and who they may become. During the last few minutes of the class I visit, Dawoud asks the students to walk into an adjoining studio where his most recent work is hanging. He has done about twenty sittings (he typically completes two sittings a day) with students from Phillips Andover, and he has tacked the prints up on the wall, testing which ones seem to fit well together. As in his early work in Harlem, "the subjects are the audience," and the students in this art history class gaze at photographs of their friends and classmates. All the recent pieces are individual images spread across six or eight panels, producing a single photograph of many parts where there is both stillness and movement. He explains the process of selection and composition to the students. "For each piece you see here I take two or three exposures. I try out the various possibilities and finally select what I want. I don't want the pieces to line up perfectly. I want to see movement in the work, a kind of flickering motion at play." Part of what Dawoud hopes to convey with the purposely imperfect alignment of the pieces is the demanding process of making the pictures. He explains, "We are devoting three hours to making this. None of us could possibly sit for that amount of time. I want to visually describe the movement and the shifting of the body."

Not only is Dawoud interested in capturing the flickering movement of the body in this work, he is also exploring ways of representing the interior lives of his subjects. The eyes of these students whose photographs hang on the wall do not look out at us; they look down or away from the camera; their aspects are pensive and introspective. Dawoud describes this new shift in his work. "I'm working now with the idea of a more internal and private space with the person. This is less a dialogue with the hypothetical viewer. When the subject is looking directly at the camera, it becomes very much about *you* the viewer. But here I'm wanting to retain the private space, allow them to be alone with their thoughts."

But Dawoud is also intent on reminding the students that this is highly interpretive, "transformative" work; "it is about the person, but it does not *literally* describe him or her." When he takes a photograph and looks through the lens of a camera, Dawoud hopes to discover something new about the person that he might never have noticed before. "I want to indulge my curiosity . . . I do not want to replicate or reproduce my experience," he explains to the students. "I want to find out something about you through the camera. I want to see how the camera transforms the space optically, physically, chemically." His voice stays even but grows more intense, "Cameras make pictures of the real world; they are *not* a substitute for that. It is a subjective construction of the real world mediated by another person."

Dawoud's work grew more interesting and satisfying when he broadened the scope of his efforts to include high school students from Lawrence, a lower-working-class community not far geographically from the privileged environment of Andover. Although he had truly enjoyed his developing relationships with the Andover students, and had felt fortunate to be able to take advantage of the place as a laboratory for his evolving work, his "social sensibilities" made him eager to extend the opportunities to less fortunate kids. "I wanted to make the work available to students beyond P.A.," he says forcefully. "The elitism and subtle arrogance in this arena did not appeal to me. It reinforced the notion that art making is for the aristocracy, and that rubbed me the wrong way."

Inviting the students from Lawrence not only meant that Dawoud got to work with a more diverse group of students, it also meant that the teenagers from both towns got to meet each other, and that the privileged prep school became linked with the working-class public school. Through these connections, Dawoud discovered another angle on his work. "I began to realize how *institutions* might establish mutually beneficial and mutually empowering experiences . . . that this could be a satisfying and rewarding experience for the people *and* the places . . . expanding minds and horizons."

He also discovered that, despite the extraordinary contrasts between these two communities and the very different life experiences of the students, there were great similarities in the ways they participated in his work and responded to his art. Whether the students were from Andover or Lawrence, they were all preoccupied with the same fundamental questions: "Who am I going to be?" and "What am I going to do with my life?" Whether the students were rich or poor, Dawoud was interested in "connecting" with them and finding a way to "create a complex and compelling photo representation of them . . . so that the audience might want to engage with them as well." Beyond the similarities in the students' questions and Dawoud's motives, he also discovered that his subjects—despite their very different life experiences—shared a common worldview; that they seemed to him "more similar than dissimilar." He observes, "There are certainly big class and geographic differences between them . . . they may be experiencing different social plateaus, but they are definitely participating in the same cultural arena. They are listening to the same music, wearing the same fashions, and seeing the same visual images."

Like the City College undergraduate in Hughes's poem, Dawoud's students begin to discover the unique and the universal; their individuality and the likenesses among them. As they gaze in the mirror, or look at each other, or see themselves in Dawoud's portraits, they begin to understand that "I am a part of you . . . and a part of you is me."

Since experiencing the pleasure and productivity of working with students from Lawrence and Andover, and building institutional relationships across class and racial lines, Dawoud has continued to design his art making in this way. In Chicago, Columbus, and Hartford he has brought together adolescents from across the social class and cultural spectrum, and continued to discover the ways in which the institutions and the people are transformed by the chance to meet, interact, and become subjects and audiences. In every setting he enters, the adults ask him about the criteria he would like them to use in choosing the students who will work with him. His response is always the same. To the teachers who often want to give him only the "best kids," he says, "I want a few kids who are interested in art, who might through this experience gain some tangible sense of art making; second, I want a few kids who are specifically interested in photography; third, I want some kids who have no clarity about their interests, who are still confused and searching. And finally, I want a few kids that they consider to be 'problem kids,' who are heading in the wrong direction." Dawoud recites the ingredients as if describing a delicious recipe for a dish that he is confident will turn out well. The passion in his voice reminds me of Kay Cottle's enthusiasm for working with heterogeneous groups of students in her classroom. Like Dawoud, she savors the diversity. "The group dynamics are crucial," Dawoud points out. "The kids get to see their peers engage in the work and each other. This can change minds and open choices."

This notion of opening minds and exploding caricatures is at the heart of Dawoud's nonjudgmental attitude. Just as he works to present "alternative images" of African-Americans, so he helps adolescents and their teachers move beyond stereotypes, categories, and facile generalizations about "teenagers." He takes me back to his own adolescence, when divisions of social class among the African-Americans in his junior high school provoked hostilities and conflict. Tastes in music carried the message of social class differences and crystallized into hardened caricatures.

"The white environment of my junior high school shaped musical tastes and signaled social class differences," recalls Dawoud. There were clear contrasts, and some mutual enmity, between the middle-class kids from Dawoud's neighborhood and the poor kids from the projects. "They were literally from the other side of the tracks. In our young black minds, *they* were the *project* kids who came on the *project* bus. Their hair was not brushed; they were often unkempt; they came to school in cut-off pants and stuff . . . and they listened to different music." Dawoud whistles a chorus of "Sergeant Pepper's Lonely Hearts' Club Band" and says, "I was listening to the Beatles, the Animals, the Stones, the Mamas and Papas when I was in junior high school. The black kids who were being bussed from the projects thought I was really weird. They were listening to the Four Tops, the Temptations, Martha and the Vandellas, the Supremes."

The musical contrasts defined by class differences remind Dawoud of a major issue that still concerns him and seems to be a source of inspiration for his work. He hears the echoes of the "project" kids calling him weird, and thinking of him as "not black" because he loved the Beatles, and says "this makes me think about the whole issue of black authenticity. I continue to be concerned about the way we tend to hold a narrow set of cultural assumptions about what is black and what isn't. It is very limiting and distorting." He sounds like the young black man in Hughes's poem who wants us to know his eclectic musical tastes—his love of "Bessie, bop, or Bach." He doesn't want us to assume that he can only dig the jazz and blues jams coming out of the Harlem clubs. He wants us to know that he is much more complex, multidimensional, and surprising than our caricature of him. Dawoud also wants to be liberated from the limits and constraints of caricature, from those who might try to define for him the boundaries of black life and black art. "I *still* listen to the Beatles."

So Dawoud finds it heartwarming and fascinating to witness the ways in which the students explode the categories in which they were placed before his work with them began. A confused "searcher" might become very focused and engaged. A troublemaker might fit comfortably and smoothly into the group. There are always welcome surprises even with a recipe that has been tried several times before. "I have never had any problems with these kids that they call problem kids," says Dawoud with an ounce of boastfulness in his voice. He tells of a sixteen-year-old kid named Reginald with whom he worked in Columbus, whom the teachers urged him not to include in the group because they predicted that he would be a destructive influence. Reginald had a big reputation for being a "bad kid," a reputation that stuck to him like glue and one that he continued to strengthen at every opportunity. He was chronically absent from school, and when he came, he brought so much disruption that teachers wished he had stayed away. His behavior in class ranged from raucous, inappropriate disruptions—shouting out vulgar language to humiliate his teachers or picking fights with classmates which would, if unchecked, escalate into full-scale brawls—to putting his head down on his desk and falling into a deep sleep. Reginald was particularly maddening to his teachers because they could see, in the swiftness of his banter and the cleverness of his manipulations, that he was a smart kid with huge potential. They often thought that if he would just channel half of the energy that he devoted to mischief and rancor into his studies, he could be a successful student. In an effort to capture his interest and his talent, his teachers were often overly solicitous, giving him second and third chances after major transgressions. But rather than show his appreciation for the teachers' special attentions, Reginald would test the limits further until he would earn another suspension from school.

When Reginald first came to the studio to work with Dawoud, he brought "that bad attitude" with him. He would either ignore Dawoud's instructions and withdraw from the class, or he would rudely cut off his peers when they were talking and then mock what they were saying. But Dawoud's presence and his response must have surprised Reginald and touched a nerve in him, because his antics were short-lived. He must have felt Dawoud's fearlessness and his affection. "There was something in this kid that I immediately liked," recalls Dawoud. "He was clearly very smart, had a great sense of humor, and he was hungry for attention." Dawoud looked him directly in his eyes; he "demanded" that he do the work; he challenged him to be successful; and he provided a lot of support. Reginald took to both his teacher and the photography, staying hours after the other students would leave, close to Dawoud's side. "We were really able to connect," says Dawoud. "He ended up being the most committed kid, the only one who showed up every day."

The memories of "connecting" with Reginald remind Dawoud again of the ways in which the camera allows for full attention to the subject. Through his lens, Dawoud sees many sides of a different person, a more complex reality. It is a view that resists caricature. He explains, "There is a real difference between what I see with my eyes and what I see through the camera." First, the camera allows you to really take a good, long look at a person in a way that would be "socially unacceptable" in ordinary interactions. "I am able to stare at the subject for two or three hours, indulging the full range of my curiosity, finding out all the things that I can't find out in normal social intercourse, and sharing that with the viewer," says Dawoud. And on the other side of the camera, the "subject" feels—often for the first time—fully seen and acknowledged, bathed in the light of Dawoud's keen interest and unending curiosity.

CHAPTER FIVE

Self-Respect

Although to be driven back upon oneself is an uneasy affair at best, rather like trying to cross a border with borrowed credentials, it seems to me now the one condition necessary for the beginnings of real self-respect. Most platitudes notwithstanding, self-deception remains the most difficult deception. The tricks that work on others count for nothing in that very well-lit back alley where one keeps assignations with oneself: no winning smiles will do here, no prettily drawn list of good intentions. One shuffles flashily but in vain through one's marked cards—the kindness done for the wrong reason, the apparent triumph which involved no real effort, the seemingly heroic act into which one had been shamed. The dismal fact is that self-respect has nothing to do with the approval of others—who are, after all, deceived easily enough; has nothing to do with reputation, which, as Rhett Butler told Scarlett O'Hara, is something people with courage can do without.

To have that sense of one's own intrinsic worth which constitutes self-respect is potentially to have everything: the ability to discriminate, to love, and to remain indifferent. To lack it is to be locked within oneself, paradoxically incapable of either love or indifference.

To assign unanswered letters their proper weight, to free us from the expectations of others, to give back to ourselves—there lies the great, the singular power of self-respect. Without it, one eventually discovers the final turn of the screw: one runs away to find oneself, and finds no one at home.

> —Joan Didion,
> "On Self-Respect" in
> *Slouching Towards Bethlehem*

I n saying that self-respect gives us "the ability to discriminate," Joan Didion suggests that it frees us for the judgments that we must make on a daily basis—what letters to answer, where and to whom our finite love and time can be directed. She expresses, with the authority and authenticity of personal experience, the potential dissonance between the view that we hold of ourselves and the views that others hold. In the absence of self-respect, this dissonance becomes so jarring that only the distorted views of others matter. At one point, Didion claims that "people with self-respect have the courage of their mistakes"—at another, with a more positive perspective, she characterizes self-respect as "the willingness to accept responsibility for one's life." Self-respect also frees us to love or "to remain indifferent," for without it love lacks the substance necessary for an authentic relationship.

The pressures and expectations of others can drive us into self-centeredness that blinds us to the authentic needs of others or a selflessness that blinds us to our own needs. Self-respect gives us the assurance to enter into relationships without feeling threatened. In such relationships—regardless of whether they are "equal"— respect flows in both directions.

David Wilkins, a professor of law at Harvard University, would appear to be someone for whom self-respect would not be an issue. A dashing, elegant man in his early forties whose charm is captivating and whose wit is winning; a distinguished legal scholar whose accomplishments have earned him an endowed chair at the Law School, who gets rave reviews from his students and his colleagues for his inspiring and exacting teaching, David Wilkins seems to have it all. His career has been meteoric: graduating with honors from Harvard College, attending Harvard Law School, editing the *Harvard Law Review*, clerking with Supreme Court Justice Thurgood Marshall, joining a prestigious corporate law firm, and finally, winning a position on the Harvard Law faculty, followed six years later by tenure.

But as Didion suggests in her essay, these symbols of lofty achievement, this chorus of adulation from the mouths of others, these "seemingly heroic acts," are often seen differently from within. Self-respect is not achieved through winning praise from others, or accumulating awards, status, and prestige. As a matter of fact—as David Wilkins knows so well—these external signs may, in fact, make one feel fraudulent. The dissonance between the applause from admirers and one's own dim internal compass can be painful.

David Wilkins is frank and articulate in tracing his arduous journey toward self-respect, a journey that has no clear and decisive destination, but one that keeps on progressing as he gains perspective and experience. His growing self-respect struggles against a family legacy of male high achievers who were filled with self-doubt, who seemed sturdy and proud on the outside but often felt empty on the inside. His father, uncles, and grandfather were stunningly successful in their chosen fields; a success that brought acclaim but not necessarily peace of mind; a success that seemed to demand the same from the next generation. A major task for David as an adult has been to untangle himself from this web of unforgiving expectation and find a way to feel at home with himself.

Much of David's teaching at the Law School is also designed to help his students avoid the emptiness of status, and a self-image exclusively defined by "the winning smiles" of others. He knows the casualties of self-deception. In the highly competitive and patriarchal environment of the Harvard Law School, where excellence is narrowly defined and hierarchies are mandatory, David works to create a classroom environment that is safe and comfortable; that allows students both to learn the strategies of survival and know that their success or failure is not a true measure of their worth. As he generously offers them his time, his wisdom, his humor, and his legal expertise, he hopes that they will feel his respect for who they are and will become; his respect for their personhood, rather than their "borrowed credentials."

Civil Procedure

Professor Wilkins enters Pound 102, one of the large lecture halls shaped like an amphitheater, at the Harvard Law School. He is wearing a black top hat, a long, flowing brown wool coat that reaches to his ankles. Underneath is a dark blue, wide pinstripe Italian-cut suit. The jacket stays closed, the clothes fit perfectly over his tall angular frame as he strides and gestures in front of the class. David is light-brown-skinned with brown wavy hair and a mustache that makes an upside-down "V" above his lips. He moves like an athlete who knows his body, expressing self-confidence through his physical ease. He arrives a few minutes before class, puts his fat *Civil Procedure* text, papers, and large seating chart down on the podium and begins to stalk silently back and forth; as if getting revved up; as if anticipating the path of his thinking for the next seventy minutes.

David's finery contrasts sharply with the one hundred and fifty students who sit in assigned seats in front of him. Many are dressed in the campus uniform of jeans, sweatshirts, sneakers; some of the men with baseball hats turned backwards. A few women are looking more sophisticated in long skirts and sweaters, slacks and jackets. I notice one older-looking, heavyset man (for the most part the students appear very young; recent college graduates, about twenty-two to twenty-four years old) who looks like one of the Grateful Dead, with frizzy blond hair pulled back in a ponytail, a couple of turquoise earrings in his left ear, a psychedelic shirt hugging his big belly, and a raggedy cowboy hat perched on his head.

He is talking to two Latino men as he saunters to his seat; their conversation is laced with legal-speak; "best efforts clauses" . . . "class actions," etc. He sits down next to a black woman whose short Afro is covered with a black beret and whose intense brown eyes look through round horn-rimmed glasses. At 8:25 A.M. many students are sipping coffee, diet Cokes, or juice, and munching on bagels and muffins.

I arrive early and perch on one of the desk chairs in the back of the lecture hall, behind the rows of stationary seats and next to the floor-to-ceiling plate glass windows. I am joined in the back by an attractive young woman dressed in black from head to toe, with a full head of black hair and a bright, friendly smile. She greets me and confesses that she is "hiding out" in the back because she hasn't done her reading. Another young woman—who turns out to have been a former graduate student of mine—sits down in the last arc of seats, sets up her PowerBook, and strikes up a conversation with me about her experience as a first-year law student: "an experience about which I have a great deal of ambivalence and anxiety in a place in which I don't feel totally comfortable." She offers an admiring comment about David, however. "Professor Wilkins is really great. He takes his work very seriously, and his standards are very high." Then more pensively she says, "He really gets what it means to be a student . . . He's empathic and compassionate."

The room has filled quickly and most of the seats are taken as David's loud, raspy voice cuts through the casual conversations. "Good morning. Good morning," he says as the room settles and grows quiet. "A couple of words about coming attractions." He announces the participation of two of his colleagues, who will co-teach with him in the next class session, and then tells them about the class party that will commemorate the conclusion of the course. "It will be in the South Dining Room from 1:30 P.M. until they throw us out. I'll do the best I can to throw an appropriate celebration." At the close of the "coming attractions," David announces the weekly luncheon ritual that accompanies his Civil Procedure course; a ritual well-known around the Law School, and one that first-year students eagerly anticipate and attend. Each Monday at noon, David goes out to lunch with ten to twelve of his students, giving "a chance for them to talk about anything they want to talk about." The students sign up and join David usually at a nearby Chinese restaurant whose prices will not be too taxing on their student budgets. Now close to the end of the semester David announces that priority for the lunch sign-up will be given to those students who have not yet had the chance to participate. As I listen to this last announcement I am struck by how clearly David wants to be in touch with his students' world, their perspective, their anxieties, their life beyond the walls of the lecture hall. He wants to see their faces and learn their first names. He wants them to "feel seen and heard." He also wants to challenge some of the rigid hierarchy that characterizes classroom interactions and shapes dialogues between professors and students.

Without pause David leaps into the academic agenda of the day, a smooth transition from the opening social announcements. "I have two objectives for today," he says. In clear, precise language, he previews the framework for the next sixty-five minutes of class. The first objective is "to lay the groundwork for how class action suits work . . . this will include everything we've said over the course of the semester and make them more *complicated*." "Mmm . . . ," he croons mischievously, "just what we need, right?"

For the next hour David mixes monologue with questioning as he paces back and forth, holding a long piece of chalk, poised for writing on the board. Occasionally he consults his big case book, but he never seems to look down at his notes. His pace is intense, often spiced with humor and witty asides; his hands and arms are always in motion. David underscores central points, marks transitions, anticipates big ideas, and tries to bring color and life to what he admits is the "dry field" of civil procedure.

"Now here is the lurking issue that I want to raise to the surface," he says as if he is uncovering a mysterious point.

Then a question: "What is *always* available?" He looks up, waits a moment, and calls on a young woman in the last row who is the only one with her hand up. "An issue of fact," says the woman. David does not pause to comment on the student's point, to offer praise, or make a judgment. He weaves her one-liner into his explanation and moves on.

Later on, however, he uses a more formal mode of questioning when he begins to examine the central case that the students have read for the day: *Hansberry vs. Lee*; a "case involving a racially restrictive covenant . . . is the rental barred by the covenant?" Now David stops, searches his seating chart, and calls out a name: "Miss Rose." The woman in black, who had hidden out in the back, sucks in her breath, blushes bright red, raises her hand. "That's me," she stammers. "I'm back here . . . I'll have to pass. I didn't read." Then under her breath she says, "The *one* time I didn't read!" She is trembling, very embarrassed by this excruciating public exposure. David murmurs in return. "Mmm . . . it's okay." But the woman looks as if she'd like to crawl into a hole. Quickly David calls on another student after checking his chart, and the young man says flatly, unapologetically, "I pass," to which David responds slightly miffed, "Aha! This is Ames week" (the first-year, Moot Court competition). On his third try—"Mr. Grant"—David finally gets a prepared response from a man in the back row and the two have an extended exchange for the next twenty minutes. The questioning is sharp and crisp, not harsh or attacking. When the student gets stuck or confused, David guides him through the argument. It is a benign but tough Socratic method; David is working just as hard as his student.

Toward the end of the class, students raise their hands to ask questions or for clarification of a point he has raised. David stops in his tracks, offers an interpretation or another angle on the argument, and then resumes his line of thinking. In response to a question asked by a woman in the front, David leans on the podium and is still for a moment, thinking. "That is an interesting question," he says. "I think the answer is yes . . . but I don't know . . . I'll find out." Then he struggles with it in front of his students, talking to himself, reflecting, reasoning, and figuring until he lands on an answer that he thinks *might* be right. Still he promises to get back to them the following week after searching out the correct response, or at least after he has given it more "rigorous thought."

"One Thing No One Knows About You"

The following Monday, when we greet the twelve students who have signed up for the last lunch of the semester with Professor Wilkins, a tall blond woman pushes through the group and whispers in my ear, "Whatever you're writing, I hope you'll describe his gorgeous suits." I nod in affirmation. There is no way to talk about this man—his persona or the theater of his teaching—without referring to his "threads." Before the student's whispered suggestion I had, in fact, asked David where he buys his "fabulous clothes." He had waved my question away nonchalantly. "Mostly in Filene's Basement," he quipped. Although I am certain that this is a man who can search out good bargains, I also suspect that he is someone who is not allergic to spending a good deal of money on material things that appeal to his sense of style.

David leads the parade of students—in yet another floor-length coat that billows out behind him—across the street and down a few blocks to the usual Chinese restaurant. A table is set up for us and everyone chooses a place; several students strategically following closely on David's heels in order to get a seat near to him. This is David's party. He barks out friendly orders regarding buffet choices and the menu, and we make quick decisions about our food so that we can get on with the main event.

When everyone is settled—but before the food arrives—David begins the ritual. He sets the tone. He asks them to introduce themselves "by your *first* and last names," "say where you are from," and "tell us one thing that no one here knows about you." He grins. "At least, one thing that you are willing to make public." He turns to the woman to his left, a pretty woman with long brown hair, a full mouth, and green eyes, who has—since we began our march from the Law School—positioned herself next to David by subtly blocking out other students. Her eyes never leave him and she doesn't skip a beat. In a husky voice she offers her name, says she is from Northern California, and that she has spent the last few years in Vienna studying to be a pastry chef. There are some silly jokes about making "torts" from some of her classmates and David follows by slowly repeating her full name, questioning her briefly about a spicy ingredient sometimes mixed into pie crusts, and offering some appreciative comments about what she refers to as "my secret past."

David follows the same sequence for all who are sitting around the table—listening intently, repeating each name, asking a thoughtful question, and making some connection or observation. The revelations are diverse and intriguing. A young man says shyly that he just got engaged and that his father-in-law-to-be was the architect of the new building that has just gone up at the Law School. "It makes me feel a bit of a connection to the place," he says softly, "like two of my worlds coming together." A woman with frizzy red hair talks about having spent several years after college working in experimental theater off-Broadway in New York City. She is missing "everything" about her old life: her friends, the city, the passion, the long hours, the artist community . . . but not the poverty, "living hand-to-mouth," or her parents' "constant disapproval and disdain." A black woman with a lean, muscular body and a peaceful countenance says she is a ballroom dancer—specializing in the tango, rumba, and samba—and she is searching for a skilled and experienced partner with whom she will be able to enter regional competitions. A Chinese-American woman glows with excitement as she reveals that she is learning to love jazz under the enthusiastic tutelage of her new boyfriend. A precise and clean-cut ex-Marine, who has just graduated from Stanford, talks about owning two boa constrictors, after being denied his "snake passion" all of his growing-up years. His mother, who raised him by herself, was "terrified of snakes" and wouldn't even let her son own a garter snake.

Everyone has a tale, some more exotic than others. But David responds to each as an invitation for interesting dialogue, making each person feel singled out and heard. This exercise—which could have fallen flat, become tedious, or caused embarrassment—turns out to be inspiring, charged by David's energy and fascinating associations. To the ballroom dancer, he describes an upcoming competition at the Ritz; to the novice jazz lover, he talks about "what's happening" at the Regatta Bar; to the actress, he describes some of the opportunities in entertainment law. Quite suddenly, as though in Dawoud's larger-than-life portraits, I begin to see twelve vivid *individuals* around the table, young people with diverse histories and rich experiences. They are no longer faceless, anxious first-year law students homogenized by their common fears and ambitions.

Once around the table, David moves into the real pleasure of the ritual. "I want to offer you all the chance to do something I always wanted to do as a law student but never got the opportunity to do," he says mysteriously, as if he is about to open a big gift. The students lean forward in their seats, their eyes intense. He tells them that they can question him about anything they would like . . . anything that comes to their minds; unfiltered, uncensored. And he promises them that he will try to answer them as honestly as he knows how. David offers up a few examples just to give them an idea of the range of possibilities, the levels of intimacy, the ways they can cross the traditional professor-student boundaries. "You can ask me my salary . . . or what I think about other professors at the Law School . . . or about my career or professional options . . . whatever you'd like." He laughs. "I only ask that we keep this fairly private . . . I used to ask students not to take stories back that might threaten my prospects for tenure. But now I have tenure, so . . ." I hear David's mixed message, which offers open access and signals trust, but also seems to ask that students recognize certain boundaries. He is opening Pandora's box only halfway; enough to invite their informality and spontaneity and feed their curiosity, but not enough to leave anyone feeling exposed. David's students receive the invitation in the way he has offered it—as a rare gift.

Almost before David has finished his introduction, the ex-Marine from Stanford leaps in: "How fast have you gotten that car of yours?" (David has a bright red Porsche 911, which everyone knows he cherishes.) "Aha," grins David, "one hundred and twenty-five on a straight strip during the daytime . . . with no other cars around." The next question comes from the pastry chef sitting next to him, who asks David his views about one of his colleagues who prominently appears in the media. David launches into an elaborate answer that refers to the activities and priorities of the various "media lawyers" on the Harvard Law faculty. He offers candid and quick evaluations of each, using the three criteria of teaching, scholarship, and "contributions to the professional community"; a kind of citizenship. I am impressed by David's candor and his courage in taking public measurement of his colleagues. But I am most impressed by the way he turns these "personal" questions that ask for the "inside story" into opportunities for teaching. His commentary does not come off sounding like gossip or whining. It sounds like instruction: fair, clear, complex, and unbiased.

Other questions follow that seem to grow in intensity and seriousness. A question about "meritocracy and affirmative action" leads to a swift reply from David about how to become a Harvard Law professor ("win the Sears Prize in the first year; become president of the *Harvard Law Review*; clerk for Felix Frankfurter [who, we all know is dead]; and join a fancy corporate firm"), none of which says "anything about your ability to become a good teacher and scholar." David admits that his own route to Harvard's faculty followed this traditional trajectory; that he is, in many respects, the "classic example" of succeeding by these rigid criteria. But he also expresses relief that some of these standards are being expanded and relaxed. "There is a shift in the credentials being looked at," he says, "and I regard that as a *healthy* shift."

The final query, from a woman student, seems very close to home, to the root of what is really causing them anxiety at the end of their first term in law school. She seems to speak for all of them when she blurts out her question: "What is the distinction between an A- and a B+ in your class?" Her question gives David an opportunity he seems to have been waiting for, the chance to assert the "relative" insignificance of grades and the "great" importance of self-respect. His voice cracks with emotion and his eyes fill with tears. He almost seems to be pleading as he says, "You know, grades are not the measure of you . . . they are not even a measure of what I think of you. They are the score you receive on a task which is really quite artificial. For four hours, one hundred and fifty people all sit in the same room . . . and participate in this particularly stylized activity." He continues along in this vein, offering them solace, support; underscoring their talents, intelligence, and skills; and assuring them that he expects *all* of them to pass the course.

His last few sentences sound like a final embrace: "This is why I have these lunches. I want to get to know something about all of you . . . not just how you perform on a test. I respect and value what I've learned about you." respects others

A Comfortable Atmosphere

David's office in Hauser, a brand-new building at the Law School, is huge and lavishly appointed. The walls look about thirteen feet high; the lighting is bright but gentle on the eyes; a full wall of windows looks out on other buildings in the Law School complex. Polished wood is everywhere and large expanses of white walls are perfect for hanging prints and pictures: a photo of Miles Davis, a Romare Bearden print, a painting of "three black men sitting on a bench" with a photograph (just above it) of the Justices of the Supreme Court. Other pieces of art—most of it reflecting African-American origins—are carefully placed, all around the office. The desk, a large wooden half-circle on a graceful pedestal, comes from Italy. "You won't believe it . . . *I* can hardly believe it . . . The Law School sent some professors over to Italy to pick out furniture," he tells me. A couple of other pieces also come from the Italian collection, provided by the Law School, and the rest of the furniture— equally snazzy—is David's choice and bought by him: an off-white couch, two sleek metal and leather chairs in red and blue, the "prize-winning" chair that David is perched on, and a tall, custom-made wooden cabinet in which he has installed fancy stereo equipment and a television. The wiring for this sophisticated sound system—at David's request—has been embedded inside the walls.

I take in this scene, awestruck by the obvious affluence and envious of the resources on display in David's office. I teach at the Graduate School of Education, one of the "poorer" schools at Harvard. My office is a quarter of the size of his, and the blinking fluorescent lights and ugly chartreuse walls offend my eyes every day. There is no sound system, no television, no designer table and chairs; just a big gray metal desk, shelves overflowing with books; piles of folders, periodicals, and papers on the floor because they will not fit into my single metal file cabinet; and two purple chairs that my students "liberated" from a building undergoing renovation because they knew their color was my favorite. But I have made this tiny space my own with a Peruvian tapestry, ancient Masai jewelry from East Africa, a kilim rug from Morocco, and family photos. I love my office, but I know that if space signifies stature and square feet are a measure of power, then on Harvard's ladder of prestige, I—a full-tenured professor sitting on an endowed chair of my own—am close to the bottom. As I take in David's digs in one of the "richest" schools in the Harvard firmament, I smile at the envy that wells up inside me, which I quickly convert into opposite feelings of relief and liberation. After all, I don't "need" these symbols of status for self-respect, these "borrowed credentials," I say to myself, slightly defensively.

We settle in one corner of the room, letting the sunlight bathe us in a glowing warmth. I sit on the leather couch with David across from me in the prize-winning chair and our work begins. Having watched him "teach" in class and over a Chinese lunch, I am eager to know what he hopes his students will learn from him; what he sees as the most important goals of his formal and informal curriculum. David begins by saying that his chief concern "is not a substantive one." For him, teaching is most importantly an effort to create a "learning atmosphere" that helps motivate students to "want to learn" and supports them in being "able to learn." Then he offers a big caveat: "I want to do that for as many people as possible given the format . . . you know, of one hundred and forty-seven students sitting in an amphitheater." "Look," he says decisively, "these students are so smart . . . left to their own devices they could figure out a whole lot . . . Teaching them the rules of civil procedure might be accomplished through directed reading . . . They can learn the data points without my support."

David's appreciation for the inherent competence of his students, his desire to nurture their confidence, mirrors Jennifer Dohrn's respect for the abilities of her mothers-to-be. With support, but "left to their own devices," these students, like the mothers, are "given back to themselves," empowered.

"My primary objective," he says switching gears, "is to help them feel comfortable and to teach them a certain way of thinking . . . what we call thinking like a lawyer." This does not involve rote memorization ("although there are a lot of rules and procedures to memorize"). Neither is it the kind of "theoretical argument" that they might have learned studying social science in college or the kind of "inductive, empirical argument that leads to a definitive answer." David admits that it is easier to say what legal thinking "is not" rather than to define what it "is." Finally, he says that it involves a kind of "analytic rigor," engaging a "particular kind of analytic structure." He smiles remembering the way his colleague Martha Minow characterizes legal thinking. "She says it is just like the game on *Sesame Street* . . . in which you have to decide which one of these is not like the other." It involves an openness to new ways of thinking *and* a reliance on former experience and skills. "At the beginning of the course, I say to my students that they will need to learn a lot that is new . . . a new language, new tools, new readings . . . but also that everything they've known before—both academic knowledge and personal experience—will be relevant . . . contracts are like promises, torts are injuries, etc." His summary sentence takes his purpose into a broader realm. "I want to create an environment in which students will become interested in learning the way the law intersects with and shapes society . . . and their place as lawyers in that process."

David seems less interested in describing "legal thinking" (*and* his efforts to teach it) than he is in talking about his wish to create a "comfortable atmosphere" within an environment that is often hostile to, and demeaning of, students. "The *genius* of legal education is the interactive stuff," he crows. "But the problem is that the structure is extremely alienating, stifling, and intimidating." David struggles against institutional norms that cause anxiety and tension among students. He challenges an entrenched social structure that is "explicitly hierarchical" and authoritarian. His first few classes, he says, are always designed to "reduce stress" and put students at ease. Curiously, David's goal—although for a class of one hundred and fifty with a set curriculum—is not unlike Dawoud Bey's, to create rapport and trust, and liberate creative thought.

"My class is the first class on the very first day of law school . . . the Tuesday following Labor Day at 8:25 in the morning. They have already read an assignment . . . they are supposed to be prepared. The first class is supposed to be substantive. They are very stiff, very frightened . . . I talk about how they must be afraid. Then I assure them that the most important thing has already happened. I say to them, 'You have one of these five hundred and fifty seats . . . the pressure is off!'" David tells them that eight thousand people apply to Harvard Law School and four thousand of those would probably have done just fine were they sitting in these same seats. Once admitted to Harvard, they can count on a "great life" of achievement. "This is a great ticket." "Of course," he explains, "there is a substantial element of luck" in gaining one of these seats of privilege, but that "they are *all* completely capable of doing the work of law school."

Given David's strenuous and heartfelt efforts to reduce student anxiety and create "a comfortable atmosphere" for his first-year students, I ask him why he calls them by their last names and why he "calls them off the seating chart" (both traditional and formal practices in legal education that would seem to emphasize hierarchy and fuel anxiety). He responds immediately. "I do this for three reasons," he says. "In keeping with this 'transparency' view of disclosing my motives, I tell them about the first two of my reasons . . . but not the third." First, he calls them by their last names—"Mr. Brown," "Ms. Green"—because he wants to emphasize that they "are becoming members of a profession . . . and there is a certain set of formalities and form related to that profession . . . this is particularly true about a course in civil procedure, which is about courtroom practice. In the court, all judges, lawyers, even witnesses, are called by their formal names." As for his rationale for "calling students off the chart," he is quick to say that he is *not* interested in checking on their preparation or humiliating them publicly if they haven't done their reading. Rather he believes that there are "many students who would not talk if they were not called upon . . . once they speak for the first time, they feel more comfortable speaking up again." He also reasons that law students need to learn to think on their feet and speak in front of groups.

David recalls my visit to his class and remembers the "extremely rare" experience of calling on two people from the chart who were *not* prepared. When the first person—"Ms. Rose"—said she had to "pass" because she had not done the reading, David remembers "not making a deal about it." I, too, recall his gentle, casual response ("it's okay"), but mostly I remember Ms. Rose's bright red face and her deep embarrassment. Even though David does not publicly chastise his students the way *his* law professors did, the atmosphere of the school fosters angst and humiliation that often overwhelm his attempts to put his students at ease.

The third reason that David offers for using the formal traditions of law teaching is an echo from his early years at Harvard when he felt less self-confident and less powerful as a teacher. In 1986, David was thirty years old and brand new to teaching; "inexperienced and unprotected." "I felt I needed to make sure that I had all the authority I could get." David recalls, "I worried that students might not give me the kind of deference I deserved or that my colleagues were getting. Being called 'Professor' seemed essential to my stance and potency as a teacher." He shakes his head with relief. "Now I know much more about what I am doing. I'm much more confident, and I probably need the formal structure less."

But David is not just thinking about his own need for status and authority when he was inexperienced and new to teaching. He is also referring to the formality and decorum that he believes are "legitimate for professors of color and women professors" in a law school culture where students are still likely to "automatically question" their competence and their authority. The skepticism of students (and colleagues) means that women and faculty of color (including the token representation of Latinos, Asians, and Native Americans on law school faculties) may feel a greater need than their white male counterparts to lean on the traditional, patriarchal forms and rituals to give them legitimacy. In Johnye Ballenger's language, they may need to attach the "handle" of "Professor" to their names in order to ensure that students will not act disrespectfully toward them. Like Johnye and David's ancestors, who like my own sought protection from the insinuating assaults of being treated like "boys" and "gals" even when they were fully grown adults, we still experience today the "legacy of slavery" in settings where our legitimacy is questioned. The titles "Professor" and "Doctor" still provide a fragile armor. "When I first began teaching," says David about students' responses to the mixture of his youth and his blackness, "I simply couldn't afford to be casual."

Remembering several of his female colleagues, David admits "actually, the gender issue may be more salient than the race issue." He catalogues some of the "horror stories"—of disrespect—that he has heard over the years from colleagues all over the country. "By far—a very large measure—I hear the worst tales from the women of color, then white women, then men of color." He recites a few "not atypical" examples: A black woman was featured in a student newspaper in a caricature that looked just like Aunt Jemima with a caption that referred to her "real place" in the kitchen. A senior African-American male professor who felt forced to resign from the Law School when his colleagues refused to tenure their first woman of color, even though they had many opportunities and more than a handful of talented and experienced candidates. The young white woman professor who suffered subtle sexist innuendoes from her male colleagues when she would occasionally challenge them—on issues of substance—in faculty meetings. The black male professor whom everyone considers an "affirmative action" hire, who won tenure even though several of his senior colleagues claimed—behind closed doors—that they were lowering their standards by admitting him into their ranks. He sits among them, knows what they are thinking, and feels unwelcome.

David's stories remind me of my own experiences as a brand-new twenty-six-year-old Assistant Professor, when my youth, my inexperience, my gender, and my race conspired to make me feel terrified and inadequate most of the time. Like most new teachers, I felt insecure about my teaching and shallow in my grasp of the intellectual substance. I was trying to stay one step ahead of my graduate students (many of whom were older, wiser, and more worldly than I), dreading the questions they would ask that might unmask my ignorance. But I also knew that my token status, as the first black woman on my faculty, also caused distortions and awkwardness in my interactions with my students. I knew that many found my presence surprising and uncomfortable; many questioned my competence. I knew that some of the questions they asked were, in fact, designed to trip me up, to expose me, to prove that I did not belong there. The mixture of my own deeply felt insecurities and their suspicions and skepticism made it hard for us to engage in the authentic work of teaching and learning.

In those early years, I, like David, leaned heavily on my professor title, developed overly formal relationships with my students, filled my classes with overprepared monologues in order to avoid the unanswerable questions and the discussions that I feared might get "out of control." Because I felt so unsure of myself, I played for the applause, for external validation, for what Didion calls the "winning smiles" of others. With time, study, practice, and maturity, I no longer need to hide behind the formalities. I no longer worry so much about the distorted views of others. I am willing to risk confrontation; I dare to name and challenge the discriminatory acts of others. David's ten years at Harvard have brought him to a similar place. He shakes his head and remarks on the symmetry that comes with time and a growing self-respect. "I think there is a kind of mutuality here. If I call my students by their first names, I've got to be prepared for them to call me by mine."

In creating a "comfortable environment" in his classroom, David begins at the beginning. "First, I need to get them to come," he says matter-of-factly. "I have never had an attendance problem . . . and I'm very proud of that." Once the students are there, he needs to "wake them up," capture their attention, and "make this a class that they want to come to." He sees the challenge as a combination of "substance and theater"; part strategy and part personality. He admits that it is his "personality" to joke, to use humor, and make frequent references to pop culture. He also believes that it is his responsibility to bring the "energy" to the classroom and advance it productively. "I understand that I really have to drive this train . . . I bring the energy and they can feed off that energy."

"It is not my personality," David says, "to be authoritarian . . . even if I wanted to act like the stern, mean law professor, I couldn't do it well. You also have to be careful because authoritarianism can backfire badly and begin to set up adversity in the classroom." Instead David relies on his ample supply of wit and storytelling. "Humor reduces tension and it often helps people remember a point." David also recognizes its deep roots in his character. "I've always used humor," he says, "as a strategy for getting people to like me." "Stories," says David, "are also important for helping to drive home a point or for bringing in examples from the real world. They also provide a context for a legal principle or argument . . . like the saga of the Agent Orange case that we are using not only offers drama, it is also embedded in a social, political, and economic context."

Whether it is humor or storytelling, David is aware of the limits of their usefulness, and uses them with style and restraint. He is, first of all, determined not to let the theater of teaching become the central agenda; theater should be in the "service of substance." Like Kay Cottle, David does not want to upstage, overshadow, or overwhelm his students. Neither does he want to let the drama take on a life of its own. "You have to watch that the performance does not get in the way . . . that you are never playing it for laughs. You don't want to script everything." David also wants to make sure that the "performance" is in good taste. "I try not to offend people, I try to be respectful . . . for example, I try not to swear in class. This, after all, is a *captive* audience. They have no choice about taking the course; nor do they choose the professor that they will take it with . . . so you need to be especially careful not to be offensive."

When David teaches he is always remembering how it felt to be a student at Harvard Law School. "I work to remember how *I* was as a student . . . all the fear and anxiety I experienced. On purpose, for example, he starts his class five minutes late, at 8:30 A.M. (rather than 8:25 A.M.) because "I could never get to class on time." And he tells his students that they should feel comfortable walking in late. "Don't feel you have to sneak in and sit in the back; come in and take your assigned seat . . . and don't *not* come at all . . . the *most* important thing is that you *come*." And on the last day of class before their final, he says to his students (in yet another effort "to take the pressure off"), "I've *never* failed a student . . . and I certainly don't intend to start now." For his anxious students, these parting words may be the most persuasive sign of David's respect; words that feel both challenging and reassuring, empowering and comforting.

His efforts at getting students to "come to class," to engage in "legal thinking," to "feel comfortable," to learn the formal rituals and procedures of the court have paid off handsomely in students' unabashed admiration of David and their appreciation of his teaching. He leaps up and grabs a handsome silver chalice off the shelf that was given to him by his very first civil procedure class. It is a "Rookie of the Year Award" and it glistens like the pride David seems to take in having achieved this honor from his *students*. At the Law School, where *teaching* is greatly valued and rewarded; where until recently "scholarship has had a tradition of being secondary to teaching"; where some of the most "brilliant Socratic method teachers have held forth, David has—in his ten years there—been considered one of the best. This normally modest man almost crows about his reputation as a teacher. "I have a reputation of being a very good teacher among my colleagues," he says. And his students consistently rate him high on student evaluations (which "everyone reads, both students *and* faculty"). "In all the years I have taught here, I have ranked among the top five in the Law School . . . and I am teaching two courses—civil procedure and legal ethics—which typically get low ratings."

When I ask David why his students rate him at the top, he admits—somewhat shyly—that they know that he "cares about them," that he "extends himself" to them, that they appreciate the "comfortable atmosphere" he creates in the classroom, and that they see that he makes himself "available in and out of the class." During his office hours, which often stretch late into the evening, David receives a parade of students who usually want to talk about a mix of personal and professional issues. "I try not to dismiss any questions as absurd or stupid, or distracting," he says. Frequently, they come for career counseling, or to discuss their ambivalence about legal training, or their wish to leave school. On occasion David has intervened with their parents or helped them find their way to professional counseling. Over time, he has grown to understand the limits of his responsibilities, the boundaries of his competence; and he has become clearer and more decisive in drawing the line with his students who are seeking his guidance and support.

Burden of Achievement

Teaching has always been the arena in which David Wilkins has felt most confident and skilled. "I always thought that I would be a good teacher," he says. "But I was *terrified* of being a scholar." He imagined that "good teaching" would flow from his experience as a law student. "You see, I was a very successful law student . . . and

I always thought it was not because I had great ideas; not because I was particularly creative or gifted. I thought my success was the result of my diligence. I knew how to persevere; how to accomplish the work." When he became a professor, David had a similar view of himself; seeing himself as a devoted and disciplined teacher, but lacking confidence in his intellectual, analytic prowess.

At first, in fact, he had felt "resentful of the idea that he had to do more than just teach." This resentment built up over time and developed into a "serious writer's block." "I had a hard time getting it out . . . I lacked confidence in my ideas. I worried that someone might not like me." "My father was very judgmental . . . as was his father . . . and it made it hard for him to be as productive as he should have been." Clearly "being liked" is a central issue for David (who seems to be universally liked, admired, and respected), and his yearning for others' approval has generational resonance. As he says these words, he seems to see visions of the men before him; pictures of strength and vulnerability, confidence and insecurity.

"There is much about my father that I don't fully understand," David begins as if "coming to know his father" is a work in progress, a central and difficult preoccupation. As soon as he decides to take on the family story ("the place from which all other experiences unfold"), his face grows somber, his voice hesitant, his sentences tentative. It is not hard to see the child in him as he begins to talk about his father.

In order to reveal his father, David must step back to trace his membership in "a very prominent black family of the 1940s." David's paternal grandfather, J. Ernest Wilkins, cast a very long shadow. A graduate of the University of Illinois (where he earned first prize for his undergraduate work in theoretical mathematics), he was warned that a black man would never be able to successfully pursue advanced studies or a research career in mathematics, so he decided, instead, to become a lawyer. In the 1920s, he attended the University of Chicago Law School and became one of the first black graduates. After practicing law in Chicago for several years, he rose to national prominence as President Eisenhower's Undersecretary of Labor.

J. Ernest Wilkins had three sons, all of whom were "amazingly bright" and precocious. "Achievement and academic success were put at a premium," says David in frank understatement. The oldest son "fulfilled his father's dream by earning his Ph.D. in applied mathematics at the University of Chicago," a degree he earned at nineteen years of age. David's eyes widen as he adds, "His mother was angry at him because if he had pushed just a little harder, he could have gotten his Ph.D. at eighteen and become the youngest *ever* to earn that degree in the history of the university."

The second son, John Robinson Wilkins, went to the University of Wisconsin at fourteen, entered the Harvard Law School at nineteen, was elevated to the *Harvard Law Review* (the third black in the history of the school), practiced law with his father in Chicago, migrated to Washington, D.C., to become the general counsel for A.I.D. under President Kennedy, and finally ended up teaching law at the University of California, Berkeley (Bolt Hall), the second tenured black professor to be hired in any department at Berkeley.

"These were the shoes my father had to follow in," says David, shaking his head. Born in 1926, called "the slow one" by his mother, David's father also went to the University of Wisconsin at fourteen, and arrived at the Harvard Law School in 1944, when he was eighteen. The Second World War broke out and he was drafted, delaying his graduation to 1949. After finishing law school, he returned to Chicago and joined his father and brother John practicing law at a small firm called "Wilkins, Wilkins, and Wilkins." Even after his father and brother had left the firm to pursue their advancing public careers in Washington, David's father practiced alone for years but continued to call the firm "Wilkins, Wilkins, and Wilkins"; probably resenting the fact that he was left holding the bag but hiding his resentment behind a dogged, bleak resignation.

"He hated every minute of it," recalls David. He was doing the work of the "traditional black practitioner . . . a solo practice in a small, out-of-the-way corner of Chicago, dealing with real estate, small black businesses, probate court." David lets out a long, anguished sigh, and then stares off into space. After a long silence, he whispers a line that he must have said many times before as he has tried to untangle this torturous story. "My father had the disposition of a poet."

Recently David received a precious package from his aunt, the widow of his Uncle John, and it contained a volume of his father's poetry that he had written during the 1940s when he was in his teens at the University of Wisconsin. David's father had been extremely close to his brother John, who seems to be the family member with whom he shared his grief, his dreams, and his soulful poetry. David pulls out a dark green leather-bound notebook that looks ancient but not at all tattered. His hands tremble as he opens the book carefully and reads the first poem he comes to. The searing, sad words speak of his loneliness, his search for himself.

David does not remember experiencing his father's pain as a young child. His father kept it well-hidden under a veneer of competence and niceness. But by the time David was an adolescent, he began to see the sadness and feel the underlying tension in his family's house. "I began to be aware of who my parents were. I began to see that things in my house were in a perpetual state of crisis, often around money. Though my father had lots of prestige—being from a very prominent and visible black family—we had very little money." David's parents carried on the fierce Wilkins family legacy of educational excellence and ambition (though David admits it was nowhere near as harsh and unforgiving as the expectations for achievement meted out by his father's parents), and sent all four of their offspring to the University of Chicago Laboratory School. At the time, David's father was making about $28,000 a year, typical for a black solo practitioner during this period, but nowhere near what was required to support four children in private schools and the rest of the trappings of a middle-class lifestyle. David recalls several times during his high school career when the school would not let him register because the previous semester bills had not been paid.

But the troubles his father faced were deeper than financial. Not only was Wilkins's law practice not lucrative, it also became clear that David's father was becoming "deeply depressed" and "paralyzed in his work." "My father was a *brilliant* lawyer, renowned among his peers for doing outstanding legal work. But, as I found out, he also had periods when he felt incapable of doing almost anything. Throughout my childhood, he was secretly struggling with his life, but never talked about his problems . . . He was a stoic." Hoping that he would be able to make a better living and measure up to the family's historic status, David's father began to entertain offers to leave his solo practice and join a large corporate law firm. This was at a time, David explains, when all the large corporate firms were looking for one reputable black to "integrate" their organization. Since corporate law firms were reputed to be among the most lucrative, many of his father's friends and family urged him to accept one of these prestigious opportunities.

David's father was the perfect prospect. He was a good-looking, light-skinned (many whites couldn't even tell that he was African-American) black man from a prominent Chicago family. In 1968, at the age of forty-two, David's father finally submitted to the pressure and joined a large law firm, making him the only black lawyer out of more than one hundred lawyers in the firm. This move "up the ladder" held no excitement or promise for him, but he hoped it would ease the family tension and be a new start.

But there was no new start. It turned out that moving to a large, all-white law firm only intensified his problems. Nothing he had done prepared him for the assaults and abuses—often veiled and oblique—that he suffered as the token black. Although he had the rank of "partner," he had neither the client base and networks, nor the experience to effectively navigate the firm's expectations. Lawyers half his age treated him with contempt. Most of his clients could not afford to pay the corporate rates. All of this magnified his own sense of depression and paralysis. "He was terrified of being uncovered as a failure." Within a few short years, his career at the firm came to an abrupt end. David received the cryptic call.

"Can you help me on Saturday?" his father asked. "I need to move some boxes." The whole move was shrouded in secrecy. When David arrived to help him carry the boxes, he discovered that his father was vacating his office and was no longer an employee of the firm.

Back in private practice, David's father's emotional and financial woes continued to deteriorate, and as his family would later find out, so did his physical health. When the small firm to which he had fled dissolved, David's mother sought her son's help. By this time, David, who was starting his own legal career in Washington, D.C., suddenly found himself taking frequent trips to Chicago to help his father resurrect the solo practice that he had abandoned more than fifteen years before. "This experience was extremely difficult for me," recalls David. "My father had many professional problems and he was suffering great psychological turmoil. As hard as it was for me to learn some of the things that were going on in my father's life, it was even harder to think how painful it must have been for him to share them with me."

Six months later, David and his family learned that the roots of his father's anguish were more complex. "A friend of the family suggested that my father's actions were consistent with a brain tumor," remembers David. His father hated hospitals and it took several weeks to persuade him to go for diagnostic testing. On the morning of the day when the tests were finally scheduled, he went into a coma from which he would never awaken. "I know that the tumor killed him," David moans, "but given the deep pain that he felt about all the turmoil in his life, and what must have been his fear of putting us all through a prolonged medical crisis, I have always felt that he really willed himself to death."

The ghosts of David's father, and his father's father, and his father's brothers are all around us as we sit talking in David's office. There is simply no way to tell his story, to talk about his style of teaching, his priorities, and dreams without reviewing these family dramas. Interestingly, David's mother's side of the family has also had a history of being ambitious, achieving, and prominent, but it is his *paternal* lineage that seems to haunt David the most, that seems to define his identity and be the source of his greatest strength and anguish. "This is all connected to me," says David, "because I've always had a tremendous need to achieve . . . I've always worried that I will be unmasked as a fraud . . . I've always had a fear of not being good enough."

I sit there looking at this handsome, sinewy man perched in his elegant office, this Professor of Law at Harvard who, at age forty-two, holds a prestigious chair, and find it difficult to believe that he feels vulnerable and unworthy. The pain in his voice and the weight of his father's story convince me that these ghosts are real. However, he has clearly chosen a different path than the one that killed his father. He will not be a stoic; he will not suffer silently. Over the last several years, he has been struggling to uncover the complex and difficult truths; he has been trying to explore the origins of his own "paralysis."

From time to time, David still experiences "fear, pain, and paralysis." When he is sitting at his computer, he will sometimes get stuck, writing the same words over and over again, feeling panicked that the essay or book chapter will not be good enough. He points to a huge, messy pile of papers, articles, notes, and books that are strewn around his desk chair, and says that these are the leftovers of a paper he has just finished. During the writing of the paper, he had been plagued by dark moments of self-doubt. Since I have recently read much of David's work, and been impressed both by the volume and the quality of his writing, I express my disbelief. "How do you push past these stuck places?" I ask. "Basically," admits David, "I fight my way through it . . . I face the challenge . . . I figure that it is better to finish than not to finish . . . But I am never satisfied with the results." At the same time as David worries about it "not being good enough," he also knows "rationally" that he is a "good writer." His publication record, the journals he has published in, the peer reviews from distinguished colleagues, should seem enough to convince him. But the doubts are deeper and they continue to cause "moments of paralysis."

Another way in which David feels the ghosts of his father's suffering is in the way he tends to relate to the people around him, both friends and strangers. "I, like my father," confesses David, "always have this feeling that I have to please everyone. My father would never say no to anyone or get angry at anyone . . . he would speak to *everyone* he passed on the street . . . all of this was because he feared he would not be acceptable to folks." David can feel the same impulses within himself, "finding things in people that will support and validate me." Now his voice is disbelieving. "I still think that part of me believes that the reason students think I am a good teacher is because I am *kind* to them." It makes me recall a statement David made a few weeks ago when I asked him about his use of humor in the classroom. He had at first listed the ways in which humor lightens dry analysis and helps students remember points, but he had finally offered a simpler truth. "I use humor to get people to like me," he had said sadly.

"Smoke and Mirrors"

It is the end of the semester, examination time, and David is feeling the "strange, ritual transition" that he always feels when he is preparing to grade his students' exams. He is uncomfortable with his shift in role, from being a supporter to being an evaluator. "I am now in this peculiar position," he says slowly, "of evaluating my students . . . In the classroom, I view myself as helping them understand and see the world in a rich and full way . . . but in grading papers, my job in part is to find which answers are better than others. It is a process we have to go through, but I am always fearful of destroying the other relationship."

This year, for the first time, David "explicitly" took on this issue in the last review session he had with students before the exam. He said three things to them about the evaluation process. First, he warned them that it was inevitably a "subjective" process; that even though in grading the papers he uses an answer key and tries to develop a fair comparative measure, there is still a lot of room for variation and interpretation. "I tell them that I am pretty confident that I will not give a C to someone who deserves an A, but the difference between an A- and a B+ is often not discernible. The grade I give will depend on a number of factors . . . whether I'm tired, what exam I read before this one." The second thing he tells them is that the grade he gives to them is no measure of who they are. "The most important thing you should know," he says, "is that the grade you get doesn't change the way I feel about you or the way you should feel about yourself. After all, this exam is just measuring one kind of thing, one narrow aspect of your intelligence." His voice is now quivering with intensity as he tells me the third part of his cautionary speech. "I say, 'I care about all of you.'"

I have, in fact, heard David say almost these exact words before, when I went to his lunch with his students. At the end of the lunch, David had offered these words of reassurance to the twelve students gathered there, and they had listened in rapt attention, seeming both relieved and comforted by the message, *and* somewhat disbelieving. At Harvard Law School, where grades and class standing are so important, where the educational culture is both competitive and combative, it must seem strange to hear David's earnest, almost pleading, soliloquy. But David means it and this year he felt compelled to "say it out loud" to his students. Although he hasn't taken a formal poll, he does feel as if his words of care and compassion may have had some calming effect. In the few chance encounters he has had with students since grading their exams, there has been an "ease" between them.

It is intriguing to hear David speak about the "narrowness" of the intellectual talents that law school tends to reward, because "school intelligence," this ability to score high on standardized tests, is an aptitude that David has in great abundance. I ask him about the origins of his obvious empathy for those who find success in school more of a struggle. His answer is not surprising because I have heard these themes echoed many times before in our conversations. But his candid and harsh self-evaluation still stuns me. He says without pause, "I feel empathy and affinity for those who struggle more with achieving in school because I always thought of myself as a fraud. It was a process of smoke and mirrors."

It is not that David lacked "validation and support" from those who mentored him, from important teachers and colleagues over the years. When he thinks of his experience as a student at the University of Chicago Lab School, for instance, he recalls a very nourishing environment. Mr. Earl Bell, the high school debate coach, was probably his most important mentor during his adolescence. He had grown up on a tobacco farm in the South, in redneck country, and he seemed to "know much more about race than anyone in Chicago." At the time, David was not only struggling over the typical traumas of adolescence, he was also "going through tough issues related to his own racial identity," and Mr. Bell seemed to understand what he was facing, and find ways of offering quiet support. "He was both demanding and generous," David recalls. "He became a kind of surrogate father to all of the kids on the team . . . but he also taught us how to frame an argument, how to present ourselves. It was very empowering." As I listen to David talk about his debate coach, I wonder how much of his own teaching has been shaped in Mr. Bell's image. I also wonder whether the debate team might have been a safe asylum from the sadness that engulfed his own father. Perhaps when he was actually engaged in debate, he might have felt especially smart and powerful.

Despite all of these wonderful aspects of life on the debate team, David decided to quit the team when he became a junior, "essentially so that I could become a black person." I am surprised and intrigued by this reason especially given that Coach Bell was one of those Southerners who seemed to "know so much about race." David takes me back to fourth grade, to his relationship with his best friend Aaron. "He was my neighbor, my rival, my confidant, my best friend. He was white. My whole world was white until I was in high school . . . all of my social life was white, and I wanted to belong desperately. I even had moments of wanting to be adopted by a white family."

Then during the summer of David's fourteenth year, he went

to an art and music camp sponsored by Hull House, the famous settlement house in Chicago. "The cabins were constructed with two wings joined by a communal bathroom. Everyone on my side was white except me. On the other wing, there were all black kids, except for one white boy who was over on the other side. I think there must have been a mistake in the room assignments. The black kids were all from the South Side of Chicago, and the white kid over there had a very rough time. Most of the white kids on my wing had no idea that I was black, so I was protected . . . I don't know what the black kids thought. One day I was walking along with the lone white kid from the other wing and he started complaining about the way he was being treated by the black kids. He was fuming, 'that nigger . . .' I listened and I said nothing."

At that moment, David decided that he had to change. He hated feeling dishonest and secretive. He felt terribly guilty for not having spoken up to the white kid. "I realized that I had been living in a cocoon. The debate team had been an all-white world." At the end of that summer, when his best friend Aaron's family moved to California, he decided to quit the team. "I decided it was time to sit at the black table. I joined the basketball team. I was interested in cementing this transformation to blackness." He smiles as he recalls the way the guys at the black table welcomed him and the way most of these guys are still his good friends twenty-five years later. "From time to time I tell them that if they had not welcomed me at the table on that first day when I walked over there, my life would have been totally different."

David graduated from high school with his black identity "cemented," having enjoyed the rigors and fun of basketball, and with a very strong academic record. "In fact," says David, "I never got the sense that my black buddies did not want me to achieve . . . just the opposite. They were proud of me." He had risen to a place of prominence as senior class president, and had already established a résumé that would be attractive to colleges. He decided to apply to Harvard after hearing about the positive experience of another boy from his school who was going there. David shakes his head in amazement. "I simply never thought about the fact that my father had gone to Harvard." Having lived with the enormous expectations inflicted by *his* parents, David's father must have wanted to spare his children the same injury. Says David, "My father never forced us in that way and it never seemed that I was choosing Harvard because of him."

Unlike high school, where the debate club and the basketball team were sources of enormous support and empowerment, Harvard College never captured David's energy or his enthusiasm. "Mostly, I felt as if I was drifting through it, as if I was not in control of my life." David wandered through the curriculum, skipping classes, studying sporadically, not seeing his advisor. He made no deep relationships with his professors and played cards. "I always thought of myself as very lazy," says David about that time. But even though he was neither inspired nor diligent, he did very well academically at Harvard. He had always known how to achieve in school, how to take tests, how to pull all-nighters before a paper was due. After four years of "drifting," David graduated *cum laude* from the college and found himself doing what his father, uncles, and grandfather had done before him: he went to law school. Again, David claims that his father's legacy at the Harvard Law School played no role in his decision to go there. "I applied to three law schools—Stanford, Yale, and Harvard—and I chose Harvard because it felt the safest, the most familiar . . . and because it had the most black students. But as I was applying, I never thought about the fact that my father had gone there."

By the time David got to law school he had decided to stop "drifting." He could no longer tolerate his own laziness. He wanted to get connected to the place; he wanted to feel passion for, and commitment to, the work, and he set out on a course of determined diligence. "The first year I went to every class. I did all the reading . . . and I found that I really liked it, that I really could do it, that I was good at it. That first year I ended up with an A- average." He went on the second year to win a prestigious spot as editor of the *Harvard Law Review*.

But David's real story of determination, a "watershed" for him at the law school, came in a course taught by the hardest taskmaster of all, Professor Phil Areeda. Professor Areeda had a well-deserved reputation as being the "most demanding," as "giving no quarter." "This was at the tail end of the era depicted in that popular movie *The Paper Chase*." Harvard Law School was changing from a fiercely competitive, autocratic system where the Socratic method reigned to a slightly more gentle and humane educational environment. Professor Areeda was from the old school. As a matter of fact, he epitomized the "old days." David explains, "You read only English cases that were decided before the beginning of the century . . . there was no attempt to be current or relevant . . . you never answered a question, you only asked another. You offered up exquisitely tortuous hypotheticals." Professor Areeda was known for demanding absolute preparation. You didn't dare go into his class without doing all of the reading. It is said that one day when a student was called on by the professor, did not know the case, and attempted to "pass" (law school speak for not being prepared), Areeda responded, "That is not an acceptable bid in this game." "He was brilliant, theatrical, and had a rich sense of humor," and yet, says David, "I never saw him intentionally humiliate students. He was always respectful. He really cared that we learn it."

Since Areeda's course was considered by everyone to be one of the toughest in the Law School, David decided it offered him the perfect opportunity to test his mettle, to see if with hard work and commitment, he would be able to excel. There was an additional incentive. "It was rumored that Areeda had never given a black person an A in his course and I was determined that I was going to get that A." David had never in his life been as motivated. He was hungry for it; he could taste success. He attended every class, was never late, and participated actively. "I subjected myself to the full measure of his probing gaze," says David, warming up to the drama of his story. The culmination of the course was a four-hour exam, a closed-book final, and David prepared for it like he had never done before. "I did the single most compulsive thing

I've ever done!" says David. "I wrote a two-hundred-fifty-page out-line of the Contracts course . . . I went through absolutely every-thing. It took three or four weeks of uninterrupted work to generate the outline. I knew Contracts backwards and forwards." David offers a dramatic pause before announcing that he got an A. "I had tried my hardest and I had succeeded! I didn't fail."

The news of David's extraordinary success was a particu-larly poignant victory for the black students, who bathed in his reflected glory. The "outline" became legendary, passed on as the best study tool for generations of students to come. "You see, because of the way Areeda taught Contracts, nothing changed." The outline never went out of print. "It was really applied effort and it brought me such a feeling of authentic accomplishment. *I* felt good and deserving all the way through. *I* knew I had excelled. The applause almost didn't matter." David links this "applied effort" that allowed him to succeed in the Contracts course to the great sat-isfaction he gets from his daily workout in the gym. "When I lift weights, it's the effort and the discipline that matter. . . the progress is visible and it comes through toil, sweat, energy. There is no way to fake it."

David uses these personal insights in his teaching, working against an institutional culture and against the deep imprints of his students' early socialization in school. He tries to convince his skep-tical students that the exams test "only one kind of intelligence." "If you get an A," he tells them, "you should be proud of your achievement, but you should also be humble. An A doesn't make you a better person. It could just be that you are good at this stuff, that it's easy for you. But virtue is in working and understanding." David pauses. "Partly I'm saying to them 'respect yourself, respect your own accomplishments.'"

David's admonition to his students seems to reflect a "grow-ing confidence" in his view of himself as a scholar; from thinking of himself as a "fraud" to beginning to see the fruits of his labors. "I see more as my eyes become more confident and adjusted," he muses. A decade ago, when David first came to teach at the Law

School, he did not worry about becoming an effective and inspiring teacher, but he did agonize over whether he would ever be able to produce good scholarship. "I was terrified I'd have no ideas," he recalls. "I never thought of myself as an intellectual. I thought that my success in school was due to the fact that I was a good mimic. I had a good memory." He was also apprehensive about producing scholarship because he had never thought of himself as a writer. "Talking was never difficult. But I always found it hard to commit myself on paper and leave myself open for other people's evaluation of me. I wanted people to love me."

The journey has been long and arduous. It took David four years to write his "first real thing" and he wrote it "over and over again." The very first piece "that broke the ice" was a short commemorative essay on Thurgood Marshall for the *Harvard Blackletter Journal*. David had clerked for "the Justice" and he wrote a piece about his famous storytelling called "Justice As Narrative: Some Personal Reflections on a Master Storyteller." Although the Marshall piece broke the logjam, David did not consider it a "serious piece of work." It did not help him feel more confident about writing. For his tenure review, David had to produce two "serious" journal articles and the process of writing was "pure agony." He sweated every moment of it, found it terrifying and threatening to his self-esteem, and produced pieces that he never really liked or thought were any good. "I just pushed my way through it," he recalls distastefully. "To help me get through it . . . I would just say to myself 'it's a piece of shit' . . . just write it. It doesn't matter. The closer I got to finishing it, the harder it was . . . because as soon as you finish it, you have to show it to people."

Despite the agony of the process, David made it through the tenure process with flying colors, his articles hailed by his colleagues as fine scholarship. Once again, however, he felt he had been able to use "smoke and mirrors" to excel in school. As soon as David completed the tenure assignments, he immediately committed himself to producing two more pieces. He was panicked that having achieved tenure he might get what one of his colleagues from another law school calls "Harvard disease," a disease that afflicts some Harvard Law professors who become "paralyzed" after getting tenure. "These are people who have always been thought of as amazingly intelligent, off the charts. The smarter you are supposed to be, the more impossible it is to live up to it."

David remembers going to a dinner several years ago to honor a revered, elderly colleague, a man whom everyone considered to be brilliant but who had gone through a long period early in his career where he was not able to produce serious scholarship. The honoree was suffering from terminal cancer and his comments that evening were poignant and painfully revealing. David can almost remember his exact words. Speaking to his colleagues, family, and friends the elder confessed, "Sometimes when you are blessed and cursed with very finely tuned critical judgment, you turn that judgment on yourself . . . and your writing stops." David has never forgotten those tortured words, and has embraced them as both inspiration and warning.

"Giving Us Back to Ourselves"

In his teaching, David tries very hard not to create a dynamic that will cause "paralysis" in his students; that will not encourage them to overdevelop the "finely tuned critical judgment" that one day might stifle their creativity and productivity. He criticizes legal training, which tends to "always make students think that they are wrong," and cites two strategies used by many of his colleagues. The first approach is to constantly "dismiss people's answers . . . to point at them, saying 'nope,' 'wrong,' and move immediately on to the next person." An only slightly less negative approach is one that is equally prevalent in law school classrooms. The professor works to get "the students to disavow their position even if it is the right answer." Over time, David believes that both of these strategies are "bad" and "reinforce a way of thinking in which nothing is ever good enough."

David is direct in his efforts to contradict these approaches that he believes diminish student effort and create a negative environment.

As he listens to students' contributions, he works to "find out what is right in what they are saying." He believes that almost always there are "multiple right answers"; that it is important to focus on "the process of reasoning toward one of many solutions"; and that he is "most interested in conveying a way of approaching problems." He wants to support an atmosphere of inquiry and exploration, and in that spirit, he "almost never tells a student that he or she is wrong." David understands the risks of being perceived as too soft or uncritical. He knows that some may fault him for not being discerning in his evaluations of students' contributions. But he would rather err in the direction of liberating people's minds, allowing students to take risks and express their point of view. And he always wants to convey his "respect for their effort and hard work."

David feels that his approach is particularly important to the women in his classes, who, he believes, do not generally thrive in the adversarial environment of law school. He sees gender as a "huge issue" in law school teaching and thinks that men tend to feel "much more comfortable in the whole classroom dynamic." He muses, "Women are rarely into challenging the professor and they tend to speak much less in class." In an effort to combat these patterns of inequality, then, David tries to avoid combative behavior and "doesn't do a lot of challenging of students." He wants to reason with them, not compete. He wants to support them, not dominate them. He wants to liberate their interpretive talents, not paralyze their thinking.

David's efforts to communicate more effectively with his women students and get the best from them remind me of Kay Cottle's response to the ways that her male and female students participate in classroom discourse. In reaching out to the boys, Kay, remembering her father's spare language, appreciates the silences. David and Kay, like the best teachers, want to liberate students' minds by opening up the channels of dialogue.

David knows, however, that his sensitivity to his students needs to be balanced against his own needs for self-protection. Since "being a man is a benefit" in law schools, and since the symbolism of "male" seems to be important to establishing authority in the class-room, David makes use of his very male qualities. "I am a particular kind of man and that gets me over. I have a loud voice; I'm very animated; I'm comfortable with talking. I'm confident and strong physically . . . all of these things help." He compares himself to one of his male colleagues who is a wonderful teacher but who is short, soft-spoken, and tentative in the classroom. Despite his brilliance, he is constantly having to defend himself against student assaults. "They go after people when they smell blood!" says David.

The only time that David remembers being attacked by these bloodsuckers was in his third year of teaching, when he was teach-ing his large course in civil procedure for the first time. "I was very nervous and extremely vulnerable," David shudders. "I got chal-lenged much more. A couple of white men tried to come after me both in class and outside of class." During his lectures, they were confrontational and rude, making gratuitous comments and esca-lating conflict. Out of class, they consumed his office hours with trivial questions designed to show him up and cause him embar-rassment. So David seeks to combine his empathic stance toward all of his students, which allows them room for self-expression, explo-ration, reasoning, and understanding, with an assured self-confidence that keeps the bloodsuckers at bay.

Despite such challenges, David does not feel that his race has been a major motivation for student attacks. In contrast to the other African-American law professors whom he knows (particu-larly the black women professors), David feels he has been spared a lot of grief. "Many black teachers tell me that they are constantly challenged by their students, questioning their competence and their legitimacy," says David, "but I don't get a lot of that." One of the reasons that David is spared is because his white civil proce-dure students may not even know he is black when they arrive in his course on the first day of their law school careers. Once the course begins and they do become aware of his blackness, his light skin and obvious "pedigree" allow them to forget that he is. "It is a skin color thing and a class thing," admits David. "I'm as Harvard blue blood as you can get. I'm obviously of middle-class origins . . . in mannerisms and sensibilities."

But even though many white students do not see David as black, this is not true for the black students who claim him as their own. As a matter of fact, each year when David speaks at the black student orientation, he speaks of the special connection that he hopes to forge with them. "I tell them that one of the reasons I am here is so I can be a resource for them, so that I can be helpful, supportive, and available," says David. And throughout the year, David tries to stay connected, offering guidance and career counseling, on occasion joining them for lunch or dinner, and participating in the meetings and gatherings of the black student union. In the classroom, David offers a more subtle—though conscious and strategic—connection to the black students. He often makes reference to "black popular culture" as a way of capturing their interest and reinforcing the importance of their presence. While acknowledging their affiliative tie to him, he insists that they become active and responsible members of the class. "I want them to know," says David, "that I have special feelings for them but that I see them as capable and committed students. I think that for black students there is actually some pride in the fact that I am a person who has such broad respect within this institution." The students can reap the benefits of some of David's glory; they can inherit some of his "blue blood" status.

With the talk of his "special connection" to black students, the conversation returns to the relationship he had with his own mother and father. "With my father there was a very distant respect," muses David. "Actually, both of my parents sort of left me alone." When he was a teenager, for example, his parents believed in his good judgment and sense of responsibility and let him "go any place" and "come home any time" just so he called and let them know where he was and when he planned to return. "They respected me and my judgment," says David, and for this "distant respect" and trust he remains grateful.

But David still seems to be longing for more, for the dimension of respect that flows through intimacy and communication.

"My conversations with my parents—particularly those with my father—often lacked emotional depth. I held myself back," he says, admitting the deep imprint of these early relationships on his continuing quest for self-respect. David sees his various relationships with students, colleagues, and friends as involving the same dimensions and dilemmas, merging them in his mind. "All of these things kind of run together for me." In all of them he describes the paradoxical feeling of being perceived as "very open" while he maintains an internal distance. "I hold myself apart. Some of that is for self-protection." David seems to be talking to himself as he ruminates about the casualties of both intimacy and distance, and arrives at a place that surprises me. "Actually," he says, "I am fighting to feel more entitled to keep myself distant. I'm fighting not to take on everyone else's burdens." He seems to be fighting the ghosts of his father when he speaks these words; fighting the need to be loved by everyone. If he can release himself from that impulse to please, he will be able to "fully own the things I say." "Different settings and different relationships require different balances," says David. "But in all of them it is a matter of ownership; a matter of feeling entitled to know and express your real feelings." In Joan Didion's words, it is "the ability to discriminate, to love, and to remain indifferent."

David's voice sounds weary. For a moment he seems much older than his years, tired of the struggle, tired of fighting the ghosts. "I'm so tired of the way in which I give so much more than I get," he sighs. Then he straightens his back and stretches tall as if preparing for battle and warns, "For most of my career, I have been very deferential to the judgments of my peers about issues relating to scholarly merit; more deferential than I think I should be. As I become more confident of my own abilities, I am starting to change that. In the last few years, I have produced as much quality scholarship as anyone on this faculty. It is time that I trusted my own judgments about what constitutes quality work. I'm tired of seeing people with fancy credentials being given exaggerated praise for mediocre work while work by nontraditional candidates is unfairly devalued or overlooked." His voice is ringing with clarity and purpose. "I am going to start insisting that if rigorous standards are applied they be applied equally." There is a decisive, assured quality in his voice as he continues, "I am trying to remember that I am entitled to judge, and judge rigorously. My scholarly achievements grant me at least that right." David's voice softens in the midst of a discovery. "As I continue to develop, I want to be able to say to people, 'This is what I need.' You can't show respect for someone else unless you are prepared to make yourself vulnerable. You can't give respect unless you have the courage to say what you need from the other person."

CHAPTER SIX

Attention

In the uncertain light of single, certain truth,
Equal in living, changingness to that light
In which I meet you, in which we sit at rest,
For a moment in the central of our being,
The vivid transparence that you bring is peace.

—Wallace Stevens,
  "Notes Toward a Supreme Fiction"

The moment described here by Wallace Stevens, "In which I meet you," is one of pure "standing in relation," to use Martin Buber's term. "Whoever says You does not have something; he has nothing. But he stands in relation." There is no "thing" that is possessed as a result of the relationship, particularly not the other; in Buber's account, relationship is a way of *being* rather than a way of *having*. In the lines quoted above, Stevens evokes the elusive beauty that can be felt, momentarily at least, when two people "meet." Often in our relationships, instead of meeting, we miss, or worse, collide with one another. In those instances when we do "meet," the image is not one of fusion, but rather of complementarity, a suspension of desire, a "transparency." Such a moment can bring peace within, T. S. Eliot's "still point of the turning world" in *Four Quartets*.

This momentary feeling of "peace" is one of both seeing and being seen. It is both timeless and transient, certain and uncertain. The meeting is also a moment of rest, a moment out of time in "the central of our being." As we hurtle through our lives, such moments are altogether too rare, and the relationships in which they occur provide a reminder of what nourishes us most profoundly, perhaps even an echo or reminder of our earliest relationships. In such moments, we feel present and acknowledged. From the earliest infant/caregiver relationship to the multiple relationships in which we find ourselves as adults, this experience of being known and valued forms both the origin and the motivation of our capacity to know and value others.

Bill Wallace, an Episcopal priest, a pastoral psychotherapist, and an AIDS activist, has witnessed the dying and death of scores of his friends, patients, and parishioners. He has participated in the painful passages, the inevitable diminishment, the anguished good-byes, and the inexorable losses. He has also cherished "moments of meeting" in relationship with the dying person; the "vivid trans-parence," the unadorned truthfulness, and the final peace. As a healer, he works against the rituals and habits of the traditional hier-archies that characterize most encounters between professionals and their clients: between doctors and patients, therapists and clients, priests and parishioners. Bill believes that these hierar-chies inhibit full engagement and limit a healer's capacity to be fully "present." He believes that the quality of *attention* is the most important dimension of respectful relationships; the way in which the healer sees the patient and allows himself to be seen; the way he joins with the patient in "wise accompaniment," not leading, but allowing himself to be led. In order for the healer to offer this benign attention, he must avoid labeling the patient—"contagious," "terminal," "addicted," "dysfunctional"—and relate to the "essence" of who he or she is as a person. He must also see the relationship as mutual and reciprocal, allowing love and care to flow in two directions.

Absence and Presence

Bill Wallace is a man who exudes both intensity and calm. Under-neath a balding head, his face is quietly handsome, his eyes pene-trating, and his body lean and relaxed. He is wearing a sweater, turtleneck, and slacks; a contrast from his formal priest's attire or his Sunday morning colorful gilded robes. Fresh from his morn-ing run, he looks both younger and older than his forty-seven years; younger in the directness and openness of his gaze, and older in the wisdom and melancholy that are immediately apparent when he begins to speak. His voice always surprises my northeastern sensibilities. Having grown up in the deep South, and having spent most of his adult life there, Bill speaks with a gentle, twangy Southern drawl and a lilting cadence. He says five like "fav," and life like "laf"; and he uses words that I rarely hear up North, like "trifling," which he makes sound long, flat, and foolish.

Bill's work and mission embrace a variety of roles that he seems to keep in balance through a combination of determined energy and meticulous organization. Although it all comes off looking graceful and smooth, underneath there is anxiety and discipline. As an AIDS activist, he has pushed for loving, respectful care for men, women, and children suffering from the ravages of the disease and facing a sure death. As a leader of the national hospice movement, he has been an institution builder and a deft politician, negotiating for resources and legislation that will allow people to die with dignity and grace. As a pastoral therapist, he has forged relationships with patients that express mutuality and symmetry, that allow support and nourishment to flow in both directions. And as a pastor he has offered spiritual guidance, prayer, and practical support to members of his congregation who are facing the celebratory moments of birth, baptism, and marriage and the traumas of illness, divorce, unemployment, alienation, and death. His thoughtful sermons each Sunday morning, from the pulpit of Emmanuel Church on Boston's Newbury Street, combine provocative, penetrating analyses of social and political events, offbeat theological interpretations, and evocative storytelling.

Bill's introspective capacities are well-honed. He begins by focusing on his own work as a patient in therapy, with his own "brokenness." "I might as well begin there. I have had a lot of practice in talking about these things recently." After twenty-five years of marriage, Bill Wallace has recently divorced. So although he has been a pastoral counselor and psychotherapist for the last fifteen years, he begins talking to me about his own role as a patient, an experience that still feels raw. "In therapy I've had to move from the position of voyeur, observer, participant—the role I have taken as therapist—to bringing all of this into my personal life. I have had to take it from a place of consideration, explicitly and devoutly in my head, to a lived life."

Bill has had other experiences in therapy; the first when he was in his early thirties, and the second a few years later, when he was in training to become a pastoral counselor and it was a required ingredient of the graduate program. The first encounter with therapy, at thirty-two, came at a time when Bill was serving as a young priest in a Lutheran parish in Southern Pines, North Carolina. It was an upper-middle-class parish that was "thriving"; a warm and comfortable place for Bill, his wife Fran, and their new baby. "I had everything that should have made me happy," says Bill sadly, "but I wasn't. I developed the mantra of 'being on a search'"; a search that caused him confusion and anxiety; that led to unrest and struggle in his marriage; and that forced him to take his first steps toward honest self-scrutiny. "I had had a naivete about reality. I had gone through college, seminary, marriage, and first child. For the first time I climbed the tallest tree and looked back."

Fran and Bill went into therapy with Leo, a Jesuit priest and a psychologist, a lovely, caring man "who honored whatever we brought to him." "As far as I'm concerned," says Bill, "Leo had the two most important things that a therapist needs in order to be in a healing relationship. The first is a gentle and respectful presence, and the second is a deep curiosity."

In the process of working with Leo, Bill made the decision to leave the safety and comforts of the Southern Pines parish and return to graduate school at Emory University in Atlanta to train in pastoral counseling. While there he studied and practiced two kinds of therapeutic approaches: "object-relations theory" and "self-psychology." Although these are complex theoretical frameworks with many aspects, Bill goes straight to the heart of them. "Object-relations theory focuses on what it means to individuate. Mother love is the crucial material. The good enough mother gives the child enough love and nourishment so that the child develops the courage first to move off the mother's lap, then to move across the room, then out the door, then across the road. But if the mother's love is either too cool or too hot, the child will be unable to successfully individuate. The father is supposed to come along when the child is four or five and help prod the child away from his mother . . . take the child fishing, hunting, or take him off to play pool or chew tobacco." Bill seems to be both describing the core of this theory and offering a parody of it, particularly when he refers to the relatively peripheral and macho role of the father.

Without pause he launches into a description of the second theory. "Self-psychology starts with the premise that everyone is a narcissist . . . this is a good kind of narcissism, the kind that allows people to feel confident. A lot of people will be wounded early in their lives, in damaging relationships with parents . . . and they do not have enough narcissistic supplies. Through the focused attention, gentle presence, and curiosity of a good therapist, they will be able to recover those narcissistic supplies. They will be able to integrate the empathy and respect of the therapist into their own sense of self."

"The therapies I chose to study," Bill continues, "were reflective of my family. In many ways my mother was too good a mother, too hot. I was too close to her apron strings . . . and my father was distant, hateful, and abusive. Through exploring and experiencing these two therapies I could begin to explain my father and my mother . . . and I could begin to grow up."

"Where did you grow up?" I ask as I try to locate the place on the map where Bill's psychological journey began, and as I search for grounding in space and time. "And who was in your family?" Bill seems a bit surprised by my abrupt inquiries that seem to interrupt his interior reflections. He has leapt into the middle of the family drama, a drama that seems to assume that I know the cast of characters and the scene. "I grew up in Albany, Georgia," he reports. "There was my father, my mother, my oldest sister Lucy (three years older), my brother Cam (thirteen months younger . . . we were very bound up together, our survival depended on our closeness), my youngest brother Jeff (seven years younger)."

Once Bill has quickly named the family, he moves back to the psychological experience of living in the shadow of a "depressed" mother and an "abusive" father. "My mother's depression caused an emptiness in my life, an early preverbal wounding. At the same time, she was too close to me because of the rotten relationship she had with my father." Despite these words, Bill's face brightens. "My mother sang in the choir at the Episcopal church in Albany," he recalls. "When I was an infant, she used to take me to choir practice and to church. She used to take me there in a kind of carrier." Bill holds his arms across his chest and begins to gently rock, as if he is holding the baby Bill in his arms. "I would be very close to her and she would dote on me. The preacher would dote on me as well." As he says this, Bill seems far away, transported back into those precious moments of maternal intimacy and adoration.

For Bill, this moment out of time—rocking in his mother's arms, close enough to feel her heart beat—anticipated the path of his life's journey and became a "quality of relationship and attention" that he would seek in his work as a pastor and therapist. He underscores the communication of love and presence that needs no language. "This was probably where I gained a preverbal, unconscious affection for the liturgy. You know, learning the liturgy is not a conscious thing. It is deeply imprinted very early."

Bill's mother had grown up in Atlanta, the daughter of a stockbroker whose luck with the market had them living in either splendor or poverty. "It was a roller-coaster existence," explains Bill. "They were a prominent family gone awry that were often poor but still had many of the affectations of blue bloods." Both of his mother's parents were alcoholics whose painful and distant relationship led to divorce when his mother was thirteen. "So my mother ended up caring for her mother, actually raising her." After the divorce, mother and daughter moved to Rockingham, North Carolina, a small cotton mill town with a population of about 8,000, a dramatic contrast from the big city life of Atlanta.

"My mother was pretty, intelligent, and very lovely," says Bill. When she arrived in Rockingham at thirteen, she was admired for her beauty and sophistication, and became a star cheerleader at the high school. Bill's father, a big football star, whose family had lived in East Rockingham, "across the tracks on the cotton mill village," met the pretty cheerleader and they soon became a couple. They were an odd couple "from totally different families"; "a blue blood partnered with someone who had hardly any social graces"; an Episcopalian who loved the liturgy and classical music with a "fire and brimstone Baptist who hated religion."

Despite, or perhaps because of, their vast differences, Bill's father and mother were immediately attracted to one another; a seemingly storybook union, the star football player with the pretty cheerleader. When Bill tries to understand the source of their attraction to one another despite the extreme contrasts in their origins, interests, and temperaments, he points to the passion. "Their relationship was held together by passion, violent passion. It kept them together through very terrible times; it still does." As a young child, Bill recalls witnessing the extremes of their passion; the brutal arguments and the fierce lovemaking; his father's harsh abuse and his mother's stoic pain.

When his parents graduated from high school, they committed themselves to "going steady" but each went off to a different college. Bill's father received a full football scholarship from Wake Forest College and left Rockingham with all the glory that small southern towns bestow on their local top athletes. But after two weeks of football practice, his father left college and returned home. "He couldn't leave his mother," says Bill. "He was too enmeshed, too tied to her apron strings." After Bill's mother's first year of college, she returned to Rockingham and fell into her suitor's passionate orbit. By summer's end they were married.

Soon after their marriage the couple moved to Salisbury, North Carolina, where Bill's father got his first real job working in a men's clothing store. His father did well selling clothes and was soon on the move with his wife and baby daughter to manage a clothing store in Savannah, Georgia. As the family grew, his father became a successful businessman. His industry and ambition were noticed by an investor who offered to put him into business in Albany, Georgia. Within months the family moved once again to Albany, where Bill's father started a store called the "Best Credit Clothing Store" on the main street of town. With four or five military bases close by, his store (which "catered to the lower end of the spectrum") found the "formula for success."

"When we moved there, I was four years old and Dad had the business on Broad Street. From that vantage point—later on as an adolescent—I watched the harshest moments of the civil rights movement . . . I witnessed the violence, the attack dogs, the fire hoses. I saw the young children being put into the paddy wagon. This experience gave me an incredible sensitivity to the social fabric and oppression of the period . . . and it gave me a huge desire to find a way to participate in the fabric of change." Bill describes Albany, Georgia, in 1965 as if he is rehearsing old film footage. Then he says something that still seems to surprise him. "For some reason, my parents were really liberal. Dad's was the only business on Broad Street that expressed any sympathy for the people involved in the struggle." His voice is disbelieving. How could this raging, abusive father have a place in his heart for the folks that all of his neighbors were calling "dirty niggers"? "I went to school in the midst of all of this. I had to hear the nigger jokes. Steve Flanigan was my best friend and he was part of the nigger-hating tradition. So I participated with my silence . . . then felt badly and guilty."

Since Bill's father's business was flourishing, the Wallace family enjoyed the comforts of money, privilege, and status. They lived in one of the lovelier neighborhoods in town, were members of the "right" social set, and employed maids in their household. I ask Bill what he remembers about the black maids and how they were treated by his family. "My father had an indifference toward them," he begins. "My mother, on the other hand, loved them. She had a kind of naivete, a bigheartedness. There was no pretense, no falseness, and the black women saw this and understood this. My mother would drink coffee with them. She enjoyed their company." Bill remembers one very important relationship that his mother had with a woman named Arlene, who was their cook. "My mother and Arlene became the best of friends." On the weekends when Arlene was not working she would often get into some "passionate partying" and she would be arrested and thrown into jail. Bill's mother would always rescue her. She'd get her out of jail, bring her home, and they would sip coffee together as Arlene would replay her raucous adventures.

Bill would often accompany his mother when she went to fetch the maids on the black side of town. He was always saddened by the poverty, by the contrasts between his fancy house and manicured neighborhood and the "shacks" that the black folks lived in. "The black part of town had clay streets, and with the rains and heat in southern Georgia, things would get very bad, just terrible conditions." But when Bill and his mother would bring the black women back home to work, their presence in the house always made it feel somehow safer and more comfortable. It was not only that the women were good company for his mother, whose life was so marked by loneliness and despair, it was also that their presence often gave Bill a sense of security and peace. "I remember one woman who I was pretty close to," recalls Bill. "I would just sit there watching her ironing. Just sitting there felt so good, being in the steady, seasoned, wise presence of this black woman."

The civil rights movement was thus being acted out with color and courage on Broad Street right before Bill's young eyes. He takes in the scene: of raging racism and venomous name-calling out of the mouths of the white folks in town (even his friends). And he absorbs the dignity, determination, and anger of the colored people who refuse to accept second-class citizenship any more. He notices that this is the only place where his father surprises him and looks like a hero. His father stands up against the prevailing prejudices of the white folks in Albany, and feels sympathy for, and identification with, the Negroes. For the first time Bill can be joined with his father in their opposition to the injustice, in their fight for equality. Time and again, Bill returns to this southern civil rights mural as touchstone and inspiration. In it, he sees the roots of his political activism for people with AIDS, his resistance to any kind of separation or hierarchy that diminishes some and advances others. He even sees in this political drama the core of his belief in therapeutic relationships that are shaped by equality and reciprocity between therapist and patient.

But it is not just the theater of the civil rights movement that seems to have influenced Bill's views on respectful encounters. It is also the more intimate image of the black woman standing at the ironing board. Her "steady, seasoned, wise presence" brought a feeling of safety and peace to a violent household. Her silent witness—black and strong—got embroidered into Bill's young psyche, into his work with his patients. He works to give them the same kind of safe place to sit, and the same kind of unspoken but focused attention.

Learning to Do Nothing

The silent, powerful presence of the black woman standing at the ironing board taught Bill lessons about the quality of attention so central to respect, lessons that he would have to make conscious and relearn in his professional training and clinical practice. During his second year at the Lutheran Seminary in Columbia, South Carolina, Bill "talked his way" into being admitted to a program in clinical pastoral counseling at the William Hall Psychiatric Research Institute, the "Ritz" of the South Carolina Department of Mental Health. This was an "excellent" interdisciplinary training program that included classes, therapeutic experience, and supervision. "I flourished," recalls Bill. "I loved the work."

For six months Bill was assigned to the ward with patients who had Huntington's chorea, a horrible disease of the nervous system in which people "wither away before your eyes, and there is nothing you can do to help them." Eventually they die; there is no way of arresting the disease. Bill was the only one on the team "who could not do anything." "The doctors and nurses could poke, prod, give medicines . . . all I could do was be present." He paints the morbid scene for me. "I'd walk into the day unit. This was one of those so-called well-appointed sixties buildings . . . concrete slabs, turquoise panels, pretty furniture, sturdy carpets . . . and I would find four or five patients sitting in the sunroom . . . just sitting there, not able to talk, drooling, shaking, wobbling, swaying back and forth, in so much pain."

When Bill first arrived on the unit, he would talk to the patients. He even tried to get them to talk to him. He recalls the frustration and disappointment of those first few weeks. "I tried talking to them, telling them stories, but it was like throwing green peas at tapioca. I didn't get anything back. They couldn't understand who I was. All they could relate to was my presence and all I could relate to was their presence. So I learned to just sit with them . . ." Bill is grinning and shaking his head as he remembers "this most important learning experience of my life": not talking, not doing anything, just being "present" with the patients. He admits that learning to "not *do* anything" was particularly difficult because he kept on hearing the echoes of his father's admonitions. "My father used to say that if you weren't *doing* something, you were no good."

Even with these strong echoes, over time Bill was able to "develop a comfort just being there." He connects this ability both to the loneliness that he learned to live with, and his search for peace and refuge amidst the chaos of his family. "I probably was able to learn to be present with these patients because I was my own comfort growing up. I was not able to look to anyone for that. I became my own resource, learning to be alone." His second reason seems to have broader origins. "I think that this incredible empathy I have for the powerless is connected to my coming from a dysfunctional family, and my deep involvement in the civil rights struggle in Albany."

The pain that has allowed Bill to feel identified with "the powerless" runs throughout our conversations. I hear of Bill's father unleashing his rage on his "favorite target," his firstborn son. The dark memories are vivid and palpable, not unlike the generational ghosts that have haunted David Wilkins's courageous quest for self-respect. In speaking of how his parents responded to his lackluster performance in elementary school, for example, Bill remembers that "my mother tried to be very supportive. She urged me on lovingly, trying to get me to do better. Dad beat up on me, calling me 'stupid,' 'ugly,' 'fat' . . . the worst things that ever came along . . . just a whole string of vitriolics. Generally, he had a shotgun approach to almost everything, spewing forth venom to the whole world. But with me, he would take out a rifle so he could aim more directly, more precisely."

Several years later, when Bill was a young man briefly working with his father in the clothing business ("we were like two bulls in a china shop"), he found it increasingly hard to tolerate his father's abusive outbreaks. He holds one horrible memory of this time above all others because it was so painful for his *mother*. "I remember when my mother's mother died on Christmas Eve. Nanny was a sad case. She had been an alcoholic for most of her life and not a particularly good mother. We were all gathered at home. The house was full of people who had come to sit with us and express their condolences. My father walked in the house and began raging, 'That god-damn fuckin' bitch died on the busiest day of the whole year.' I'll never forget it as long as I live. My mother was so hurt, so embarrassed. That day I stood up to him. I barrel-chested him." Fighting back, feeling his father's wrath, not allowing himself to be the helpless victim; all of these seem to be at the root of his growing capacity to give comfort to others and to be comfortable "just being present."

Once he learned how to "do nothing," the attention that Bill offered the sunroom patients at the William Hall Institute did not anticipate response or reciprocity. They could not return his smiles, his conversation, even his eye contact; and Bill had to discover within himself the selfless, generous gesture that does not expect or demand reaction. This is a rare and difficult discipline. I suspect that we all offer our smiles expecting ones in return. We coo at babies on airplanes *because* their eager babbling will bring us pleasure. Sustaining attention when you know that no audible or visible response is possible, but when you believe that your presence is needed and experienced, is another matter; and it is a crucial dimension of respectful witness.

Bill's experience of "learning not to *do* anything" is echoed in Kay Cottle's dawning feeling of helplessness when her mother, in her mid-eighties, began the slow decline into Alzheimer's. First forgetting and losing things, then experiencing confusion and disorientation, she would find herself in places, not knowing how she got there. As the disease progressed, Kay knew their mother/daughter relationship had to change. "For all of those years, I got respect *from* her . . . which led to my respect *for* her. The way I believe you express your respect is by allowing people to do the right thing, to make their own decisions. *But how could I exhibit this kind of respect for her when she was becoming childlike?* This was overwhelmingly tragic, just heartbreaking, to see my mother that way."

Kay struggled mightily with finding a way to help, with discovering a way to give back to this woman who had given her so much. Over time—painful step by painful step—Kay began to recognize that she was trying to *do* too much; that there was no way that she could halt the march of this dreadful disease. She learned that less was more; that she needed to stop "doing" and begin to "just *be* in her presence"; that in the silence was the discourse. Kay's story switches to the present tense as if she is living it now. "My mother doesn't grasp what I am saying. The Alzheimer's and the stroke have knocked it all out of her, and she has lost her power, lost her capacity to think or communicate, the connections are shot, broken . . . But I caress her face and she smiles. In this simple act she has the capacity to be reassured." Over time, Kay felt a shift inside herself, in the way she viewed her mother, in her expectations. The revelation came on slowly. It didn't erase the pain or the feelings of loss, but it did give her some relief, and occasionally offered her moments of joy. "I began to realize," she says, looking off into the distance, "that I could show her respect in very simple, uncomplicated ways . . . that my *physical* presence was important . . . just being there with her. The simple act of walking outside and feeling the moist breeze, looking at the cats, or making her a meal . . . just being present with her."

Bill's story of "just being present" with the patients in the sunroom is also reminiscent of Johnye Ballenger's experience as a young medical student, when she witnessed the loving care of the senior resident who could not "do" anything more for the dying woman. His final healing act was an ordinary gesture of love and care, offering the dying woman his full attention.

As a mother—a hardworking, devoted mother with a full-time career—I have always puzzled over this question of "attention" and "presence" in relation to my children, particularly over the distinction child development experts often make between the "quality" and the "quantity" of time that parents spend with their children. "Quality" time is considered more productive and supportive of healthy child development than the actual "quantity" of hours spent with one's children. I confess that the "experts'" advice and counsel have been a welcome justification for my schedule and temperament. What is most important, they say, is the "quality" time you spend with your child; the focused attention, the dynamic interactions, the feeling of being "all there" and "completely present." "Quality" implies limited but precious engagement; not like the diffuse, unstructured, limitless hours of "quantity" time.

But even though I have received, and acted upon, the wisdom of experts who were saying what I wanted to hear, something in me has always felt guilty for, and anxious about, the long hours spent away from my growing children. Something in me has always known that "quality" time does not always respond to tight scheduling, and that "quantity" time should not receive such easy dismissal. The promise and potential of "quantity" time with our children; a time to just "be" together; a kind of attention that neither expects nor demands response; the permission to just sit side by side, eyes *not* meeting, allowing each person to be engaged in his or her own activity or be deeply immersed in his or her own thoughts; just *feeling* the diffuse light, just taking the time to be present.

The feeling of respect Bill experienced in the "seasoned and wise presence" of the black woman ironing takes me back to my childhood, to an encounter that has had reverberations in the ways I seek to "see" and listen to others in my adult life. The summer of my eighth birthday, my family was visited by a seventy-year-old black woman, a professor of sociology, an old and dear friend. A woman of warmth and dignity, she always seemed to have secret treasures hidden under her smooth exterior. On this visit, she brought charcoals and a sketch pad. Midafternoon, with the sun high in the sky, she asked me to sit for her in the rock garden behind our house. I chose a medium-sized boulder, perched myself upon it in an awkward, contrived pose, and tried to keep absolutely still. This suddenly static image disturbed the artist, who asked me to talk to her and feel comfortable about moving. She could never capture me, she explained, if I became statue-like. Movement was part of my being.

Her well-worn, strong, and knowing hands moved quickly and confidently across the paper. She seemed totally relaxed and unselfconscious, her fingers a smooth extension of the charcoal. Her deep calm soothed me and made me feel relaxed. But what I remember most clearly was the wonderful, glowing sensation I got from being attended to so fully. There were no distractions. I was the only one in her gaze. My image filled her eyes, and the sound of the chalk stroking the paper was palpable. The audible senses translated into tactile ones. After the warmth of this human encounter, the artistic product was almost forgettable. I do not recall whether I liked the portrait or not. I do remember feeling that there were no sharp lines, only fuzzy impressions, and that I was rendered in motion, on the move. This fast-working artist whipped the page out of her sketch pad after less than an hour and gave it to me with one admonition: "Always remember you're beautiful," she said firmly. To which I responded—beaming with pleasure and momentary embarrassment—"Now I *know* I'm somebody!"

In the process of recording the image, the artist had made me feel "seen" in a way that I had never felt seen before, fully attended to, wrapped up in an empathic gaze. I learned that an essential ingredient of creating a portrait was the process of human interaction. I suspect that the penetrating quality of the artist's attention that I experienced as a child must have been much like the "stare" that Dawoud Bey's "patient" camera permits.

Almost thirty years later, I had an experience that brought back the sensations that I had felt when, at eight, I was the only one present in the artist's eyes; when her full attention magnified the sun's golden light. Only this time, I was on the other side of the palette. Talking with a student at one of the high schools I was portraying in my book *The Good High School*, I was trying to understand the quality of her experience there. This is what I wrote in my field notes that day.

> Maria, a fifteen-year-old Puerto Rican girl with a head full of unruly curls, clear penetrating eyes, and a raucous laugh, agrees to talk to me about her freshman year at John F. Kennedy High. We sit on the floor in the hall with our backs up against the metal lockers, our legs stretched out in front of us, and our faces turned sideways toward one another. The tape recorder is resting on Maria's lap. She seems to forget about it immediately as she talks to me about her friends, her family, her school, and her dreams. Once I get used to her lilting Spanish accent, I relax and give her my full attention—our eyes connecting, our heads nodding in unison, our voices in synchrony. At the conclusion of our hour-long conversation, Maria's eyes fill with tears and she asks me, out of the blue, "Do you know what this feels like to me . . . this talk you're having with me?" "No," I respond, surprised by the tears and the sudden urgency in her voice. "It feels like it feels when my grandmother brushes my hair," she says. "Real soft, real gentle . . . you know, safe." In that moment, we both feel "real close"—an unexpected intimacy, a connection neither of us anticipated and one we will never forget.

Bill's early experience of receiving full attention—sitting in the peaceful presence of the woman ironing, feeling the rhythm and music of the liturgy next to his mother's body—must have felt a lot like the warmth and pleasure I experienced being at the center of the artist's generous gaze or the intimacy Maria felt as we talked that brought back her grandmother's loving touch.

This Is What We Can Do

Several years after his internship at the William Hall Institute, when Bill had already graduated from seminary, become an ordained minister, and pastored congregations in Savannah, Georgia, and Southern Pines, North Carolina, he decided to head to Emory University in Atlanta for graduate training in pastoral counseling. Ever since he had entered the seminary, Bill had always struggled with two equally powerful commitments: his devotion to activism and service and his appetite for intellectual engagement. Even though he enjoyed the spiritual work, the leadership, the entrepreneurship, and the relationship building that were part of pastoring a parish, he always yearned for the more contemplative life of the academy and the political commitments of "the movement."

In both Georgia and North Carolina, Bill had become active in the hospice movement as a way of moving beyond the confines of parish life and offering service to the community, and as a way of becoming engaged with the issues of death and dying. Despite the fact that he had never had anyone among his family or close friends die, there was something about the work that brought him comfort and satisfaction. "This was something that I was deeply drawn to," says Bill, not questioning his motives, "work that I felt very comfortable doing." At that time, the hospice movement was a relatively new initiative in the United States, recently transplanted from Great Britain, and its philosophical, political, and spiritual tenets were very attractive to Bill. Beginning as a volunteer—"accompanying" one young man who was dying of cancer—he quickly became more deeply and widely involved, joining the local board of directors and then working at the state and national levels.

The graduate program in pastoral counseling at Emory University married many of the desires and goals that Bill had always experienced as unyielding dichotomies. The interdisciplinary program balanced clinical work and academics, and combined courses and training in the medical school, the divinity school, and the psychology department. Bill loved every minute he spent there. After two years of graduate training, which included "four hundred hours of clinical supervision that was exciting, challenging, and wonderful," Bill was offered the opportunity of running the hospice program at Grady Hospital in Atlanta. Even though accepting the offer meant that he would have to discontinue his graduate training, and not conclude the Ph.D. program, Bill jumped at the opportunity. His face is now beaming. "This was something I truly loved doing. This was the best job I ever had."

The Grady job was irresistible in the way it "brought together so much" that he cared about. It combined "healing, advocacy, and liberation work." As a matter of fact, the mission statement was explicit in its reference to giving "service to the indigent poor." Not only was Bill "seduced" by the blend of advocacy and healing, he also loved the combination of teaching and supervision of students, all within an interdisciplinary framework. Because this was a new program, he was also able to grow the institution and give it his imprint. "This was great, passionate work," exclaims Bill. "We gave it our heart and soul and the program flourished." One of Bill's greatest thrills and proudest moments was when, after a "process of advocacy and politics," he and a few of his colleagues were able to get a state Medicaid Benefit bill passed that allowed the indigent poor full access to hospice care.

Up until 1983, hospice work had been completely voluntary. But with the passage of national and state legislation, hospice became "an arm of the health care system" and it became "legitimized as a movement and a service." In fact, it was not only that hospice was brought under the umbrella of the national and state health systems, it was also that it began to transform the practice of medicine more generally. "The hospice movement taught medicine how to care for dying people," explains Bill. "It was a holistic program that brought together nursing, social work, physical therapy, psychology, political advocacy, and spiritual work."

One innovation of the Grady program was its work in the black, largely poor community surrounding the hospital. Up until this time, hospice had been "a mostly white middle-class movement" that had not served poor communities or African-American neighborhoods. The Grady program reached out to these communities, recognizing their needs, but also seeing the ways in which these communities offered important lessons in "caring for their own."

Bill and his colleagues wanted to push the boundaries of hospice care to communities that it had not yet reached, much in the way that Jennifer Dohrn expanded midwifery services, which had largely been limited to highly educated, middle-class women. In reaching out to new populations, the interdisciplinary team at Grady Hospital initially had to face the reluctance and skepticism of community folks who were uneasy with, or unclear about, their strategies and their mission. The Grady people also began to see how much they had to learn from folks and how those lessons needed to be incorporated into their hospice work. Respectful care required that they teach *and* learn, and that they recognize both the opportunities and the constraints of their caregiving.

Bill loved the Monday morning ritual of going out into the community to do home visits, clinical work that he held onto despite his heavy administrative duties, because he believed practice and policy should always inform one another. His partner on these home visits was Vivian Granger, a black woman and an oncology nurse. Bill often felt like the student. "Vivian taught me so much about life," he begins. "We would have five appointments in the morning and we would be going into some of the most brutal and tragic situations. . . . We'd go into the projects and sit down with the people who were dying. And, of course, I would want to say things that would make them happy and hopeful. But Vivian would always start by saying all the things that we were *not* able to do. 'Don't expect this and don't expect that.' At first, her approach scared me . . . this setting of the terms and the limits. But then she'd say 'This is what we *can* do.' This was a much more honest, respectful, and ultimately productive approach." The program, for example, could not become the primary caregiver, but it could "support whatever family dynamics were in place," prescribe medicines, offer visits from social workers, help with activities of daily living, help patients sign up for food stamps and gain access to other neighborhood, city, and state resources.

Bill recounts one of the many inspiring stories of their work in this community. "I'll never forget our visit to a seventy-five-year-old black woman. She was extremely depressed. Of course, she would not have put it that way. She would have said that she was 'broken-hearted.' In her agony she had almost turned fetal. They had tried everything . . . medicines, talk therapy. On one of our Monday morning visits Vivian and I sat with her and Vivian asked her, 'Precious, what hurts most?' And the woman told us, 'For fifty years I have cooked Sunday dinner for my family. Now I can't do that any more and I have no reason to live.' So we got an occupational therapist to come in on Sundays to help her make Sunday dinner. She blossomed and died a peaceful death."

Teachers of Presence

"AIDS patients die a spiritual death before they die a biological death," says Bill, searching for a way to begin to describe the dynamics of his pastoral and therapeutic work with dying patients. His voice is tentative. Perhaps it is hard to name feelings and behavior that by now come naturally and feel almost intuitive. Or perhaps Bill's hesitancy grows out of the fact that the work of sustaining healing relationships often sounds fairly "mundane" and ordinary, not unlike describing any attentive encounter. "The health care systems do not relate to the essence of who they are as people, but rather they seem to relate to the accidents of their illness," continues Bill. "AIDS sufferers are described as 'contagious,' 'terminal,' 'addicted,' 'poor,' and 'on the margins.' The care is arranged around these adjectives rather than around the person." In an essay he recently wrote entitled "Care of the Dying," Bill Wallace describes the categories that distort the vision and insight of caregivers and dehumanize their patients.

> The boundaries of diagnosis and treatment are drawn in order that those seeking help may be broken down into manageable and comprehensible categories of meaning able to be examined and fixed. The one seeking help is de-mystified, and therefore, discounted as a person for control's sake. The healer, by such reductionistic behavior, is able to stay perched above the more messy, unpredictable, indefinable phenomenon aroused by any kind of relationship with her, particularly a mutual one . . . The dehumanization of persons by medicine's orientation to the accidents rather than the essence of their beings was brought home to me by Ted's shaming confession: "Well, Father Wallace, I failed my last chemotherapy treatment. I guess I'm now ready for hospice." To which I replied, "I wonder, Ted, if you might consider that the chemotherapy failed you."

"I see myself as moving through the categories in order to connect with and give honor to the person," says Bill. "What do you actually say and do?" I ask him. Bill's face seems to go blank for a moment as he searches for a way to name his approach. Finally, he offers a very simple and profound reply. "I follow my *curiosity* about the person in very *specific* ways."

The word "curiosity" comes up again and again in Bill's descriptions of his work. Bill sees authentic curiosity as the bedrock of respectful relationships. The caring person must possess a desire to know; the questions must be genuine; and the patient must feel the focused attention and probing interest. Such questions tend to be very ordinary and "specific," rarely abstract or esoteric. Bill mentions a few questions that he might use to begin to make contact with an AIDS patient coming to the clinic, although each of these would have to be inspired and shaped by the moment, the person, and the context. "What is the hardest thing about being here today? Who is not here that you would want to be here with you today?" Or maybe Bill might begin by noticing, and remarking on, the person's clothing, a piece of jewelry, or something else that would reveal his interest in "their being."

Bill considers himself fortunate that as a "pastoral psychotherapist" he is not burdened by the expectations that most people have of medical professionals, nor by the mystique and skepticism that often shroud patients' perceptions of psychiatrists and psychologists. Bill does admit that people's views of him, and their willingness to engage him, are obviously influenced by their perspectives on religion or their attitudes toward priests. "I am at the mercy of their view of religion." But somehow these barriers seem less formidable, more easily navigated, than the ones enforced in most relationships between doctors and patients, or psychologists and their clients. "As a pastoral psychotherapist I am to some extent stripped of an agenda. I just have myself . . . and it is a helpless self."

"What do you mean by 'helpless'?" I ask. "You must be ready to give up power and control," responds Bill. "You must be willing to be changed and shaped. You must be open to relationship." To drive home his point about "mutuality" and "openness," Bill cites the work of Shirley Holzer Jaffrey, a grief counselor, who says that the hospice professional—who hopes to offer respectful care and witness—must practice what she calls "heroic helplessness." Bill writes:

> Heroic helplessness is when the caregiver faces the limitations of her ability to make well and chooses not to sprint back to a job on more solid ground, that is, intensive care or home infusion nursing. She stays put after hitting, several months into the job, what I call the hospice wall. She comes to terms with the fact

that her helplessness, finally, is the most she has to offer, the precious source of empathic connection which fades unhealthy distinctions between healer and healed. She comes to understand Will Campbell's definition of where two or three are gathered: "The church is one cat in one ditch and one nobody of a son-of-a-bitch trying to pull her out."

Bill is reminded of a recent experience he had working with some medical residents at Tufts University trying to get them to role-play their encounters with patients. He wanted to encourage the residents to be more "respectful and honoring" of their patients and to "feel more at ease with them." He asked them to participate in what seemed like a very straightforward and simple exercise: to role-play their coming out and welcoming the patients in the waiting area before "going back into their inner sanctums." Bill shakes his head, remembering how difficult this was for these young doctors to do; how awkward they were, how out of their element they seemed. "They found this simple act almost impossible to do. It was very hard for them to move away from, and out of, the aura of professionalism, across the boundary of authority." Absent the mantle of professional hierarchy and absent the tools of technology, the residents had nothing to guide their encounters with patients. They felt "exposed and vulnerable. The more strongly people are attached to the external signs of professional status, the more vulnerable they are. They feel threatened by the prospect of being changed themselves . . . and you must be ready to change if you are going to meet in a respectful relationship with patients."

"As you know," Bill continues, "there is this boundary war in psychotherapy. Does the healer get healed in the process of therapy? Is the healer's life changed?" By now I hear these as rhetorical questions. Then he admits to the inspiration and provocation he derives from doing psychotherapy with patients. "I have a very selfish motivation for doing this work. I am moved to a deeper, more painful awareness of myself." At this moment, Bill sounds like

Jennifer Dohrn, who claims that midwifery is not only an act of healing and service, it also allows her "to become more *me*." From Bill and Jennifer's perspective, then, mutuality and reciprocity are at the core of respectful healing relationships; boundaries are dynamic and negotiable, and they are drawn and redrawn in the service of developing and growing the relationship.

It is not only that the healer *and* the healed must both be open to, and ready for, transformation as their relationship grows, it is also that, in the process of dying, the patient is likely to become the "teacher of presence," the one who leads and models full attention. Bill's essay "Care of the Dying" describes the healer's journey as one of "accompaniment"; listening and learning, attending and responding.

> Persons situated in the experience of dying who seek help are the exemplary teachers of presence. For the situation dying persons bring to the helper is not something the helper can fix, chart a direction out of, or claim expertise in regard to. We all die and each person dies in her own way. One can see that the illness metaphor which permeates the trades of most helpers and prescribes the outcome of cure is of little value in the face of death, and, when followed, leaves the helper all thumbs. The helper, if she is to heal, must assent to the less fantastic metaphor of accompaniment. The climb up to the mountain of this metaphor is rugged and steep because few of the guilds within the helping professions give much credence to it. It can be a lonely journey with few markers along the way.

The "boundary wars" being waged within the psychotherapeutic community are also at the center of a broader cultural controversy. "Society says that the most individuated person is to be respected; that rugged individualism is to be most valued," says Bill. "But I see the respectful person *in relationship*; committed to interdependence." In therapeutic encounters this interdependence can develop only when the traditional doctor-patient hierarchy is dismantled, and when the doctor is willing to be changed. What clients are really asking for," continues Bill, "is a safe setting, a containing environment. They come helpless and out of control . . . and they need to be accompanied. You can provide that without the parent-child or teacher-child dynamic."

Again, some of the ways Bill describes a hospice caregiver could also be said of a midwife: "With dying patients you must give up agency and control. *They* are the boss. They tell *you* what is important, what they need, what they value, what is appropriate. We must become responsive to them . . . we are at the mercy of the dying person's (I hate to use this word) agenda. It is really a revolution." When Bill says "revolution," his voice is strong and clear. I ask him to describe what it is that dying people usually "want"; what they are yearning for from the healers who are listening to their wishes. His response is clear and immediate. "Dying people want to live their lives the way that they've always lived them. People don't fear biological cessation; they fear what dying will do to life the way they have known and experienced it."

Bill recalls a resident at the AIDS homes on Mission Hill where he worked who would go outside each day and just sit in the truck of the resident director for about an hour "just to feel the rightness and ordinariness of life moving on." And he remembers the response of an AIDS patient he had in therapy whom he asked, "What is the hardest thing about dying?" His answer: "When I go out to a meal with my friends, they won't let me pick up the check." Both of these memories of people on the edge of death underscore for Bill both the "revolution" that is needed in the ways therapists work with their patients, and the "ordinariness" that the dying people are aching for. Dying people want to be in control, but they are asking for power over a specific, personal, mundane world of their own. "Dying people have nothing to protect," muses Bill. "They don't measure the consequences of their actions."

With "nothing to protect," dying people tend to be very open and honest about their feelings and needs, and healers must not only follow their lead, they must also respond with clarity. "The folks who are most successful working with AIDS patients tend to be folks who are very matter of fact . . . who are very clear . . . there is no bullshit," says Bill. "Well, how do you train people to be this way?" I ask. "I think you can't train for respect or care," responds Bill. "You either have it or you don't." He must see the puzzled look on my face. I am wondering how a man who has spent so much of *his* life training to do this work—and training others to do it—would take the position that the therapist's respectful regard is essentially untrainable. "If it is there, you can hone it," admits Bill. "How?" I ask, still pressing. "You need to get them to know themselves better. This is deeply personal work. I want them to see that they are more like the persons that they are caring for than they are different from them. The empathic connections are vital. It is about the therapist and the patient connecting inner worlds."

Agape

In comparing his attitudes toward therapeutic and pastoral encounters, Bill says simply, "The difference is in degree rather than in kind. Just as in therapy, you want to convey that the person can share the deepest concerns of her heart to a curious and respectful ear." Again Bill stresses the essential empathic connection. "In conveying that respectful demeanor, you somehow need to reveal that you too struggle with some of these issues in your own life. You too are asking the essential questions rather than dispensing the answers."

Bill feels that parishioners observe the way their pastor handles his pain very carefully, watching for his insight, self-knowledge, and generosity. "If parishioners see that you have a kindly disposition toward your own humanity, then they are likely to think that they will be kindly received as well in terms of whatever vulnerabilities and anguish they may bring to you." But it is important that the priest not think of himself as the sole source of solace, the only person who can listen, empathize, and heal. Everyone in the community is a potential resource, and most often Bill thinks of himself as a "matchmaker," as the person who identifies the resources and orchestrates connections. He offers an example. "If a woman comes to me with a shadow on her mammogram, I need to try to connect her with another woman in the parish to whom that happened two weeks earlier."

I ask Bill Wallace how he conveys this kind of empathy in his sermons. He immediately refers to the storytelling. He begins by recognizing that, depending on how it is used, storytelling can be both inspiring and dangerous, both empathic and narcissistic. He asks, "Does the conveyor use stories to create connections, or does the story use the person? Are you venting or are you offering a gift? Who is getting the benefit of this story?" He recalls a humiliating moment in his early clinical training at the psychiatric research institute when he gave a presentation full of anguished autobiographical references. "I got up and talked about how my life was dark and out of control." Perhaps his public disclosures offered Bill a moment of catharsis, but his words left the audience cold, feeling disconnected, feeling like uncomfortable voyeurs. His supervisor's evaluation was harsh but to the point. "You just don't take down your pants in the pulpit," he admonished. Bill explains, "There is a thin line between mutuality and need. You have to be in charge of your story, find a way to keep it contained. You don't project your own needs and expectations onto those who are listening. It is important not to communicate the yearning, to keep a respectful distance." Empathy requires mutuality and connection, but also restraint and distance.

Bill's notion of "containing the story" and finding a "respectful distance" is one that concerns many teacher and student relationships. Kay Cottle must make sure that her stories do not overpower or overwhelm her students' stories; that she must never use her classroom as a stage for acting out her "autobiographical drama," but as a place where "lives connect" in their common quest for learning and understanding. As a law professor, David Wilkins is also restrained and strategic in his use of storytelling in his classes. He uses stories to humanize and concretize legal abstractions; to drive home important points and make them memorable; sometimes to add humor. But, like Bill and Kay, he tries never to let the "theater" of stories or the narcissism and needs of the storyteller dominate; stories should be used in the service of ideas and concepts, not for self-indulgence. "Know your own story first," says Bill, "and keep it in focus so it can be helpful. Your story contains the other person's story. But never make your story the center of therapy."

Negotiating this "thin line" requires maturity and worldliness. Although Bill says, "I can't imagine anyone being a healer before they are thirty-three or thirty-four, and that's even young," he recognizes that the kind of maturity he is speaking about is rarely measured in chronological years. "It helps to have gone through the bowel of the elephant and taken good notes along the way in order to develop the kind of wisdom you need to do this work."

The kind of healing involved in therapeutic work, Bill explains, "is as simple as making time to be present to the moment. It is crucial to be 'in the room.' With every word, gesture, silence, you are saying, 'This is your time, our time. We are open to what happens.'" He is speaking about the quality of attention, an openness of heart and mind, a willingness to be vulnerable, a deep curiosity on the part of the healer. He is talking about respect that grows out of mutuality, connection, and engagement in relationship, but one that also honors boundaries and privacy. "In this work, I follow my own curiosity respectfully . . . in a way that doesn't violate the patient's personhood."

"Does curiosity ever turn into voyeurism?" I ask, wondering how Bill draws that "thin line" that all of us engaged in inquiry and intervention inevitably face in our work. He shakes his head in full understanding and responds, "It is not *if* . . . it is *when* voyeurism shows itself. There is always the danger of slipping into that." But Bill believes that when curiosity bleeds into voyeurism it is a sign that "there is a blind spot in your own field of self-awareness." Voyeurism is not about attending to the needs of others; it is a way of "feeding your own hunger." This is why Bill thinks that it is crucial that therapists and healers be involved in ongoing supervision, critique, and self-scrutiny. To avoid the "blind spots" they must never work in isolation, never feel that they are omnipotent. "We are not really our own best listeners," says Bill. "We have to do this work in community."

Not only do healers need to work within the context of a "community" of critics, they also need to work with a certain moral stance. "The morality of this respectful work is that you are there to support the wholeness and healing of the person." He refers to the Christian term *agape*, meaning a kind of deep, selfless love. "You must," says Bill, "expect nothing in return. You must be clear that you do not *need* this relationship. The mutuality is serendipitous and discovered, not sought after and expected."

"Respectful work means wise accompaniment," Bill says again. "This is a broken world. Hope is about reconciliation and connection. The way we transcend our brokenness is to share it. This is the connecting tissue of community. The person in crisis wants to know that the healer knows her story implicitly and explicitly; that it is unique and fascinating; that the healer is listening at this time and in this moment to only her story. *But* the person in crisis also wants to be assured that the healer has heard it all before."

Death

Bill has recently provided such wise accompaniment to grieving parents. Richard, their nineteen-year-old son, had waged a courageous sixteen-month battle with leukemia, until all the medical treatments had been exhausted and his body finally had to give up and let go. Bill had received the call from Richard's father at 4:00 in the morning telling him that his son had died an hour earlier. He had risen from bed and gone immediately over to the hospital to sit with the family. As Bill tells this story—still raw from the anguish and the loss—he takes his glasses off, closes his eyes, and rubs his swollen eye sockets. The story pours out of him, unedited.

Richard had discovered his illness after returning from hiking the Appalachian Trail feeling exhausted and weak. He had taken a year off after high school, and was preparing to go to Indiana University to combine studies in the liberal arts with musical training. Instead of going off to college, he spent most of the next fifteen months at the Dana-Farber Institute in Boston, with his parents at his bedside. His twin brother Samuel had also postponed the first year of college so that he could be close to Richard while he battled the illness.

Last summer, Richard had been at the point of death, but somehow—through his strength of spirit and the doctors' aggressive and vigilant care—he had managed to survive, even recover enough to leave the hospital. He left Boston and headed home to be with his family in Vermont. He built a log cabin out in the woods, got a new dog, and had a meditative, "Thoreau-like" experience. Bill received amazing letters from Richard in which he talked about dying and the way he was living every moment he had left.

But after a couple of months Richard was back in the hospital, this time to stay. The doctors tried everything to keep him alive, while his mother, a surgeon, watched helplessly as her son's health declined; knowing too much about his physical condition, but feeling impotent to save him. His doctors refused to give up; they exhausted every treatment. Even when he failed the traditional criteria for bone marrow transplant, they tried another experimental method to keep him alive. With every attempt, the doctors kept saying, "There is still something we can try," and with each desperate move, Richard grew more exhausted.

Bill visited Richard often, both in the hospital and during his brief time in the Vermont woods. He had met Richard's godfather and father one Sunday when they had visited Emmanuel Church. They had not come looking for religious instruction; they had come to hear the healing music of Bach. As it happened, that morning Bill had preached a sermon about death. At the end of the service, Richard's father was moved to tell the priest about his son, and Bill asked whether he might visit Richard in the hospital. A couple of days later, Bill went to Dana-Farber to meet Richard. Although Bill felt the usual jitters as he approached Richard's room, he was immediately struck by how comfortable he felt being there. Somehow, there was never any awkwardness with Richard. "He never acted victimized," Bill recalls. "He never said, 'Why me?' . . . There was certainly sadness, and some fear. But he talked about the sadness of never being able to be a father . . . or the fear of never becoming an old man; not the fear of dying."

I am trying to get a picture of Richard, so I ask Bill to tell me what he looked like. My question seems to come as a surprise, almost as if Richard's physical body were not important. It was—and is—his spirit that was so moving and memorable. But, after a moment, Bill does manage to piece together a physical description. "He was tall with red hair and lots of freckles and very long fingers, which must have been one of the reasons he was such a fine cellist," says Bill. "He had very deep eyes and a face that exuded a gentle curiosity about life." Bill is silent for a long time, and continues. "He seemed to be able to see through mask and persona . . . through all the external stuff . . ." He shakes his head. "Other people said the same thing about him. He had a face that somehow communicated that you could be known by him." Bill seems to be describing the ways in which his "being present" with Richard made *him* feel seen and acknowledged. The healer was being healed. The dying person was offering a lesson in living. "You know," Bill suddenly remembers, "I actually only saw his red hair once, when I visited him in Vermont. The rest of the time he was bald."

Richard, who had started playing the cello at nine, had become an "incredible cellist," possessed of a passion and a musicality that was rare for someone so young. But his gifts and interests did not stop with his prodigious music. "He loved nature, poetry, drama," recalls Bill. "He was a wonderful, sensitive writer." Those who had heard Richard play the cello saw the same qualities in him that Bill felt when he sat with him in the hospital. "People, other musicians, told me how *relational* his playing was." He explains, "You know, you can be a technically proficient artist, even dazzling . . . but where you really take the leap is when your art becomes relational . . . when you are able to make connections and communicate."

I recall the many times that Bill has talked about "being present" with a dying person, and I ask him to tell me what he talked about with Richard. "I don't say much, really," he responds tentatively, searching for a way to convey the feeling of the moment, when words will not do. "Active attention is not about shutting up or not talking. It is more about attitude . . . One of the most important aspects of presence is revealing a gentle curiosity about that person." He repeats the quality—of gentle curiosity—that he has always felt as central to *Richard's* attitude and temperament. "You want to give someone the permission to talk about his dying." Bill's voice gets stronger, more certain. "I want to let Richard know that he does not have to take care of me . . . He doesn't have to use up any of his spiritual or psychic energy on taking care of me." He recalls a comment made by Richard's godfather, who had said that Richard often felt relieved when Bill visited because he "didn't have to *do* anything."

Bill believes that giving people permission to talk about dying, and letting them feel that they don't have to protect you from their anguish and their truths, requires that you know yourself well, "that you have a good deal of self-respect and self-knowledge." He presents the difficult paradox: "You need to know your own demons, your own inner workings, your own brokenness. Yet, you have to use that very brokenness to create an invitation for connection with the person." Bill wants me to know that this is not easy to accomplish. Even with Richard, with whom he felt most fluid, and genuinely comfortable, he would often leave his room "feeling all thumbs," "disjointed and awkward."

One of the ways in which Bill gives people "permission" to talk about death and dying is to ask them questions that others would never dare to ask, and to ask about things that are very ordinary, "very concrete." "Most people feel that the questions I might ask are utterly violating, too intrusive, rude . . . But the thing is that the person is just *dying* to express these things, just wanting the chance to tell the story." "So what sorts of things did you ask

Richard?" I inquire, wanting Bill to become more "concrete." His response is immediate. "I might ask him, for instance, 'What particular dream do you fear not having realized now that you are dying?' ... or 'I know it's painful to talk about, but what do you feel you most missed in not being able to play at Interlochen [a music festival where he had spent several summers] last summer?'" He elaborates, "You need to ask about those things which no one else has the guts to ask about or listen to. If you ask a question shaped by a lot of forethought and design, then you are probably asking a question to make *you* feel better, not one that gives the person the space to feel and express himself." He uses a "terrible metaphor" to underscore the dynamic quality of "active attention." "It's like judo," he says. "You use the strength of the other person . . . to join the dance."

Knowing that he has just returned from spending several hours with Richard's parents, I ask him to tell me about how he found a way to "be present" with them in their loss and grief. First he describes the anguish of anticipation that he experienced driving up to visit them. "You know, as much as I've been doing this . . . writing about it, teaching about it . . . I still find myself driving along thinking to myself, What the hell am I going to say to them! . . . But, in fact, it turned out to be an exceedingly moving day."

For hours the three of them had talked about Richard, reminiscing, weeping, laughing, grieving; looking at his things, remembering his gorgeous music making, reading his letters and his poetry. At one point, Bill asked a question that triggered the "long story" of his dying; the story that will be told over and over again—in the next months and years—as Richard's parents search for some shred of solace, some measure of resolution. Bill had asked Richard's mother what had happened between 9:00 on Tuesday evening and 3:00 the next morning, when Richard died. "I told Richard's mom that I had lost track of an important piece of what happened," recalls Bill. Richard's mother received the question like a gift, and "she walked through *every* minute of what happened during those hours."

She told Bill about going for a walk with her son around 9:00 P.M., enjoying the lovely garden in the hospital courtyard, the smell of the flowers, the feel of the air, Richard's meandering talk, his frailty, and his stoicism. She told about hugging him good-bye and returning to Shannon House, the place where they had been living while Richard was receiving his treatments; about going to bed feeling unsettled and fearful, but finally falling asleep . . . only to be awakened at 11:00 P.M. by a call from the nurse telling her that Richard was failing. She told him that she and her husband had gotten dressed in seconds, gone out into the night, and hailed a cab. They had been picked up by a Haitian cab driver, who asked them why they were going to the hospital so late at night. She told the driver that her son was very ill, and that they had just received a call saying that he had gotten worse. She told him about the driver's words that touched her soul, and gave her comfort. "God never sleep," he had said quietly.

"Somehow," says Bill, "through all of this terrifying time, this is what she held onto . . . 'God never sleep.'" Richard's mother continued to trace the minutes—move by move, feeling by feeling—until her beloved child took his last breath. She spoke; Bill listened; and her healing began.

"It is awful to see a mother lose a child," Bill says with such feeling that it seems as though he has lost his own son. "Do you think you had a special connection to him; that Richard's death was more painful to you than most?" I ask. "Well, I love music and I always wanted to be a cellist," he says only half joking, "and that was certainly a powerful connection." He grows very pensive. "Also, I admired him having it so together at nineteen years old." Now he seems to be talking to no one in particular. Maybe to the spirit surrounding us. Maybe to the God who never sleeps. "Even though he was so young, Richard was able to complete his life . . . to come full circle. He lived the whole cycle."

"At the still point," says Eliot in *Four Quartets*, "there is the dance." Birth and death join at such moments, inviting our full attention. "For the dying and, I believe, the living," says Bill in conclusion, "the immediate moment is the most significant. Now is always."

Some Roots of Respect

Behar, Ruth. *The Vulnerable Observer: Anthropology That Breaks Your Heart,* Boston: Beacon Press, 1996.

These six essays reflect on the nature of ethnographic observation and the qualities necessary for authenticity and passion in "seeing." Behar, a Latina, a professor of anthropology at the University of Michigan, and a self-described "woman on the border," looks at what she calls the strange business of "humans observing other humans in order to write about them." Critical to this work is an examination of "the central dilemma of all efforts at witnessing"—that "tender-minded tough-mindedness" required both to see the observed clearly and to recognize the impact of the experience on the observer. Behar muses,

> As a storyteller opens her heart to a story listener, recount-
> ing hurts that cut deep and raw into the gullies of the self,
> do you, the observer, stay behind the lens of the camera,
> switch on the tape recorder, keep pen in hand? Are there
> limits "of respect, piety, pathos" that should not be
> crossed, even to leave a record?

Other interesting examinations of the witnessing of relationships are Michael Jackson's *That Path Towards a Clearing: Radical Empiricism and Ethnographic Inquiry* (Bloomington: Indiana University Press, 1989), Renato Resaldo's *Culture and Truth* (Boston: Beacon Press, 1989), and Sara Lawrence-Lightfoot and Jessica Hoffman Davis's *The Art and Science of Portraiture* (San Francisco: Jossey-Bass, 1997).

Buber, Martin. *I and Thou* (1923). New York: Macmillan Library Reference, 1978.

Martin Buber (1878–1965), the German philosopher, theologian and political leader, has been described by a biographer as regarding "every encounter a focal point for human growth." Buber's "philosophy of dialogue" views human existence in relation to the other in two fundamentally different kinds of relations: "I-It" and "I-Thou." An I-It relation is the everyday relationship of human beings toward the things around them, one in which individuals regard other human beings from a distance, as parts of the environment, or as links in "chains of causality." In the I-Thou relation, the individual enters into relation with the other with his or her whole and innermost being, in a meeting of real dialogue. For Buber, these human meetings are only a reflection of the human meeting with God.

Chernin, Kim. *In My Mother's House: A Daughter's Story*. New York: HarperCollins, 1983.

In this brave and moving memoir, the author tells the story of conflict, confrontation, and reconciliation among four generations of Chernin women. She speaks about the anguish of secrets and misunderstandings between mothers and daughters, the power of forgiveness, and the mutual respect that intimacy and autonomy require. My own work, *Balm in Gilead: Journey of a Healer* (Addison-Wesley, 1988) is also, in part, about the journey of self-discovery embarked on in portraying my mother's life and work.

Didion, Joan. "On Self-Respect." In *Slouching Towards Bethlehem*. New York: Touchstone, 1968.

In this early essay, Didion recalls a certain lost moment of innocence when, at nineteen, she failed to be elected to Phi Beta Kappa, an academic honor society. Describing this era in which she realized that "the same cause-effect relationships which hampered others" also applied to her, she considers the importance of self-respect, which has little to do with the outer world's evaluation of us but is about "a separate peace, a private reconciliation." Didion acknowledges the hard truth that "anything worth having [in life] has its price" and that only self-respect gives us the ability to see clearly: the wisdom to "discriminate, to love and to remain indifferent."

Harris, George W. *Dignity and Vulnerability: Strength and Quality of Character.* Berkeley: University of California Press, 1997.

In this work, Harris, a contemporary philosopher, examines definitions of respect in relation to our ability as humans to sympathize. He considers four features of respect and sympathy, concluding ultimately that it is not simply enough to respect others, in the traditional Kantian sense, but that respect demands something more: sympathetic emotional engagement.

Jacobs, Jonathan. *Practical Realism and Moral Psychology.* Washington: Georgetown University Press, 1995.

Jacobs, a contemporary philosopher, looks at the concept of respect for persons as it binds us in a common moral world. Jacobs describes how respect motivates and controls practical human action: "To respect people is to acknowledge that they are equal participants in a common ethical world and that objective considerations of good are to direct our attitude and actions." Jacobs also distinguishes self-respect from self-love. He writes, "Self-respect is a recognition that it is important that one's choices, purposes, and policies of action answer to a sound conception of what is good."

Jordan, Judith V. "A Relational Perspective on Self Esteem." Paper no. 7. Wellesley College, Stone Center, 1994.

Building on the work of Carol Gilligan, Jean Baker Miller, and others, Jordan describes how constructions of "separate selves" in our culture often mean a preoccupation with competition and who is better than whom. This cultural preoccupation, reinforced by our dominant theories of moral development, bears significantly on our treatment of respect. To exhibit the kinds of respect that the individuals in the book do, one must move away from "traditional standards of worth" to a more relational model, in which "trying to feel good about oneself emphasizes a person's capacity to form good connections and to be empathic. [It] involves a sense of commonality with the other person." Commonality and connection are at the center of the definition of respect sought in this book.

Josselson, Ruthellen. *The Space Between Us: Exploring the Dimensions of Human Relationships.* Thousand Oaks: Sage Publications, 1996.

As a corrective to psychology's focus on the self, Josselson, along with other contemporary psychologists, seeks to establish a context in which therapy "takes place within a web." Many individuals in this book echo Josselson's sense of "moving with":

> This "moving with" (as opposed to "getting ahead of" or "gaining control of") others has not been encouraged. It is clear that we have come to the edge of our capacity as a species to wield power over one another or to solve problems with force and domination. Either we live interdependently or we all vanish. Our survival necessitates seeing what connects us, looking at what occupies that space between.

Kant, Immanuel. *Critique of Pure Reason.* (1782). Boston: Charles E. Tuttle Co., 1993.

Any exploration of the concept of respect must have in its background an examination of the work of Immanuel Kant (1724–1804). Kant's assertion that people share a dignity and are owed respect by virtue of being moral agents who are capable of using their reason to formulate and follow moral laws underlies many of our contemporary moral and legal views. In terms of our conceptions of human beings as practical moral reasoners and entitled to respect based on their reasoning capacities, Kant's views are profoundly influential.

Lawrence-Lightfoot, Sara. *I've Known Rivers: Lives of Loss and Liberation*. Reading, MA: Addison-Wesley, 1994.

Using a mode of portraiture that I call human archaeology, I explore the life journeys of six successful African-Americans in their middle years. *Rivers* tells two tales: the first chronicles the life stories of each of the protagonists, and the second traces the evolution of our relationships. In the opening chapter, I speak about the many complex roles I played as these relationships developed over time: relationships of respect and reciprocity, skepticism and appreciation, of trust and alliance:

> As I listen to these extraordinary women and men tell their life stories, I play many roles. I am a mirror that reflects back their pain, their fears, and their victories. I am also the inquirer who asks the sometimes difficult questions, who searches for evidence and patterns. I am the companion on the journey, bringing my own story to the encounter, making possible an interpretive collaboration. I am the audience who listens, laughs, weeps, and applauds. I am the spider woman spinning their tales. Occasionally, I am a therapist who offers catharsis, support, and challenge, and who keeps track of emotional minefields. Most absorbing to me is the role of the human archaeologist who uncovers the layers of mask and inhibition in search of a more authentic representation of life experience.

Lickona, Thomas. *Educating for Character: How Our Schools Can Teach Respect and Responsibility*. New York: Bantam, 1991.

In this book, Lickona makes a case for the importance of moral reflection in primary and secondary school teacher training, in classroom management, and within the larger curriculum. Lickona considers two "great" neglected moral values: respect and responsibility, which in his view "constitute the core of a universal, public morality." Building on the work of Lawrence Kohlberg, Lickona makes a philosophical distinction between respect and responsibility. He writes that respect is a prohibitive moral code that delineates our negative obligations to each other (he notes that " 'Thou shalt not murder' has a precision that 'Love your neighbor' does not"), whereas responsibility:

> supplies the vital giving side of morality. Where respect says "Don't hurt," responsibility says "Do help." Over the long haul it calls us to try, in whatever way we can, to nurture and support each other, alleviate suffering, and make the world a better place for all.

Readers will note that both these "codes" underlie the actions of individuals in this book.

Lickona, Thomas. *Raising Good Children: Helping Your Child Through the Stages of Moral Development.* New York: Bantam, 1983.

Here Lickona explains that a morality of respect, which he defines as respect for ourselves, for other people, and for all forms of life and the environment, "doesn't burst forth, fully formed [but] instead develops slowly," and with great effort on the part of parents, caregivers, and educators. Lickona believes simply that "morality is respect." He adds, "Moral development, like all other forms of human development, begins in love."

Martin, Jane Roland. *The Schoolhome: Rethinking Schools for Changing Families.* Cambridge: Harvard University Press, 1992.

Drawing heavily on the work of Maria Montessori and her Casa dei Bambini, created for Rome's urban poor at the turn of the century, and on the work of the educational philosopher John Dewey, Martin emphasizes that, in young children, respect and caring are derived "not from possessiveness but from attachment" to their schools, their classmates, and the natural world. Martin's belief that "the ability to take the point of view of another is a basic element of morality itself" is critical to the definition of respect explored in this work.

May, Rollo. *The Art of Counseling.* Nashville: Abbington, 1939.

This pioneering work examines the place of empathy in the therapist's shaping of affirmative, "constructive," and "upbuilding relationships." May claims that empathy is the opposite of egocentricity and that the therapist must be ready to both witness and experience change, to move beyond self-reminiscence to a place of deep understanding and connection.

Miller, Jean Baker. "Connections, Disconnections and Violations." Paper no. 33. Wellesley College, Stone Center, 1988.

Jean Baker Miller, director of education at the Stone Center at Wellesley College and author of many highly regarded works on women's development, considers the characteristics of growth-fostering relationships, as opposed to relationships that lead to a sense of disconnection from others. Baker identifies five characteristics of mutually empowering relationships. She notes that these are relationships which are energizing and "zesty"; in which both parties are active participants; which provide clarity and knowledge for both parties; which enhance the self-worth of both parties; and which create connection, spurring the desire for more connection. The characteristics of the mutually empowering relationships Miller describes mirror in quality the respectful relationships forged by the individuals in *Respect*.

Rogers, Carl. *Counseling and Psychotherapy*. Cambridge, MA: Riverside Press, 1942.

In this classic work, Rogers stresses the importance of the supportive, healing qualities of empathy in therapeutic encounters but also underscores the insights and generative knowledge that emerge during empathic exchange. Like the healers and teachers in this book, Rogers describes the counselor's role as one of encouragement and responsiveness, talk and silence. "The primary technique which leads to insight on the part of the client," says Rogers, "is one which demands the utmost in self-restraint on the counselor's part."

Sacks, Oliver. *The Man Who Mistook His Wife For a Hat*. New York: Summit, 1985.

In recounting clinical tales from his medical practice, neurologist Sacks underscores the power of storytelling as an essential dimension of building respectful relationships between doctors and patients and offering healing care. He laments the decline of "richly human clinical tales; the combining of narrative and science" in modern neurology; a field that has become increasingly routinized, codified, and impersonal. Sacks claims that efforts to increase the rigor and the science of neurology in the last century have led to caricatures and distortions in seeing, hearing, and healing the patient. Like several of the people in *Respect,* Sacks sees respect carried in the "intersection of fact and fable." Storytelling is one vehicle for creating the symmetry and for mining the information so central to healing.

Shakespeare, William. *The Comedy of Errors* (written in 1594, first printed in 1623). New York: Viking Penguin, 1978.

In this work from Shakespeare's early period we are given a glimpse of a comic but poignant attempt to dismantle hierarchy in respectful relationships some four hundred years ago. At the conclusion of *The Comedy of Errors,* two sets of identical twins, separated in infancy, are reunited after much confusion and threat of impending tragedy. As the play ends, one pair of twins remain on stage. As they prepare to exit, they try to decide which one should go first, taking the position of greater honor in a society based on strict observance of primogeniture, the authority of the first-born son. Faced with a dilemma, since neither knows which is the elder, one says,

> We came into the world like brother and brother;
> And now let's go hand in hand, not one before the other.

A vision of mutual respect, departing hand in hand, the twins remind us that the differential respect bestowed by cultures on individuals, whether based on birth order, class, race, gender, or something else equally arbitrary, belies the principle of the essential value of every human being.

Shakespeare, William. *The Merchant of Venice* (written between 1596 and 1598, first printed in 1600). Brent Stirling, ed. New York: Viking Penguin, 1972.

In a familiar passage from *The Merchant of Venice,* Portia reminds Shylock that one cannot be compelled to show mercy:

> The quality of mercy is not strain'd,
> It droppeth as the gentle rain from heaven
> Upon the place beneath . . .

Beginning a series of images that reinforce the divine nature of mercy, Portia asserts the healing and generative qualities of mercy, especially when practiced by someone in power, someone who has the "right" to assert authority. Portia reminds Shylock that the effects of mercy are reciprocal:

> it is twice blest,
> It blesseth him that gives and him that takes, . . .

Portia reminds us that mercy resembles respect more than pity; the person in a position to show mercy in one situation will be the person in need of mercy in another, just as a person who shows respect needs respect. Extending this idea of reciprocity, Portia presents the paradox that to refrain from asserting the authority one possesses can demonstrate greater strength. The mercy that Portia recommends to Shylock resembles respect: it cannot be compelled; it must be given freely. If given freely, it enriches the life of both the giver and receiver. It originates in the heart, not with the position of the giver. It embodies a spiritual dimension that transcends a dry and literal principle of justice.

Truitt, Anne. *Daybook: The Journal of an Artist.* New York: Penguin, 1983.

At the age of forty-two, Truitt began to keep a journal as a way of coming to terms with "the artist in herself." In seven years of journal entries, she examines the evolution of her artistic work in the context of her life story and of her relationships with family and friends, past and present. Her self-reflections chart a journey toward self-respect—one that is both difficult and hopeful, solitary and communal. Anyone interested in respectful relations with self and others can learn from the sustained honesty of this journal.

Index

About the Author

S ara Lawrence-Lightfoot, a sociologist, is Professor of Education at Harvard University. She is the author of *Balm in Gilead: Journey of a Healer,* which won a Christopher Award, given for "literary merit and humanitarian achievement." She is also the author of several other books, including *I've Known Rivers: Lives of Loss and Liberation, Worlds Apart: Relationships Between Families and Schools,* and *The Good High School: Portraits of Character and Culture.* Professor Lawrence-Lightfoot has been a Fellow at the Bunting Institute at Radcliffe College and at the Center for Advanced Study in the Behavioral Sciences at Stanford University. She is the recipient of Harvard's George Ledlie Prize for research that "makes the most valuable contribution to science" and the prestigious MacArthur Prize Award.